The Living Tradition

FRANCES STEVENS

The Living Tradition

The social and educational assumptions
of the grammar school

RADIUS BOOK / HUTCHINSON

HUTCHINSON & CO (*Publishers*) LTD
3 Fitzroy Square, London W1

London Melbourne Sydney Auckland
Wellington Johannesburg Cape Town
and agencies throughout the world

First published December 1960
This edition August 1972

Printed in Great Britain by litho on smooth wove paper
by Anchor Press, and bound by Wm. Brendon,
both of Tiptree, Essex

ISBN 0 09 112420 4 (cased)
112421 2 (paper)

Contents

CONTENTS

All this is true, if time stood still; which, contrariwise, moveth so round, that a froward retention of custom is as turbulent a thing as an innovation.

Francis Bacon: *Of Innovations*

But education decays when, in the individual human beings who, at their maturity, have to bear responsibility, the historically transmitted substance has crumbled. Anxiety about this substance is tantamount to a consciousness that there is peril of its being absolutely lost. In such circumstances, a man will look backwards, and will have his children taught as absolute that which he himself no longer regards as such. Another will reject this historical tradition, and will have education carried on as if it had no relationship with time at all, and consisted only of training for technical skill, the acquisition of realist knowledge, and information that will enable a child to take up a position towards the contemporary world. Every one knows that he who moulds children moulds the future.

Karl Jaspers: *Man in the Modern Age*

Acknowledgements

I should like to thank Professor W. R. Niblett
and Professor J. W. Tibble, both of whom read my
manuscript and made constructive criticisms; my
colleague Dr. K. Lovell, who suggested what
numerical material was likely to be significant;
and members of my family, who helped me in the
tedious work of counting and tabulating.

June 1960   FRANCES STEVENS

Introduction to the Third Edition

Is there still a living tradition?

The quotations from Francis Bacon and Karl Jaspers which preface this book are more apposite than ever. Ten or twelve years ago, the struggle between innovation and froward retention of custom constituted one of the most important tensions in education, particularly for the guardians of the academic tradition. Now, the tension is near breaking point – has, indeed, in places, already broken – not only in the world of mere learning but also in conduct, attitudes and values. As for Jaspers's words, written over twenty years ago, they are a prophetically accurate description of what is happening today. The historically transmitted substance has crumbled. Feeling this, some parents (and perhaps some teachers) wish to have the young taught as absolute that which they themselves no longer regard as such. Others undoubtedly reject the historical tradition and 'will have education carried on as if it had no relationship with time at all, and consisted only of training for technical skills, the acquisition of realist knowledge, and information that will enable a child to take up a position towards the contemporary world'. Well, why not? Perhaps indeed there are no absolutes. Situational ethics, action painting, descriptive grammer, modern mathematics, electronic music – these have been only a few of the manifestations of a half-deliberate abandonment of certainty, the as yet unverified hypothesis of an undescried epicentre. It may be that the embracing of insecurity is the task of our time and that the historically transmitted substance must be relinquished. If so it is more necessary that teachers should ask themselves what they are teaching, and why.

The phrase 'the living tradition' was intended to refer not to the actual institution of the maintained grammar school but to a tradition of learning and disciplined thinking which it inherited almost by chance. The tradition, which very quickly transcended the instrumental functions of the school, was primarily curricular, but gathered about it associations which ranged from ethical principles and standards of behaviour to matters such as dress and even irrational rituals. At its worst it favoured pedantry and a complacent conformity: at its best it could foster 'a sense of history, the imaginative leap that carries the sciences as well as the arts, appreciation of both the comedy and the tragedy of the human situation, and a capacity for disinterestedness' (see page 255). In theory, it could be maintained, among other traditions, in the comprehensive school as well, and in my more recent book *The New Inheritors* I have given some attention to its place in such a school. *The Living Tradition* is however an examination of the type of school which was expressly concerned with its maintenance.

Since this book was first published, many changes have taken place both in the educational system and in the climate of educational thought. Comprehensive schools have greatly increased in number, at an accelerated pace since Circular 10/65 required local authorities to submit plans for organizing secondary education in their areas on comprehensive lines. Over this period the concept of comprehensive education, and indeed of secondary education, has become very much differentiated. Comprehensive schools are normal, but the '11 to 18' school is no longer the dominant type. There are various developments of the two-tier system. Sixth form colleges have grown in number, variety and size. At the other end of the age range, it has been seriously questioned whether eleven is the best age for the change to secondary education; consequently – in accordance partly with theories of development and partly with administrative convenience - 'middle' schools, with an age range of 8 to 12 or 9 to 13, are being established in increasing numbers. Opinion has also moved strongly and decisively in favour of co-education. When this book was written, the greater number of grammar schools were for boys or girls only. The early comprehensive schools, too, were often single-sex schools. Nowadays, a new comprehensive school is, almost without question, co-educational; and in areas where grammar schools remain there is a tendency to amalgamate boys' and girls' schools.

In 1960 I was still naive. Myself of working-class origin, reared as a child in the kind of socialism that extended from Keir Hardie to George Lansbury, valuing memories of the ardent Ellen Wilkinson and the humble and visionary George Tomlinson as Ministers of Education, I had yet to learn that the epithet 'middle-class' automatically meant 'bad'. It had not occurred to me that the 'bourgeois virtues' of patience, perseverance and the like could ever be discredited. Unheroic they might be, even faintly comical on occasion; but that they should be denied as goods – that was inconceivable. So, too, the acquisition of refined sensibilities, width of vision and depth of knowledge (see page 259) seemed to be a manifest function of education, though not the only one. My close contact with schools of many kinds in the course of work at an emergency training college had made me, at a very early stage in its development, enthusiastic about the idea of the common school; but a brief acquaintance with common schools in the United States, followed by a few years' experience as head of a grammar school in which many underprivileged children struggled to reconcile the pressures of their environment with the demands of learning, moderated this enthusiasm. (They did not, however, entirely destroy it – hence a certain ambiguity which critics correctly sensed in *The Living Tradition* and which I made no effort to conceal or eliminate.)

Chapter 14 (*Academic and Social Assumptions*) represents an attempt to draw together and enumerate various elements of the tradition. At the time of writing it seemed that this tradition, always changing but still recognisable, was, though imperfect, an unquestionable and unquestioned good. It was not for everybody, but must be made accessible to to all who either clearly were equipped to profit by it or had a passionate desire to possess it (in its essentials, that is – not in its accidental accretions). The only important problem was how to ensure that it was made most accessible and most effective. One might argue whether the selective or the comprehensive system were the better means of achieving accessibility and effectiveness: one did not doubt that it was worth acquiring.

1960 is several ages away. When I was working on the book I was able to write (page 226):

'There is talk currently in America of the selection and training of men – and perhaps women – destined to be "astronauts".'

While visiting the schools I met children who were distressed by reports that a dog had died in Russian space exploration. Today, all over the world, people will scarcely pause to follow the progress of a spacecraft, or watch the actions of men on the moon, unless a threatened disaster, such as nearly befell Apollo 13, sets on a cosmic stage the common drama of man's effort to survive. The decade of the sixties has been the time of the panic-stricken wave of reform that swept through American education in the wake of the Sputnik; the time of 'Nuffield' science teaching (or its equivalent), 'new math', modern linguistics; of the rapid increase of language laboratories, closed-circuit television and programmed learning; of the development of computer-assisted learning; of the growing influence of curricular policy and practice of behaviourist theories. 'One impulse from a vernal wood' has little substance under the the hard lights of modern education. (Of course, there are not so many vernal woods.)

By 1960 the angry young man was known, and teddy boys had appeared on the social scene. (See page 175.) But Carnaby Street had not become a world-wide symbol, pop singers had not received the M.B.E., pornography as a subject had not received explicit and respectful attention from writers in serious newspapers and academic speakers on Radio Three. The peaceful demonstrations of Negroes in America had aroused a generous indignation in some of the boys and girls encountered in the the survey; but coloured immigrants had made little noticeable impact on English society, and the voice of Enoch Powell had yet to be heard. There were only faint indications of the desperate decade to come – the decade of the escalation and prolongation of the Vietnam war; of the rise and falls of regimes in Africa; of the assassinations of John and Robert Kennedy and of Martin Luther King; of student protest from Tokyo to the Sorbonne, of sit-ins and violence; the decade, too, of drug-addiction and of strange cults.

The blood-dimmed tide is loosed; and everywhere
The ceremony of innocence is drowned.

Those who study education should also note the appropriation by esoteric movements of what had seemed limpid and positive, very much of the daylight world. Thus, Tolkien's *The Lord of the Rings,* which children have appreciated for its romantic wonder and adults for its nobility and profundity, has become a sacred text for San Francisco hippies.

In England the comprehensive school has developed in a rapidly changing educational environment. The new universities have been established. Colleges of Advanced Technology have become universities. Large and elaborate polytechnics have appeared, often absorbing older and very diverse institutions. Training colleges have become colleges of education; the Bachelor of Education degree has been instituted, and some colleges have established research fellowships: one can see foreshadowed something like the rise of state colleges in the U.S.A. The Schools Council, through its enquiries, its research projects and its publications on subjects which range from school counselling to mathematics in primary schools, has exercised a strong influence of curriculum and organization. Local authorities have set up teachers' centres. The in-service training of teachers, through the agencies of the Department of Education and Science, of university schools of education, and of local authorities, has very greatly increased, though not to an extent at all commensurate with the need. The Certificate of Secondary Education has stimulated much curricular discussion amongst teachers and has formed interesting relationships with the General Certificate of Education. It has also to some extent blurred distinction between 'grammar' and 'modern' curricula in the schools. The whole public examination system is under anxious review, and, since the rejection of proposals for 'Q' and 'F' level examinations in the sixth form, American-type standardized tests have been viewed with increasing though not universal favour.

Inside the schools, more and more boys and girls are entering the sixth form. The 'unacademic' sixth-former has arrived. Sixth forms themselves exist alongside alternative institutions, in the various forms of further education provided by local authorities. During the decade the principle of 'unstreamed' teaching-groups, first worked out and observed in primary schools, has been applied to many comprehensive schools, this at the precise time when Americans are much concerned with programmes for the gifted, and when the intelligent child in the States is more likely than ever before to be pulled out and pushed along.

The day of the small school is over. With increase in size have come important changes in the functions and status of the staff and of the head. One of the headmasters questioned in the *Living Tradition* survey said that the head's function would change entirely if schools became very big. This has undoubtedly happened. The head of a school today has a difficult task – to be an efficient manager and good public relations man (for neither of which roles has his academic training or successful teaching experience necessarily fitted him) while tradition still requires him to be a pastor. Nor has the infra-structure of the school yet developed in such a way as to compensate. Moreover, the uneasy compromise between executive efficiency and personal communication, which is also to some extent the problem of every teacher, has been reached – not, of course, by accident – at the very time when the conflicts and instability of society place adolescents under great strain. Understandably, then, the importance of the trained school counsellor, which the old grammar school amateur would have been apt to deny, is increasingly recognized.

Speaking at the 1968 Convention of the National Council of Teachers of English in Milwaukee, Dr. Buckminster Fuller pointed out how much more the modern child knows – and knows effortlessly – than do his teachers. 'He knows that he is living on a spacecraft . . . He knows that he does not inhabit a Euclidean universe . . .' Some of the moral, aesthetic and political principles which could still be appealed to in 1960 may be comparable to those of a Euclidean universe. Thrift, for example, may have no moral significance, or even a negative one. The economist is likely to say that it is commendable or not according to the inflationary or deflationary state of the economy at a given time, while a Marxist sees the inculcation of it as a device to keep the poorer classes depressed and acquiescent. Again, in my Introduction to the second edition of *The Living Tradition* in 1962 I expressed genuine surprise that Brian Jackson and Dennis Marsden had seemed to question the value of 'the tacit assumption of contracts of mutual responsibility between individuals and between an individual and his society'. But perhaps they were aware of a social topology which I had not grasped. Looking more particularly at the tradition, one sees that scholarship is of its essence. But in 1971 a professor of education, speaking to a conference of sixth form teachers, could confidently invite members to agree with him that 'our aim is not scholarship'. In the same year, during a talk on the music of Lennox Berkeley in the BBC series *Talking About Music,* Anthony Hopkins mentioned that a French critic, listening to this composer's *Divertimento,* had said, 'It's such *civilised* music.' Commenting ruefully that civilised music was against the grain of the time, the speaker likened it to a well dressed and nicely spoken schoolboy who finds himself at a hippie pop festival.

But the argument of *The Living Tradition* reduces itself to its essence in the last sentence:

'For education becomes in the deepest sense comprehensive not through administration, but in the unity of a single civilized perception.'

In this book I gave some account of the development of state secondary education. I examined carefully, according to the evidence I was able to obtain, the assumptions of both pupils and staff in maintained grammar schools at the end of the first half-century, noting important changes in in the types of each group after the Second World War. Some of the assumptions appeared to be good – others ignoble or even dangerous. I did not attempt to conceal my observation that some teachers were ill equipped, even academically, to meet the challenges of the time, and that many were blind and resistant to the need for an immense enlargement of their human experience and sympathies. It puzzled some critics and angered others that I could report so candidly and yet appear to 'defend' the grammar school, and I was at times discomfited, since I felt myself in intuitive accord with my enenies rather than my friends. But my reply – even to myself – was always twofold. First, I had no grounds for believing that most of the defects I noticed would necessarily be remedied in a comprehensive system. Secondly, I had not started from a prepared position, and it was only on balance, and after serious reflection, that I concluded that the grammar school as an institution ought to be preserved. It was always the non-neighbourhood school, covering the whole social range, that I had in mind. I knew from deep experience how difficult was the schooling of the intelligence of the new inheritors.

I believe, however, that the development of recent years is now irreversible. The slowing-down of the rate of change which has followed the advent of a Conservative government is on the whole to be regretted, since the grammar schools which remain are mostly in districts where the 'first generation' is no great problem, and where grammar schools are too readily associated with the less democratic of the social values. Rather, I suggest, we must now accept the change and ask ourselves what place, if any, the living tradition has in the comprehensive school. Perhaps it has none – but it should not be abandoned out of mere thoughtlessness. My recent observations, in this country and in the United States and Australia, leave me with misgivings about the common school in those very areas which one had hoped would be its justification. Nowhere have I yet found convincing evidence that the known relationship between social class and academic achievement has been appreciably modified, or that the very intelligent are less apt to stay with their intellectual peers, outside the classroom as well as in it. I also find that the 'grammar school' or 'college preparatory' curriculum has excessive prestige in the programme of studies, and a social prestige which ought by now to have become totally irrelevant.

The Living Tradition can claim historical interest as a picture of an important sector of English secondary education at a critical stage in its development. It may also make its contribution towards deciding whether the tradition itself has a place in the contemporary world, and, if so, how best to embody it in the comprehensive school. It is comparatively easy to train the elite of a meritocracy: it is not easy to create and preserve a fellowship of learning.

PART ONE

Towards an Appraisal

I

A Changing Pattern

A grammar school should provide one place at least in
the modern community where the virtues of hard work at
sometimes uncongenial tasks are preached.

A SENIOR FRENCH MASTER

I think we should have the privelage but not the homework.

A SCHOOLBOY AGED TWELVE

To think is difficult, and usually painful. We press buttons, drink our
pasteurized milk, are conditioned by 'commercials', hope to win the
pools, ride powerful motor-cycles, stay in holiday camps, listen to
juke-boxes, possess ciné-projectors and tape-recorders and read the
illustrated papers. We buy packaged goods. We are born and die in
hospital, and manage to avoid in the interim too close a proximity to
disturbing questions of human existence. Why then should we, who
'have never had it so good', seek the arduous disciplines with which
education has traditionally been concerned?

> On a huge hill,
> Cragged, and steep, Truth stands, and hee that will
> Reach her, about must, and about must goe;
> And what the hills suddennes resists, winne so.

Let the hived-off minority do our thinking and speculating for us and
let us, relieved of the necessity of decision, enjoy its products. It is not
in such a climate that a common passion for learning is likely to be
born.

Yet, to a naïve observer, this passion might seem to exist. Throughout
the twentieth century, but with growing momentum since the Second
World War, there has been a movement to make generally accessible a
type of education formerly reserved for the few: the rich, the outstandingly intelligent and – occasionally – the limited but striving. First were
removed the more obvious barriers of class, though concealed barriers

15

still remained. In 1920 the brilliant son of a factory worker could not go to Eton; but he could win a scholarship to the municipal secondary school. Next went the barrier of money. Free places in secondary schools became available in increasing numbers up to the end of the 1930s, and after 1944 no local authority retained fee-paying places. Now the barrier of 'intelligence' is cracking – strangely enough, in one sense, since the earlier barriers were removed ostensibly in order to preserve it.

One of the less foreseen consequences of the 1944 Education Act was to force an open recognition of the fact not only that a few people were in some absolute sense clever but that many people were more intelligent than many others. This fact has always been empirically known but need not be acknowledged as long as there are circumstances to mask it. When from several streets or from a whole village only one child in a year gains access to a higher education we may be envious, but do not necessarily feel a personal challenge. He is clever and therefore different; or he is unusually, even unnaturally, industrious; or he has parents who are in a better position or who choose to deny themselves many comforts in order to afford school fees. It is an unfair world: but we do not doubt our own or our children's capacities to succeed 'if we had the chance'. When, however, the chance is offered us, then we are challenged. We do not interpret equality of opportunity as the right of access to one form of a highly diversified but uniformly esteemed system of secondary education. On the contrary, we refuse to give 'parity of esteem' and demand instead access to the minority school of the past. Is this evidence of a disinterested passion for learning? Far from it. Though we should like 'the privelage but not the homework', we are no more eager than we ever were to wrestle with ideas. We are beginning to demand that if our children do not learn Latin they shall at least be placed in a school where foreign languages – or, more important, mathematics and physics – are taught. But if a school that exists to profess such a curriculum is found to be unsuitable for the majority, destroy it!

> When nobody is anyone
> Then everyone's some-bódy.

The object of this popular love-hate is, of course, the maintained grammar school. Fruit of sixty years of change, survivor of two world wars and the years of economic depression, social unifier, provider of members of every profession and nurse of scholars, statesmen, scientists and writers of the first order, the grammar school is an institution that even its critics acknowledge to have been extraordinarily successful. Yet it will be quite in keeping with the fashion of the time if this school dies not of its faults, of which there are many, but of its virtues.

What is the grammar school, so keenly desired by so many, yet threatened with extinction because it is manifestly for the few? On first trying to answer the question one is tempted to conclude that it is not only indefinable but perhaps non-existent. Here, for instance, is a boys' school which traces its ancestry from the Middle Ages, when the Guild of the Holy Cross made some provision for secular education. Reconstituted as a grammar school in the reign of Edward VI, it now ranks as a boys' day public school. But it is also a 'direct grant' grammar school – that is, it charges fees to some of its pupils, admits some on its own scholarships, and receives a financial grant from the Ministry of Education (not from the local authority) in return for admitting a certain number of pupils to free places. Its sister school – for the foundation, as the Latin inscription on the new buildings engagingly states, was later 'graced by the addition of girls' – is in much the same position. Both schools admit through a highly selective procedure children of very good intellectual ability, follow a concentrated programme designed to encourage scholarly attitudes of mind and distinguished academic achievement, and expect to send a very large proportion of their pupils to universities.

In contrast to this is a school in a thickly-populated industrial area. Founded in 1919, it formerly held a position of modest privilege in the district, admitting its proportion of scholarship pupils and having its other places filled by those children whose parents could afford the low fees and who desired, from social or educational motives, to give them the benefit of what was then the only secondary education available. Today the population of this school is changing. Some of the children who would formerly have held fee-paying places are in the secondary modern school. A few local children are being sent to the 'direct grant' grammar school in the same town by parents who, in consequence of higher wages, can now afford to pay fees which their own parents would not have been able to pay. A number of children at present in the school would not have been there in former times, because their parents would have been too poor to send them, or even not sufficiently interested to let them take the special-place examination. Some of these children settle down, profit by their new opportunities and do well. Others cannot adjust themselves to the more stringent demands of the grammar school, and are not supported by parental encouragement. They grow restless in the middle school and may want to leave before they have completed their programme, particularly if there is financial anxiety at home, or if they have seen their friends from secondary modern schools now out in the world, leading an apparently less exacting life and perhaps at the same time earning attractive wages.

Another school, situated in the residential part of a town which is a harbour and holiday resort, was formerly a girls' private school of good standing. Its curriculum was arduous and forward-looking in the pioneer days of girls' education, but it also paid attention to the accomplishments, good manners and graceful deportment which were then valued so highly as feminine attributes. Though this school has long since been under the control of the local authority, much of its former social prestige remains, and its tradition is strong enough to impose on present pupils something of that regard for both academic success and social ease which characterized it in former years.

Yet another – a boys' school in the industrial Midlands – has only since 1946 been classified as a grammar school. Formerly a vigorous and successful senior school, it has spent the last fourteen years gradually changing its character. In 1953 it had, for the first time, a small upper sixth, formed from those boys who were in its first 'grammar school' entry. Its old senior-school population worked itself out in the first few years, and all pupils are now admitted through the selective entrance examination. During the post-war years the school eagerly sought to acquire all the marks of a grammar school. More specialists were appointed to the staff. The curriculum – for a proportion of the pupils only, at first – became more verbal and abstract. The chance to take the examination for the General Certificate of Education was welcomed and much stress was laid on success in this external examination, for it was to be the proof to the outside world that the school could challenge comparison, as far as instruction was concerned, with neighbouring grammar schools. Other badges of grammar-school status were also acquired. Uniform was introduced, and painstaking but not entirely successful efforts made to ensure the observance of its regulations. The school now plays other grammar schools at games, and sends its representatives to all inter-grammar-school functions. The house system, embryonic in senior-school days, has been greatly developed. Much stress has been laid on 'loyalty to the school' and 'school spirit' and every care taken to impress upon senior members of the school the idea of leadership, and a sense of their responsibility to the school and to society. All these measures have had their effect. The school population is now more homogeneous, some pupils have won fairly conspicuous success in sport or examinations, and many boys, well informed, reliable and self-respecting, have caused employers to praise the training they have received. Notwithstanding its considerable achievement, however, the school is as yet unsure of its status. Because of its lack of tradition, and also because it is still housed in old elementary-school buildings, it is usually placed last on the list of grammar-school choices. The speech of its pupils is rough, some of the younger boys are difficult to control and unpolished in their social behaviour, and there are comparatively few pupils who, through their own imagination or because of home tradition, come with much sense of the value of culture or see education at first as anything but a possible avenue to a better-paid job. The headmaster and staff have an uphill struggle, and their undercurrent of anxiety and defensiveness has at least two unfortunate results: in the attempt to promote 'school spirit' and develop leadership there is a tendency to make the more conscientious boys a little too grave and responsible; and, because the school is still to some extent on trial and anxious to justify itself by academic success, some of the less able are pushed rather too hard towards a standard of attainment they cannot achieve without strain.

Before 1902 there were several day grammar schools for boys and a very few for girls.[1] They varied in quality and status, but the best had much in common with the public boarding-schools – indeed, they were often the older foundations – and were regarded as day public schools. Many of them had scholarship places, and it is true that from the Middle Ages there had been in English education a tradition of provision for the poor scholar. Nevertheless, the number of poor children who received higher education was almost negligible.[2] This education, taking the country as a whole, was almost entirely the privilege of the upper classes and substantial middle classes. Thus it was not merely the consequence of material prosperity or social prestige: it was also, with its accompaniments of speech and manners as well as of scholarship, closely identified with their enviable status, and therefore gave those few who were not born to such an education, but acquired it, a clear mark of having 'arrived'.

After 1902 the gauge of the educational ladder was gradually widened.

[1] The North London Collegiate School was founded in 1850. In 1872 the Girls' Public Day School Trust was established.

[2] 'It would be wrong to picture the endowed grammar schools of England at that time as upper class or middle class preserves to which a mere handful of elementary school boys were admitted . . . The justifiable complaint was not that they were socially exclusive, but that there were not really enough of them, so that only about four or five pupils per thousand in elementary schools were able to pass to the grammar schools, a figure which may be contrasted with the two hundred per thousand for whom there are grammar schools today.' *15–18* (The Crowther Report), Ministry of Education, 1960.

The new secondary school was open to a large number of fairly intelligent children whose parents possessed moderate means, and to the intelligent minority of the poor. Many children who might have profited by a secondary education were, however, still excluded. These were chiefly children of good intelligence whose attainment was not quite high enough to enable them to win a scholarship and whose parents could not afford to pay fees. There were also a very few exceptionally able children who, because of family circumstances, would have to leave school and begin earning as soon as possible and whose parents were in any case too poor to afford the expenses incidental to the holding of even a scholarship place. These children seldom sat for the scholarship examination. They left school early, and became the highly skilled artisans, the intelligent and book-loving shop assistants of their generation.

Given this predominantly middle-class population,[1] the maintained secondary school worked out its patterns, sometimes markedly individual but also possessing clearly discernible common qualities – the bourgeois qualities of hard work, ambition, good sense and strict morality, and to varying extents the more aristocratic qualities of scholarly accomplishment, social poise, athletic prowess and leadership cultivated hitherto in the public schools and ancient grammar schools that were at first its only model. The new secondary schools were not quite at ease, for they were conscious of their lack of history and their need to justify the hopes placed in them.[2] They were, however, fortified by the optimism of the public and by the knowledge that they were fulfilling a very evident need. They were also fortunate in being able to attract a very fine body of teachers, men and women educated in the older schools and universities, who found in secondary-school teaching an outlet for their intellectual abilities and who usually brought to their work a civilized and scholarly attitude which set the tone of the schools.[3]

[1] Predominantly but not exclusively. Though too few in number, many even of the earlier secondary schools had fairly large proportions of free places. Moreover, some of the fee-paying parents were of the working classes.

[2] 'In education . . . there is a certain antagonism between quantity and quality . . . A few thoroughly good Secondary Schools are better . . . than a larger number of schools which are of imperfect efficiency, because defective in premises and equipment, in quality of teaching staff or in scope of instruction. In the efforts which are being made by Local Authorities towards a full supply of Provided Secondary Schools this danger has to be very seriously kept in mind.' *Report of the Board of Education for the Year 1908–1909*. Subsequent reports mentioned inefficient schools and some girls' schools in particular that were little more than finishing-schools.

[3] Qualifications varied. Some teachers had not graduated. An elderly headmaster interviewed in the course of this inquiry said: 'The teachers at my secondary school were ex-elementary schoolboys. They had to learn – and they learnt fast.' But many also were of the kind described.

Children taught by these masters and mistresses not only acquired information and skills: they also often became infected by their enthusiasm for learning, and caught from them some grace, perception of beauty or discriminating taste which was not invariably present in their homes but which they and their parents were generally anxious to acquire. Here and there the secondary school had its rough customers – the uncouth, the resistant, the unteachable or even the delinquent – but a large number of those who began as 'odd men out' came under the social and intellectual pressures of the school and eventually conformed fairly well to its demands. Besides, since the secondary school was recognized as holding a position of privilege, the head had one ultimate sanction for those who would not or could not conform. Expulsion was seldom used, seldom even mentioned or thought of; but the possibility of it exerted a silent influence.

For curriculum the secondary schools turned to the classical and mathematical tradition, with its 'modern' additions, of the older schools. From the first, however, they modified and abbreviated the traditional programme of studies[1] and admitted more modern subjects, partly no doubt because their pupils inhabited a more practical and less leisurely world than did the pupils of public schools, and partly because they were conscious of the increasingly complex and varied demands of the society in which the children would live and find employment when they left school. Anxious to establish themselves academically, they welcomed the public examinations of the university bodies, which established a common standard.[2] Performance in these examinations, for the majority of secondary schools, came to be an important criterion of success. To parents the award of the certificate meant that their children had profited by the good teaching they had received; to the schools, a high proportion of examination successes meant that they were teaching on the right lines and could hold up their heads in the company of other secondary schools.

The new schools had a rather slow and doubtful start, but gradually faith was built up from without and self-confidence from within. Teachers knew that, whatever they did in the preliminary stages of the course, the later hurdles were fixed. Children knew that they were expected to work hard and that the tangible reward of hard work would be a certificate, in itself a delightful and enviable badge of ability and success, but also probably a passport to desirable employment. Thus was established a

[1] Greek, for example, was seldom an important element of the curriculum.
[2] The first School and Higher School Certificate examinations were held in 1917. For many years before this, however, the Universities of Oxford and Cambridge had conducted local examinations.

tradition of sound work which earned respect for the quality of secondary-school education, especially when an increasing number of pupils proceeded to the older universities, sometimes with open scholarships which they had won in competition with pupils from public schools. The municipal secondary schools provided almost the entire population of the newer universities, whose development was contemporaneous with their own.

There was, however, in the old fee-paying days, a significant dualism in the work of the secondary school, implicit from the outset in the mode of entry. The scholarship examination was difficult: the examination for fee-payers was much easier and, for children who came up from the preparatory departments which were attached to many schools, often almost nominal. Consequently the range of intellectual capacity was very wide. Not all scholarship-holders, of course, fulfilled their earlier promise, and there were some highly intelligent children among the fee-payers; but in general the scholarship pupils were in 'A' forms, the fee-paying pupils in 'B' and 'C' forms. In one typical 'A' form of the late 1920s in a 'two-stream' school, only six out of thirty pupils were fee-payers, and they had been transferred from the top of a 'B' form.

The curriculum was necessarily modified to suit the varied intellectual powers of the pupils, for most schools would have found it impossible to keep up even a pretence of equality. The School Certificate, too, offered a fairly wide variety of options. The necessity of passing in a language other than English sometimes caused difficulty, but many children even in 'C' forms could be taught, by means of extra lessons, sufficient French to reach the low pass mark. Pupils in 'A' forms were usually expected to gain something approximating to a matriculation certificate,[1] passing in predominantly 'academic' subjects at credit level or above. The others mostly had an easier choice and passed at a lower level. Sometimes, indeed, they found even the pass standard too high for them, and in some schools (not the majority) there was a small form each year consisting of pupils not considered suitable to take the examination.

The interesting thing was that these last-mentioned pupils more frequently than not stayed at school to complete their course. Most of their parents no doubt considered themselves bound by the agreement they had signed. Many, too, probably attached some value to the modicum of book-learning their children were able to absorb, and a great deal to

---

[1] The possibility of fulfilling minimum entrance requirements to universities on the result of the School Certificate examination meant that the popular idea of the function of the examination was confused, and the matriculation exemption was regarded as intrinsically superior, rather than as exemplifying one important but limited purpose of the School Certificate.

the social tone of the school. Nevertheless, as secondary schools became more and more geared to external examinations such pupils felt increasingly inferior, and became apathetic and lazy. By the 1940s it seemed urgently necessary to restore their self-esteem, if only by putting them back into the examination 'stream'.

In many secondary schools the pupils of 'C' forms constituted something of a problem. They formed at least a third of the school population, and could not be ignored. But the secondary school had chosen from the first to play for academic success, to emulate the older schools, and to keep up the pretence that it existed in order to prepare pupils for university. In fact no more than a minority ever proceeded to universities, but this minority was regarded as the *raison d'être* of the school, the curriculum of which therefore ultimately took its colour from university requirements. In most schools this academic bias was taken for granted, and less intelligent pupils whose parents had chosen a secondary education for them were expected to conform. Some concessions, of course, were made. Such pupils did not study difficult subjects like Latin. They usually dropped mathematics (substituting for it arithmetic) and took no more than one scientific subject. If they showed aptitude for a subject such as art, they studied it for examination purposes in place of a subject which exacted a more rigorous mental discipline. For the common subjects, however, such as English and history, they followed much the same course as did the 'A' forms, except that they went more slowly, covered less ground, and did their work less well. The school usually would not risk lowering its standards by making too many concessions to its less able pupils. They were taught, moreover, by specialists who, though often good and stimulating teachers, had been drawn into teaching largely through love of their subject, and measured their success by the degree to which their pupils' work approximated to their own preconceived standard of achievement in it. For all but the most able of their pupils the syllabuses of public examinations represented a rather formidable body of knowledge, and required the mastery of some difficult intellectual conceptions. With 'B' and 'C' forms, therefore, they sometimes yielded to the temptation to substitute memory for understanding and provided their pupils with notes, summaries and ready-made opinions, which were reproduced with fair accuracy and perhaps some understanding in examination papers.

In conduct and demeanour, as well as in work, the less able pupils sometimes caused difficulty. Older teachers will have memories of those overgrown boys and girls (they always seemed to be big!) for whom booklearning had no attraction, who could not concentrate, whose work was weak and inaccurate, who were bored and sometimes insolent, and who expended a great part of their abundant energies in restlessness and noise or in distracting the attention of their companions. Yet there were many unacademic children who seemed to thrive on what in theory should have been an unsuitable type of education. They appeared to enjoy their work, incomprehensible as some of it must have been, they were on good terms with their fellows and their teachers, they took a pride in their school and they sometimes enriched it with valuable social qualities. Moreover, the school usually in the end forced them to show some respect for a world of the mind to which they could have been little drawn by temperament.

The society of the secondary school evolved, with some individual exceptions and variants, and certain geographical differences, according to a characteristic mode. It was at first a somewhat heterogeneous society, and every effort was made to give it coherence by building a tradition and developing a sense of *esprit de corps*. In girls' schools and many boys' schools uniform was obligatory, partly as a means of obliterating differences in wealth and social standing, partly as an outward symbol of unity and of pride in the school. School mottoes were devised, school shields inscribed, and school songs composed – of pious sentiment and usually negligible literary value, as is characteristic of the genre. As already stated, hard work was expected and academic success valued. Games were important, though not as important as in the public school. A prefect system was developed, designed in the best schools not to provide nurse-maids or policemen for the lower forms but to encourage real initiative, responsibility and leadership. The house system, borrowed from boarding-school education, was used as a stimulus to work and games through the fostering of a competitive yet corporate spirit; it also sometimes provided older pupils with opportunities for organization, and allowed smaller social groups within the community to acquire their own reputations and patterns of success in sport, games, music and other activities. School societies of many kinds developed, and members of staff gave generously of their out-of-school time to encouraging these societies or to coaching games. All these activities, supplemented by the growth of old-pupils' associations with their accompanying benefactions to the school and customs designed to perpetuate tradition, tended to create a compact school community, aware of itself and bound together by partly real and partly artificial loyalties.

The secondary school was not a completely closed society. For one thing, it was a day school, whose pupils were returned every evening and week-end to the influences of the social forces exercised by family and neighbourhood. Within the school, too, one form at least of wider social awareness was fostered: pupils were trained to remember those less fortunate than themselves, and to look on their advantages and privileges as a trust. This bourgeois counterpart of *noblesse oblige* was emphasized in various ways. Regular contributions were made to school funds for charities, and the proceeds of Christmas services or harvest festivals used for the relief of the poor and the sick. Some schools went farther: for instance, they 'adopted' elementary schools in poor districts, giving Christmas presents to the children and organizing parties and picnics for them. Such contacts aroused the social sympathies and consciences of boys and girls and were the starting-point of many careers in medicine, teaching, nursing and other forms of social service. During the Second World War the tradition of service bore its fruit, and a large amount of useful and frequently courageous work in hospitals and elsewhere was done by pupils of secondary schools.

This conception of voluntary unpaid service to the community, so successfully inculcated by some schools, was – and is, where it survives – a most valuable bulwark against the rising tide of materialist preoccupations. Yet all these doctrines and practices, admirable and wholly desirable though they were, stressed the difference even while promoting the contact. The secondary school, in fact, was consciously though not arrogantly superior. Its world – the schools of which played one another at games, debated with one another and attended one another's concerts and plays – was a well-defined world, inhabited sometimes with slight condescension by the older grammar school and with diffidence or aggressiveness by some new and struggling schools, but on the whole self-contained and recognizing its members by many tacit acceptances and rejections, some superficial, some of fundamental significance.

A strict standard of behaviour, both inside and outside the school, was expected. Morals, in the conventional sense, were taken for granted; the parents of any pupil known certainly to be an undesirable influence would be asked to remove him. Within the school such phenomena as stealing were very rare indeed; other forms of dishonesty such as lying and cheating were actively discouraged and, if not entirely eliminated, kept to a minimum. In this, as in other matters, the school depended on clearly-defined standards the validity of which was unquestioned.

The secondary school, then, was a respected institution, based on a set of assumptions evolved out of the tacit agreement on aims and purposes which existed between the teachers and the sections of society for which they provided. Education was felt to be a good thing. At the lowest level it was seen as a passport to material advancement or social acceptability; at the highest there was a hint of absolute values, a reflection of nineteenth-century dreams of liberal education. The children were bound to be influenced by this unanimity. Boys and girls have a natural and salutary resistance to the pedagogue, but they are also eager to perceive and acquire the values of the adult world, or that section of it in which they move. Beneath all fluctuations of pattern, and normal manifestations of naughtiness or recalcitrance, most of them unconsciously acquiesced in their elders' assumption that secondary education was something to be worked for and valued.

It might be thought that the influences and development so far surveyed were conducive to a complacent and joyless uniformity. Certainly there was a discernible strain of primness, and evidence of standards rather anxiously imposed and received, in some secondary schools. But fortunately there were factors, some of them powerful, working in the opposite direction. First, and perhaps most important, was the fact that though the secondary schools were within a national system they were also to a high degree autonomous. Several schools soon earned a distinctive reputation under the influence of a fervently convinced headmaster or headmistress. A boys' school, for example, developed a strong tradition of character, initiative and intellectual flexibility through serious and arduous exploration entailing fairly severe trials of physical endurance. A girls' school forty years ago was investigating the possibilities of dance, drama and creative writing. The list could be almost indefinitely continued. Though sharing common characteristics, these schools were among themselves intensely and even fiercely individual. And if the heads were strong individualists, so were the staffs. Eccentrics – and there seemed to be some in every school – might have been laughed at or feared, but were often felt to add lustre to the school. Moreover, if they were scholars with a passion for their subject they could kindle that passion in a clever pupil and, by submitting him to the utmost rigours of intellectual discipline, train him to be a thinker and a student.

Another factor mitigated the potential severity of what might otherwise have been a too consciously prescribed régime. This was the easy relationship which usually developed between pupils and staff. It must be remembered that teachers derived, though often unconsciously, considerable support from the expectations of society. Those virtues of application, industry and honesty, that belief in the value of sound instruction, were the accepted values of the middle-class world which was ruffled but not disintegrated by the experiences of the First World War. Such difficulties as they encountered largely consisted of the relatively restricted and familiar resistances of children to their elders, not those which are deeply rooted in an almost wholly different set of social assumptions. Here and there was a child who, they recognized with a shock, had to be trained from the beginning; but such a pupil was rare enough for teachers to be able to devote some extra time and thought to him, while the social forces of the school, and of the community outside, were working strongly to bring him within the accepted circle, or in the last resort to pronounce him unacceptable. The standards of the secondary school, therefore, were not exactly an artificial mould, except in the sense that all training for civilization is an artificial mould for the primitive being within the child. They corresponded with the aspirations, if not the invariable practice, of the rising classes. Though there was little compromise in teachers' demands, and probably little self-questioning, they were able to be on good and friendly terms with their pupils. They were dealing with children who spoke the same language as themselves, or whose parents earnestly wanted them to learn it. Consequently the discipline of the secondary school, though firm, was usually not harsh, and indeed at its best was a model of humane, gentle and sane relationship.

This, then, is the picture of the secondary school as it developed during the earlier part of the century. Before 1944 it was already becoming modified. As stated above, certain local authorities had early abolished fees. Some made this move prematurely, and had to reinstate a fee-paying system. Others made it in the later 1930s and maintained free secondary education, so that the 1944 Act might not at first seem to have made a great difference to them. The majority of secondary schools, however, retained fee-paying places (even if they had diminished the number), and some preparatory departments continued to exist, right up to 1944. Moreover, even where all places had become free, an important principle had remained. Though the abolition of fees meant that a certain number of the less clever children who would formerly have obtained admission was excluded, the secondary school still usually remained the deliberate choice of those who sent their children to it. No doubt there was some pressure from primary-school teachers, when parental apathy existed, to enable a promising child to take the selection examination. In general, however, the fact that a child took the examination meant that his parents strongly and consciously desired a secondary education for him. When he entered the school, they expected it to provide a distinctive and markedly superior type of education which would exact from him hard intellectual effort and conformity to its conventions of dress, behaviour and general outlook; and they were themselves prepared to make, in his interest, considerable sacrifices of time, money and personal convenience over a period of years.

By 1940 reform seemed overdue. On one side were the secondary schools, providing an academic education for a minority of the nation's children. Such education, with its gaze fixed ultimately on the universities and the professions, was manifestly designed for the intelligent. Yet in a good number of districts it was being given to many children of only mediocre ability whose parents could afford to pay for it, and denied to children who were their intellectual superiors but whose parents were too poor, too timidly class-conscious or too apathetic to send them as fee-payers. In some districts the only children from the poorer classes able to obtain this education were of exceptional ability, and, moreover, children of unusually discerning and self-sacrificing parents. On the other side – if we disregard the large number of unreorganized elementary schools – were the senior schools, containing children who represented every degree of mental ability except the very highest, most of whose representatives had gone to the secondary school. A few even of these remained within the elementary system, where circumstances had prevented the child from taking a scholarship place. The curriculum of these schools, far from depending on university standards and old heritages of scholarship, was painfully growing up from below, adding, by a slow and uncertain process of accretion, new deposits to a structure which had originated in the requirements of mere literacy and computation and which had indeed in its nineteenth-century days shown a reluctance to admit any elements that might make the poor discontented with their lot or raise them above their station.[1] Between these two parts of the national system was a small indeterminate territory represented by the selective central school.

Founded rather optimistically from 1911 onwards to provide a further education than that of the senior schools for children supposedly intelligent but not bookish, some central schools had succeeded in fulfilling most of the original intention and were giving a good general education, often with a bias in the older forms towards commercial or technical studies. Many more, however, like their predecessors the higher grade and higher elementary schools, tended to become increasingly academic as

[1] The ruling of the Government Auditor, Mr. T. B. Cockerton, in 1900 – that it was illegal for school boards to use public money to support higher grade schools – while it was one of the precipitating causes of the 1902 Education Act, also showed clearly that elementary education was officially restricted still to the elements of education.

they met with success, took external examinations, and probably hoped
for the apotheosis of recognition as secondary schools. Though interesting,
these schools formed only a small part of the major situation, the essential
problem of which was the antithesis between senior and secondary
schools.

The policy followed, which of course owed much to the Spens an
Norwood Reports, was a rational application of the doctrine of equalit
of opportunity. The secondary school was giving, so the argument ra
an education suitable for the intelligent, yet it contained many childr
not clever enough to profit by it. These children not only kept out oth
more suitable, pupils: they themselves would find more happiness a
self-fulfilment in a less academic type of education. The senior sch
contained many who were capable of meeting much more exact
intellectual demands, and were either longing for the opportunitie
secondary education or sinking into boredom and mischief because
were insufficiently stretched. Such misplacement, and such wastag
intellectual resources, could not be allowed to continue, especially
an obvious remedy was at hand. First, secondary education (in th
sense) must be denied to no one possessing the capacity to profit
a capacity understood to be roughly equivalent to mental ability. Sec
education must no longer be divided into 'elementary' and 'secor
perpetuating a class distinction which had ceased to be tolerable
term 'secondary', which had come to connote 'middle-class and aca
must be given the more logical meaning of 'post-primary', and
new sense would represent the whole field of education for childr
eleven, differentiated according to the ability and aptitude of th
This policy became law and accomplished an educational re
overnight.[2] In some areas, where it completed a process which ha
been at work for a number of years, the shock was at first scar
in others it was violent: throughout the country it created a di
and disequilibrium the effects of which were and are profoun
still difficult to assess.

The first effect among the public at large was one of mild ex
Education, which has seldom had major news value, can

[1] It had been deprecated by the Hadow Report of 1927 and the Spens R
both of which advocated an educational division, based on age alone, int
secondary stages.
[2] The 1944 Education Act did not stipulate how secondary education shoul
Most authorities, however, following the Norwood Report, kept a potent
system of grammar/technical/modern schools, though in fact the technical
developed in comparatively few areas. Since fees and special places were nov
had of course to devise means of selection for all types of secondary school.

acquiring it in the days succeeding the Butler Act. The imminent end of
the war, and the dreams which many people had of a time of relaxation,
leisure and plenty, coincided with the growing conviction which had
penetrated dimly even to the unreflecting: that our destiny lay with the
coming generation, and that education, rightly developed (not perverted
as in Hitler's Germany) offered the best hope of preventing future follies,
crimes and disasters. Evacuation, too, had shocked the public conscience,
and education was vaguely seen as a possible instrument of social reform.
The exhilaration, however, was short-lived. Scarcity of teachers, inadequacy of buildings and lack of 'secondary' tradition prevented many
senior schools from getting off to the flying start of post-war optimism.
'Secondary school, indeed!' said a head teacher in the Midlands who was
struggling with the difficulties of hideous, noisy, inadequate and insanitary
buildings; the legacy of illiteracy left by evacuation; pupils many of
whose families were well acquainted with the police-court and the proba-
tion officer; and a too small staff, which included a newly-qualified girl of
nineteen. 'I've told my children not to have any such nonsense. If they
can learn to be a decent senior school that's quite good enough for me.'

Some parents, too, who had previously regarded the secondary school
with envious but ill-defined admiration and had not been averse to the
idea that their child would now acquire a secondary education without
having had the trouble of winning it, were surprised and disillusioned
when they found that apparently the new secondary school was still the
old senior school in all but name. Others, chagrined to discover that they
could no longer purchase the old kind of secondary education for their
children, though able and willing to do so, sent them to private schools or,
with bitterness and reluctance, to the secondary modern school. Despite
many encouragements and favours, this school faced a hard battle against
odds to achieve its new status. The battle, which is still going on, is full of
interest to the educational observer. Our attention, however, must be
turned to the grammar school, which has undergone a change of at least
equivalent importance.

It might perhaps have been expected that, whatever the difficulties of the secondary modern school, the grammar school after
1944 would suffer no disturbance in its progress, and might indeed proceed
the faster for being relieved of the burden of its least intelligent pupils.
In fact, the changes, marked or unobtrusive, which have come upon the
grammar-school world in the last sixteen years have made it as a whole less
self-confident, less optimistic, less sure of its objectives, more defensive
and more vulnerable. It has to examine and assess these changes if it is to

survive to meet the challenge of the day and to preserve for a new population the benefit of the old secondary school.

One effect of the Act was to introduce, even among grammar schools themselves, sharp distinctions between one kind of school and another. These distinctions are based first on the degree of independence of the schools. After 1944, those schools which possessed some endowments (not always large) were faced with an important decision concerning their future. They might indeed apply for the desirable direct-grant status; many of them did so but were denied it, for direct grant was given only to a strictly limited number of schools, and some which had possessed that status now actually lost it. The endowed schools then had to choose between 'going independent' and facing the financial risks attendant on a complete absence of Ministry aid, or sinking their pride and allowing themselves, endowments and all, to be fully maintained by the local authority. As things turned out, if a school had any financial resources to speak of the risks of choosing independence were less than had been feared,[1] for the prestige of any schools with pretensions to exclusiveness tended to increase, while middle-class parents whose children had failed to 'pass' the selection examination eagerly seized whatever chance existed of obtaining a fee-paying place in an independent school, thus rescuing from extinction, or even bringing into being, some schools that gave an education much inferior to that provided by most local authorities. Independent schools, of course, retain full control over their finances and the admission of pupils and thus cannot be said to come within the State-maintained system. Direct-grant schools are virtually independent but are within that system. They too control the admission of their pupils, all but the highly intelligent minority admitted to free places, who would in any case usually be desirable pupils on the schools' own criteria. These schools preserve a pupil population very much like that which they had before 1944.

In some ways the Act flattened out distinctions in the maintained grammar schools, which have now lost many little individual privileges they once possessed, and are under the much closer surveillance of local authorities. New distinctions, however, have come to be emphasized. Let us consider two boys' grammar schools, A and B, in a city which possesses three such schools. In former days school A charged considerably higher fees than did school B. There was thus a fairly well marked class distinction between the two schools. As school A was more expensive,

---

[1] Nevertheless, when the direct-grant list was reopened in 1956, many good schools which had previously chosen independence were eager to be placed on the list.

and therefore more desirable to many, it tended to receive the more intelligent of the scholarship boys. But it also received a wide range of intellectual capacities among its fee-payers, since its exclusiveness in this field was more dependent on money than on brains. School B had its own assets. True, it did not usually receive the outstanding scholarship boys, but most scholarship children had at least good intelligence. Among its fee-payers were those whose parents could just afford its low fees and chose it in preference to the elementary school, sometimes for reasons of petty snobbery, but more often from a sober and genuine desire to buy, perhaps through their own sacrifices, the best possible education for their child. Such parents wanted their children to do well, assisted them to conform to the school's requirements, and trusted and valued the school for the education it had to give.

Now, not only does school A still possess the few intelligences at the very top, as it did in the past: the average level of intelligence in the school has also risen. For, no longer deterred by monetary considerations and delighted by the thought that A, so inaccessible in the past, may now be open to their children, most parents put it as their first choice among the grammar schools. When the results are announced, A finds that it has perhaps three times as many applicants as it can take. It is thus able to admit a highly selected entry, and is fast becoming as exclusive as before. (The exclusiveness is now of brains rather than money, though money still counts in a school where certain things are *de rigueur*). School B at the same time has lost many of its former loyal fee-paying clientèle who no longer qualify for entry, and also the equivalent of its former scholarship boys, most of whom will have gone to school A, having passed the examination at a level approximately that of the top of A's former fee-payers. It still receives a few boys who, through family tradition or because of their parents' real regard for some qualities of the school, have made it their first choice. For many boys, however, it will be the second or third choice. Consequently it will receive many pupils who are placed low by the selection examination. Among them will be some who are vexed and discouraged at having failed to gain admission to the school of their choice and others to whom, and to whose families, the idea of grammar-school education is so strange that they enter the school with few expectations and few potential loyalties. Among these are the boys who will be the unteachables of the middle school or the premature leavers in the fourth year, while the parents of several boys now unwillingly attending the secondary modern school would have given all they could to obtain for their children the education that school B had to offer, and would have seen to it that they pursued their school studies as far as possible.

Indeterminate as the category of grammar school may be, and varied as are its actual examples, the idea of a grammar-school education continues to be immensely attractive to many people. Those who before 1944 advocated the reform of the secondary-school system usually envisaged a new system, the component parts of which would be distinguishable from one another but recognized as variants of a single concept. That is, in the terms 'secondary grammar', 'secondary technical' and 'secondary modern' the second word would be parenthetical and subsidiary to the first; or, if the rather clumsy terms were abbreviated, they would be to the words 'grammar', 'technical' and 'modern', with the general and unifying word 'secondary' always understood. This, however, was to ask people to accept a theory first and then make it work in practice, a procedure alien to pragmatic English tastes. What happened was that both the general public and the grammar schools abandoned the word 'secondary' without a struggle in the term 'secondary grammar school'. The schools themselves found no difficulty in doing this. 'Grammar' had always been an honourable and an older alternative to 'secondary'. Technical schools had never had the word 'secondary' firmly attached to them and, when they began admitting children at the age of eleven, were felt to be sufficiently identifiable as technical schools: some, however, proclaimed the selective nature of their entry by calling themselves 'technical high' schools. The word 'secondary' was thus almost from the beginning reserved for the rest – the former senior and central schools – which, at first labelled 'secondary modern', are now becoming increasingly known simply as 'secondary'. (A well-known publisher of educational textbooks recognizes the *fait accompli* by publishing two lists, one for 'secondary' and one for 'grammar' schools.) Secondary modern schools, therefore, acquired the prestige label just in time to find that it was no longer a prestige label. The public and the grammar school saw to it that there should still remain a privileged institution within the State system.

This verbal development is so simple and so well known that to draw attention to it would be futile but for the fact that it points to something beyond terminology. In the eyes of the theorist it seems both stupid and annoying that the public substitutes the word 'grammar' for 'secondary', keeping its concept of a superior school unaltered; and that it persists in regarding the selection examination, ostensibly distributive in function, as competitive, and continues to talk of 'scholarships' though all places in maintained grammar schools have long since been free. Can 'equality of opportunity' and 'parity of esteem', so long elusive, be made present realities only through a system of comprehensive schools: or, if comprehensive schools became the rule rather than the exception, would the pressure for an exclusive type of education break out in a new form? Is the desire for a grammar-school education due only to snobbery or acquisitiveness – my need to feel socially superior to my neighbour or to beat him to a better job – or is there in it a blind and dumb recognition of the existence of a domain of thought and values in some fashion essential to the good life, the way to which and through which is strenuous and difficult? Is the grammar school an extravagance we cannot now afford – or must a nation no longer rich in the nineteenth-century sense concentrate its resources of intelligence in such a school, in order to protect and develop the powers of execution and of leadership necessary if it is to preserve its material standard of living and its capacity for economic competition with other countries? If the grammar school is to remain, what should be its size, and what percentage of children should it admit? Assuming the desirability of grammar-school education, should the number of available places be increased, or should such education, in order to preserve its academic quality, be restricted everywhere to less than the present national average of about 19 per cent of a given age group?[1] Is there anything except the mere name that links the great diversity of schools at present labelled 'grammar'? Should the grammar schools of the future become more diverse or more uniform? Has the task of the grammar school changed? Must those who teach in it question their former assumptions and become more flexible in order to meet more satisfactorily the needs of new elements in their population, or do the strength and value of the grammar school lie in its conservatism? Any attempt to give even a partial answer to such questions entails a careful examination of present-day assumptions and attitudes.

---

[1] The Ministry of Education Report on Education in 1958 gives the number of 12-year-old pupils in maintained grammar schools and grammar 'streams' in bilateral and multilateral schools as 102,673 out of a total of 564,021 in maintained secondary schools of all kinds. It is not possible to reach an exact percentage, as direct-grant and independent schools have not been counted, and some of the 17,201 12-year-old pupils in comprehensive schools would have been receiving a grammar-school type of education.

2

The Grammar-School Paradox

In woods, in waves, in warres, she wonts to dwell,
And wil be found with perill and with paine:
Ne can the man that moulds in ydle cell
Unto her happy mansion attaine:
Before her gate high God did Sweate ordaine,
And wakefull watches ever to abide;
But easy is the way and passage plaine
To pleasures pallace: it may soon be spide,
And day and night her dores to all stand open wide.

Spenser: *The Faerie Queene.*

TEACHERS of the '30s on the whole knew their task. In curricular
terms it was to train their pupils up to the age of about sixteen for
the School Certificate at the two levels described in Chapter 1,
and afterwards for the Higher School Certificate and university entrance
examinations. The public-examination system set a standard and goal for
the curriculum. It was also constructed with some realistic appreciation of
the pupils' varied powers, though this appreciation was shown more in
the exceedingly wide range of the graded pass mark than in the character
of the syllabus, which tended to be heavy and factual. In mathematics,
for example, much emphasis was laid on 'bookwork'; in history on
accounts of events, and of the causes of this and the consequences of that;
in English on a study of set books which demanded detailed knowledge of
the text and usually much learning of explanatory notes and comments.
There were, it is true, reforming influences at work, seeking to test
capacity for thought and action rather than rote learning, and the examination was modified as time went on by such things as, in geography,
considerable emphasis on map-reading and the introduction of a new type
of answer-book. To the end of the period, however, it remained broadly
true that a pupil could gain a creditable School Certificate by means of
industrious learning even if this were unaccompanied by a great deal of
insight.

To say this is not to suggest that the pre-war secondary school was a place of mere cramming. Given good teachers and clever children, and there were plenty of both, it was possible to make a curriculum geared to this examination significant and valuable. A really brilliant teacher could even then elude examination pressure without penalizing the children. To many of the less able pupils, though, the curriculum must have presented itself as a mass of 'knowledge to be acquired and facts to be stored',[1] a programme which demanded much application and power of memory, and allowed little time for relaxation. And even this considerable task grew more difficult for teachers and pupils as additional subject-matter came to be seen desirable for secondary-school study. Some of the additions made were to examination syllabuses, as 'social history' increased in importance, or scientific knowledge became more complex and more difficult. Some took the form of extra periods devoted to such topics as civics, art appreciation, or philosophy, for which, in proportion as they were thought desirable, room had to be found in the already crowded timetable.

Critics were not wanting. In the very early years of secondary education, A. N. Whitehead[2] had pointed out the futility and danger of inert ideas and said that the merely well-informed man was the most useless bore on God's earth. By 1941 Sir Richard Livingstone[3] could write of the bursting portmanteau of the secondary school, and ask pertinently whether a child of fourteen could be said to be capable of learning the meaning, in any true sense of the word, of the Treaty of Utrecht. But within the schools the programme was seldom seriously questioned. There was indeed much to recommend it to both teachers and pupils. It is always satisfactory to have a clearly defined assignment, however difficult: once this has been seen and accepted (and to teach in a secondary school was *ipso facto* to accept it) energies can be bent with single-minded concentration to the work. Teachers who maintained the régime of the '30s were themselves the products of a similar régime, which most of them had accepted and enjoyed. It is in any case difficult to dissociate oneself from early disciplines and not regard them as a datum of life, or at least of a certain kind of life.

And these teachers were the successful ones. They were, perhaps, the

---

[1] 'The curriculum of the primary school is to be thought of in terms of activity and experience rather than of knowledge to be acquired and facts to be stored.' Board of Education report on *The Primary School, 1931* (quoted in the Spens Report, p. 152).

[2] *The Aims of Education*, by A. N. Whitehead (Lecture delivered in 1912).

[3] *The Future in Education*, by Sir Richard Livingstone (Cambridge University Press, 1941).

natural scholars, to whom the disciplines had never been difficult; or they had triumphed over the difficulties after a hard struggle, and therefore unconsciously depended for their self-esteem upon remaining on easy terms with their old adversaries; or – but this was rare – they had only imperfectly won their victory, and must seek constant reassurance through the minor triumphs of their pupils. Some of the pupils were as able as their teachers, or abler. They apparently justified the programme by their easy success, which was in reality largely due to the capacity of the intelligent in every generation to make learning-material significant for themselves. Others were very much less clever; some indeed would never catch the rhythm of the French tongue, or truly understand the principle of division by fractions. But by patient and skilful teaching – and much of it was very skilful – they could be brought to learn the forms of French verbs and the rules of agreement. They could be taught the motions of division by fractions, and much more complicated manœuvres than these. They could tabulate and learn the effects of the Industrial Revolution or give an account of the Battle of Trafalgar. Provided pupils wished to learn, and were even moderately intelligent, the staff could teach them almost anything; almost anything, that is, in the form in which it could be tested by public examination.

But why should a pupil wish to learn? For, in spite of Dr. Johnson and the Argonauts, every child is not willing to give all he has to acquire knowledge, at any rate in the form in which teachers dispense it. Yet teachers in secondary schools, though they had their pedagogical troubles, could on the whole count on the acquiescence of their pupils. This was because, while no public outcry was heard in those days about selection procedures, a silent and most effective method of selection was constantly in operation, ensuring for the schools pupils who, however varied in other respects, were a much more homogeneous group in their acceptance of the teaching-situation than, except in a small number of schools, the grammar-school population has ever been since 1944. Scholarship-holders represented a minority of their age-group and of their class. They had struggled to get into the school, and it was in their interest to accept its conditions. Parents supported them. In those years of recurrent depressions and unemployment they desperately wanted white-collar work for their children, partly because it was better paid and more secure, partly because it offered the child a release from the grim physical conditions of their own life. The child had a foot on the rung of the ladder and was not going to be dislodged if he or his parents could prevent it. In the world, as they knew it,

Those that were up themselves kept others low;
Those that were low themselves held others hard;
Ne suffered them to ryse or greater grow;
But every one did strive his fellow downe to throw.

The competition was bitter indeed. Not even a secondary-school education could guarantee economic security. Of the candidates who presented
themselves on a typical day in 1933 to be interviewed for one job in a
warehouse at 17s. 6d. a week, twenty had matriculated. It was not sufficient to be well educated – you must excel. It was also a bosses' world.
If you were ever to penetrate it, it was not enough to be good at your
books. You must speak the bosses' language. Small wonder that the
scholarship children tried hard.

Fee-payers' children were also predisposed to acquiescence. Perhaps
they did not feel so directly the fierce economic strains to which the
scholarship children were exposed. Yet their situation was not so very
different. The hazards were there, in the background, menacing all. If
the scholarship-holders were struggling to gain a position, they were
struggling to maintain one. In addition, and perhaps more strongly
motivating them to fit in, was the fact that at school they were for the
most part in a familar world, the middle-class world of their parents. To
question the assumptions of the school was similar, though in a less
degree, to questioning those of the home. Finally, most powerful argument
of all, perhaps: their parents paid for them, and no one is going to pay
for what he does not value. These parents wanted their child to accept the
school. If necessary, they put pressure on him to do so. He must at least
try. If, despite the efforts of home and school, he made not the slightest
attempt to adjust himself, they would remove him. Therefore, in both
fee-payers' and scholarship children the teacher, though he was largely
unconscious of the fact, was perpetually teaching an acquiescent residue.

Of course this picture is over-simplified: it is also a 'still' of what was in
reality an unfolding drama. The examination syllabus was not invariably
quite so heavy, nor were teachers quite so rigidly bound by it, as has been
suggested. Children and their families were not always conscious of being
driven. In any case, as Mrs. Floud[1] and her colleagues have pointed out,
economic conditions in the '30s were very different in, for example,
Watford and Middlesbrough. Scholarship children did not always come
from back-to-back houses, nor were all fathers unemployed. Children
in the school were not all consciously motivated by ambition or fear.

---

[1] *Social Class and Educational Opportunity*, by E. Floud, A. H. Halsey and F. M. Martin
(Heinemann, 1956).

As for 'acquiescence', some teachers would have had difficulty in recognizing it, for they met their share of lazy, resistant, and mischievous children. The relationship between social conditions and educational assumptions has also been made to seem more direct than in fact it was, and the persons involved more conscious of their motives than most people ever are. Nevertheless, it remains true that many forces of the time conspired to make the secondary school an acknowledged repository of established values; the best agent of upward social mobility (in the previous generation it had shared this role with the evening class and the Workers' Educational Association); and the best insurance against unemployment and poverty. The wind that blew strongly in Middlesbrough was felt faintly even in Watford, and the climate of the time was favourable to the secondary school.

It must not be forgotten that teachers also were highly selected. In the '30s it was not at all uncommon for young graduates with good honours degrees and usually with professional training to be unemployed for a time, or to accept of necessity posts hundreds of miles from their homes, or to go into elementary schools.[1] This meant that heads and governing bodies were able to exercise a fine degree of discrimination when appointing a new member of staff, and could construct staffs very carefully calculated both to provide the right teaching-balance and also to perpetuate the attitudes and traditions most desired. A teacher could be, and indeed often was, rejected because of wearing the wrong shoes, or showing too little interest in games. Understandably, teachers tended to show a meticulous observance of protocol. They wrote carefully conventional letters of application; they stayed in a post for what the head considered a reasonable length of time; they gave due notice of their intention to leave. It is not suggested that their own inclinations in any way ran counter to such a procedure: only that the times were conducive to professional correctitude.

The school situation probably seems now to have been more stable than in fact it was. Throughout the whole period of State secondary education there have been forces making for change, and in the 1930s they were gathering momentum. Events abroad and at home – the Third Reich, the Spanish Civil War, Abyssinia, the Abdication, the 'King and Country' resolution in the Oxford Union, the growing number of refugees – from all these flowed powerful ripples that rocked the complacency of

[1] 'Though the number of graduates (19,600) in the grant-earning secondary schools is very much larger than the number (11,800) in the elementary schools the number of trained graduates in each type of school is approximately the same: 12,300 in the secondary schools and 11,800 in the elementary schools.' *The McNair Report*, 1944.

the school. Teachers might still read Kipling with their classes: outside
was the world of the Hollow Men, and a contemporary poet was writing

> Oh hush thee, my baby,
> Thy cradle's in pawn.

Team spirit, loyalty to the school, pride in its symbols, might be fostered;
but if, in the thought of the time, the public school itself was not sacro-
sanct – if the old school tie was becoming an object of derision – so much
the more vulnerable was the secondary school. Mass influences, too, were
beginning to be felt in earnest, with the incipient Americanization of the
Press and entertainment.[1] Even the composition of the school population
was altering, for the increasing number of free places opened the doors to
'new' children who, as older teachers began to realize with alarm, could
neither be taught nor controlled as easily as their predecessors. The world
was changing. But the rate of acceleration was still manageable by the
human consciousness; it was possible for working purposes to make
assumptions which would be constant for the five or seven years of a
pupil's life; and when war came, though it necessarily brought violent
disruptions and compelled undreamed-of adaptations, in some respects it
actually created a moratorium, in which both staff and children were
disposed on the whole to emphasize the conservative properties of school,
and (in face of the inevitable modifications caused by war) to hold fast
to what was stable and reassuring.

The war ended. One by one the lights came on. Optimism and dis-
illusionment, self-restraint and ruthless hedonism, made a strangely mixed
pattern in the web of the contemporary consciousness. Abroad, a schoolmaster from Shanghai said to an Englishwoman in America: 'All the world
is looking to Britain; no other country can show such magnificent self-
discipline.' An Indian official at the United Nations Headquarters
commented that the moral leadership of this country had never stood so
high. At home 'Austerity' Cripps fought a losing battle. Now that the
immediate danger was past, the reaction was too strong. The wave of
idealism that had carried both the Welfare State and the Education Act
receded, leaving the new social structure and the new educational system
existent certainly, but hardly buoyant.

The doors of the grammar school were opened wide at a time when,
even had its structure and population continued unchanged, it would

---

[1] 'Europe has not been Americanized . . . The triumph of the masses and the magnificent
uprising of the vital level have come about in Europe for internal reasons . . . But it so
happens that the result coincides with the most marked aspect of American life.' Ortega
y Gasset in *The Revolt of the Masses*, 1930.

with difficulty have remained a stable institution. Staffs had lost their resilience. Whether they had been in an evacuation or a reception area, they had had to deal with the upheaval, emotional even more than physical, caused by the evacuation. Later, many of them had endured the long strain of air raids, often beset by domestic difficulties, and at school attempting to do advanced work under dangerous and bizarre conditions. Women had taught in boys' schools, many of their colleagues being elderly men who bore too many responsibilities. In both boys' and girls' schools the size of classes had swollen almost unendurably, and standards of learning had declined in consequence. For pupils as well as staff the alarms of war and sorrows of bereavement had undermined the old securities. When the former teachers came back, some were lost for ever to other professions, and others did not easily readjust themselves to their old work. Many found it an anticlimax; nearly all discovered that in a hundred ways the school to which they returned was not the school they had left. Most nebulous, but perhaps most important of all: belief in progress, which had inspired the nineteenth-century development of education, had finally died; and the eschatological Christian outlook which perhaps alone could have provided a compensatory sense of significance was not sufficiently strong to be effective.

Less optimism. Less faith, hope or charity. But also less adversity. As the last of rationing ended and the period of inflation began – with almost full employment and goods returning to the shops – the time was ripe for the fruition of what Ortega y Gasset had seen beginning in European society two decades earlier:

> The common man, finding himself in a world so excellent technically and socially, believes that it has been produced by nature, and never thinks of the personal efforts of highly endowed individuals which the creation of this world presupposed. Still less will he admit the notion that all these faculties still require the support of certain difficult human virtues, the least failure of which would cause the rapid disappearance of the whole magnificent edifice.

In the English tradition there has long been a place for the industrious apprentice and the honest merchant, both of whose virtues were harnessed to satisfyingly tangible rewards. The principles of these folklore figures, together with the lingering imperative of Christian ethics, made it comparatively easy for a respectable family to accept, even to receive as unacknowledged and perhaps unrecognized assumptions, the somewhat severe and strenuous demands of the grammar school. Now, however, when a good general education is not so clearly an economic asset, when the inherent philistinism of the average Englishman can no longer be overcome by an appeal to either his principles or his pocket, these demands operate with a greatly weakened force. Many grammar-school teachers are at present inclined to look back wistfully to the days when they drew most of their pupils from middle-class homes. It is doubtful whether they have yet begun to realize that even with their former clients they can no longer rest on an implicit identity of expectations, and must therefore without delay re-examine their own assumptions and rediscover, or if necessary re-create, a basis for their academic, behavioural and ethical demands.

It is not merely that older drives, taboos and values have largely disappeared. If the school operated amid conscious frustrations and deprivations, if the sense of loss were poignant, education might be eagerly welcomed as providing a sense of purpose and a refuge from boredom. But despair and loneliness are seldom explicit, and often masquerade as their opposites. People need never be alone. Exotic luxuries of the past are now commonplace. Recreation and entertainment may be had cheaply and readily. At the same time the element of rationality is largely missing from human endeavour. In a system of highly standardized wages and salaries the slacker, provided he keeps above a low minimum, will not be penalized, and his industrious colleague will not be rewarded – if he hopes to make a fortune he must look to the Stock Exchange or the pools. Wonder, except in the excitement of a gamble with chance, has been destroyed. Great works of literature, art and music may be obtained in cheap editions, reproductions or hi-fi recording. But even if accessible as never before, the high products of thought and creative achievement have not to an appreciable extent enriched, though they have in a sense reached, the communal consciousness. They have become the province of a sophisticated minority who, being neither common men nor the acknowledged leaders of society, tend to be suspected by both, not without reason, of preciosity and decadence. Members of this minority are conscious of their alienation, and often adopt the role of prophet, eccentric or 'outsider'. To the average person the very mechanisms of our civilization, even its creature comforts or its life-savers – its television, radio, transport, heating, lighting, its isotopes and antibiotics – come as end-products. They are accepted without understanding.

The attributes of creditable achievement in modern England are ease, enjoyment of end-products, and publicity. The socially approved attitude is to be tolerant and non-committal. Yet these characteristics are, as

Riesman[1] in America and Hoggart[2] in England have pointed out, inextricably mingled with residual but still strong ideals of persistence, thrift, ambition and rectitude. In such circumstances the grammar school may well feel like Thor in the hall of the giants, when, taking a pull at the drinking-horn, he found that he was trying to drain the fathomless ocean. And teachers are themselves part of the situation. Among them, as in all professions, can be found a minority of the lazy, inefficient or cynical. With these we need not here concern ourselves. Most of the rest, whatever their years, are of the older, 'inner-directed' type – conscientious, strenuous, and somewhat intolerant. But there is a sprinkling of other attitudes, especially among young teachers. The new-style teacher (and it must be remembered that many, perhaps most, young teachers are 'old-style') is pleasant, easy, not so acutely conscious of standards nor so zealous for their maintenance.

In this changed society the role of the school as an institution has also been modified. During the war the school was obviously the most convenient and suitable body to carry out the feeding-arrangements for children. It was perhaps appropriate that after the war it should continue as an instrument of the Welfare State, especially since it became an increasingly common custom in most sections of society for both parents to go out to work. Some of the consequences of this development in the function of the school are well known: we have heard much of the burden of teachers' extra 'duties', and indeed they are a serious item in an already heavy programme. There are, however, deeper consequences than this. The school now takes responsibility for its children during many more hours of the day. It even – most symbolic of actions – gives them milk, thus underlining its appropriation of quasi-parental functions. Have we sufficiently considered what this means in the personal development of the child? Have we, moreover, examined its implications in terms of collaboration between school and parents – and not necessarily through the machinery of parent-teacher associations? It is true that the grammar school had long been accustomed in a small way to providing meals for its pupils, and it might in consequence have been expected to assume more easily than other schools the parental role. But it must be remembered that before the war there was much more certainty on the part of both home and school about what was desirable in work and behaviour, and a much closer identity of aims. There was consequently no need for the school to emphasize to the child its paternal and maternal

---

[1] *The Lonely Crowd*, by David Riesman (Yale University Press, 1950).
[2] *The Uses of Literacy*, by Richard Hoggart (Chatto and Windus, 1956).

aspects. Indeed, it would hardly be going too far to say that at the pre-war school dinner the parents remained the real though unseen authority, of which the school was the accredited agent.

In the post-war world the situation is different. When school and home represent so many divergent attitudes, the school's overt assumptions of parental authority must often sharpen the conflict in a child's mind. It should be remembered that we are not yet considering the 'new' members of the school population: for them the discrepancy must be greater still. But even for the 'old' – that is, virtually, for those whose parents themselves attended grammar schools – the miming of the parental part on such occasions as meals paradoxically only becomes significant when they are no longer ready to accept it without question in its wider significance: that is, in all the implications of the school's curriculum, rules and general outlook.

It is evident that, even with a population composed in much the same way as before, the grammar school would have had a great problem of readjustment as it tried to cope with changed conditions. At this very moment, however, came the greatest challenge of all. The Act required local authorities to provide schools sufficient in number, character and equipment to afford for all pupils such variety of instruction as might be desirable in view of their different ages, abilities and aptitudes. It was not difficult to deal with the first of the 'three A's', for it was already generally accepted that secondary education should begin at eleven years of age. 'Aptitude' was and has remained a somewhat vague concept, though tentative concessions have been made to it here and there in attempts to identify a 'technical-school' type.[1] The second 'A' was extremely important. In fact, the most revolutionary consequence of the Act for grammar schools was the assumption by local authorities that ability (usually as measured by an intelligence test, and tests in English and arithmetic) was now the only criterion of fitness for grammar-school education. This meant that the former qualities of grammar-school pupils, which might be approximately defined as high intelligence *or* middle-class social and intellectual aspirations, gave place to those more appropriately defined as intelligence, not necessarily of the very highest, and not necessarily associated with social or intellectual aspirations. In consequence, the pupils of only moderate ability who were formerly in secondary schools and whose attitude – or whose parents' attitude – was one of positive co-operation with what the school was felt to stand for, disappeared from the grammar school. These pupils, representing perhaps a quarter of the

[1] For example, by introducing 'spatial' tests into selection procedures.

total grammar-school population,[1] were replaced in part by a different minority, represented to some extent by a type of child who would not formerly have attempted to enter a secondary school; who, though possessed of at least fairly good intelligence, sometimes came not knowing the ropes, and having few clear expectations or cultural ambitions. The school has not yet learnt how to deal with this type and there is still among teachers a fairly widespread resentment of the educational parvenus.

There is another side to the picture. In the first few years after the 1944 Act, when the working of a tripartite system seemed to be the obvious way of applying its principles, the tendency was, understandably, to concentrate on the new member of the trio – the secondary modern school – and to do everything possible to give it prestige and provide the conditions conducive to its successful development as an exciting venture. To be sure, people actually working in modern schools were not over-conscious of being in a privileged position. They saw too-large classes, inexperienced teachers, and a school population which, far from being rapturously aware that the gates of learning were suddenly opened to it, was on the contrary disposed to resist with all its might the imposition of an extra year of school life. Many senior elementary schools had been housed in disgraceful conditions, as some modern schools still are. The public also obstinately refused to accord 'parity of esteem' to all secondary schools. So the modern-school teachers had their hands full. To grammar-school staffs, however, the situation looked very different. Knowing that they were the recognized transmitters of the learned tradition, and considering, with some justice, that they had not only upheld many social services but had performed the hard task of maintaining the qualities of scholarliness, industry and probity when the world was disintegrating around them, they felt themselves to be left out in the cold and indeed actively discredited. If there was money to spare, it was

---

[1] Figures for pupils admitted to secondary (grammar) schools during the year ended 31st July, 1938, were analysed by the Board of Education as follows:
   (i) Ex-elementary school pupils:
      (a) Paying full fees: 26·6 per cent.
      (b) Paying partial fees: 8·3 per cent.
      (c) Paying no fees: 44·5 per cent.
   (ii) Other pupils:
      (a) Paying full fees: 19·6 per cent.
      (b) Paying partial fees: 0·5 per cent.
      (c) Paying no fees: 0·5 per cent.
(Note that ex-elementary school pupils constitute nearly 80 per cent. of the whole, and out-number those from other schools even in fee-paying places.)

It is impossible to estimate accurately what proportion of the fee-payers would not have gained admission after 1944, but about half – i.e. between a fifth and a quarter of the whole entry – is a reasonable guess.

almost invariably lavished on primary or secondary modern schools. And 'lavished' was the word. Many a grammar school, using its assembly hall for gym, music lessons, drama, and indoor games on a wet day, lacking a spacious library, and struggling to run a full science course with two ludicrously inadequate laboratories, had to watch the erection of a palace complete with changing-rooms, stage, and well-furnished library. Most bitter of all, it saw magnificent laboratories that seemed more than likely to remain unexploited because, as it appeared at that time, there were in most modern schools neither children intelligent enough to learn nor staffs sufficiently well-informed to teach the complex and advanced experimental work which such costly equipment was so admirably designed to promote.

Privilege was undermined in other ways. The basic salary scale, introduced with the avowed intention of creating parity of esteem and of encouraging highly-qualified teachers to work in all types of school, undoubtedly caused great bitterness. Almost as important was the equalization of holidays. Perhaps in some ways most significant of all was the much-increased direct control of school matters by local authorities.[1] The stature of heads was diminished by a few inches when they began to receive circular letters from the Education Office impersonally addressed to 'The Head Teacher'.[2] In time they grew accustomed to the lower altitude, but their resentment at having to fill in forms in triplicate or ask official permission for the use of their own classrooms for out-of-school activities was not all caused rationally by the considerable amount of extra routine work which these activities entailed. They also felt, and were correct in feeling, that however necessary such measures might seem to be in the interests of the greatest happiness of the greatest number, the autonomy of their own schools was seriously threatened. This threat was accentuated when some local authorities introduced the policy of grouping several secondary schools under a common board of governors.

Scarcely had the schools begun to adjust themselves to these new conditions when they had to deal with yet another change, the replacement of the old School and Higher School Certificates by the General Certificate of Education. The grammar school's attitude to public examinations will be analysed in a later chapter, and an attempt made to explain

[1] This was, of course, largely a consequence of the application of a single code for secondary education.
[2] 'The terms teacher and Head Teacher are normally applied to the staffs of elementary schools, and the words master (mistress) and Head Master (Head Mistress) to the staffs of secondary schools. We regard this distinction as objectionable . . .' *The McNair Report*, 1944.

why the recommendations of the Norwood Report, out of which the new examination grew, have never been fully realized. It is sufficient here to say that most grammar schools did not feel the pioneering spirit which, however short-lived, had affected other forms of education; that in 1950 all but a few school staffs were too busy trying to maintain standards and integrate the many conflicting elements of their situation to have energy to spare for large and venturesome experiments; and that with the removal of the familiar examination it seemed to many that their last security had vanished. Understandably, the average school immediately set about making the new examination serve a purpose as indistinguishable as possible from that of the old.

The grammar school, manned like all mortal institutions by fallible human beings who are themselves a prey to the uncertainties of the time, is in a peculiarly exposed position. It has already been pointed out that in itself an elaborate education (as distinct from an efficient training) is no longer, except for the few, an economic asset. We must also recognize that it has ceased to have social prestige. The Barbarians, as Matthew Arnold observed, have never been wholly devoted to culture. But they possessed 'a kind of image or shadow of sweetness', which was to him one attribute of culture, and one that the pre-war secondary school, with its care for manners, strove unpretentiously to maintain. Sweetness now confers no social cachet. Even if membership of aristocratic society were desired, which in the egalitarian temper of the age it scarcely is, that society is not now distinguished by its grace, its eloquence or its affability; and the grammar school is far from being able or willing to cultivate the studied gaucherie, the brusque throw-away brevity of statement, by which these qualities have been replaced. The young, however, have their ideals of social grace and beauty – in Hollywood and in the glossy magazines. They have their highly conventionalized language and dress. It is the dress of duffel coats and jeans; the language of the Tommy Steele and Elvis Presley fans. Let us hear a fourteen-year old-grammar-school girl:

I like anything that is lively and care-free and detest Orchestral music and dull plays and the B.B.C. programmes on Television.

I like going to the pictures and getting into an 'X' or an 'A' film on my own . . . I sometimes get bored in church, especially when I have to wait for Communion and the bass singer in the quoir is near me.

I like designing clothes and drawing although I am not very good at it. I like to wear nice clothes but I would much rather have Jeans and Gondalier shirts or duffle coats. I like any shoes with stiletto heels which are *really* high and tight split skirts, although Left Bank styles do not suit me or the district. I like to go abroad for my holidays and Italy is the best country, and Venice is the best place to go, because it is the only city in the world that I like. I would like to go on a World Tour, one that lasts about 18 months, if I had the money, but £75,000 is a sum to aim at and so is the 64,000 question on I.T.V. I dislike sensible clothes like, tweed costumes and brogues. My favorite dishes are, (apart from Christmas fare), Roast Beef and Yorkshire Pudding, fish and chips, spaggetti, baked beans, black coffee and champagne.

If decorum has little social prestige, still less has erudition. The pedant, it is true, has never been considered truly well bred, and the pure scholar has tended, in England at any rate, to be regarded with patronizing or somewhat uneasy approval. It has generally been preferred that learning should have a certain elegantly amateur quality. But from Sir Philip Sidney to Cardinal Newman it was the perfectly acceptable, indeed desirable, attribute of a gentleman. In the last century, when a public-school education was one of the marks of having arrived, it was an advantage, as a proof of that education, to be able to cap Latin verses. If the grammar school conferred this ability on its pupils, so much the nearer had it brought them to the world of the ruling class. In modern England, however, the near-ostracism of the intellectual, as of the creative artist, is obvious. In the century of the common man, the egg-head is one who has committed the solecism of being cleverer than his fellows. True, the immensely powerful scientists are respected and feared for their manifest control of things and events

> . . . his dominion that exceeds in this
> Stretcheth as far as doth the mind of man.

Because of this dominion and of its one-dimensional social acceptability, science can appeal to the power-loving individual who lives within most boys, if not most girls. But mere learning, learning that has no manipulative function: to acquire this through strenuous discipline, in a world whose resources are at one's disposal for the dropping of coin, is clearly both eccentric and futile.

Girls' education is significantly affected by the contemporary spirit. The recession of social approbation of learning came just when the idea of higher education for girls had, after a long struggle, ceased to be a novelty; when at last it seemed as though the woman with a fully culti-vated mind might no longer pay the price of being thought odd or slightly unfeminine. At present it is not merely the learned woman who risks a degree of social disapproval: it is the learned person – man or woman. But the girl, who even when circumstances are propitious is predestined to conflict and generally ready in the last resort to sacrifice her intelligence to her feminine needs, feels more keenly than her brother the anti-intellectual spirit of the day.

Whitehead defined culture as activity of mind and receptiveness to beauty and humane feeling. The public may not desire this culture as an absolute good, and the possession of it may not be a passport to either wealth or power; but the need for highly specialized intellects is undoubtedly recognized, and expertness, particularly in the field of applied science, rewarded. What it may mean for civilization if even the profession of absolute values ceases to be made we can as yet only conjecture. Sometimes it seems possible that the greatest intellects of our time may eventually establish a new encyclopedism; this is supported by the fact that among the most perceptive and skilled in letters, philosophy and the arts today are men trained in scientific disciplines.[1] At other times the vision of George Orwell,[2] that the only ultimate scope for the assertion of our humanity will be found in the primitive instincts, as expressed in the involuntary gesture of a mother to protect her child, seems more likely to be realized.

For the school the bias of the age means quite simply that in effective contemporary opinion education is that which leads to control of the physical world and the manipulation of its resources in commerce or industry. If any support of this statement be needed it can be found in the establishment of the Industrial Fund for the Advancement of Scientific Education in schools,[3] and in the rapid expansion in all universities of provisions for pure science and technology. This in turn means that there is everywhere a huge pressure on the more intelligent, impelling them towards scientific studies. Though a few of the great schools have long been well known for their cultivation of science, pressure of this kind and degree is a comparatively new phenomenon. It is a matter of common observation that whereas a generation ago the really able boys and girls in most sixth forms were classicists, now they are on the science side. (This remark is less completely true of girls than of boys, but it is nevertheless generally applicable to both sexes.) In theory such a development need not of itself deeply modify the cultural assumptions of a school. Actually, it is almost bound to do so, and for several reasons.

In the first place, the study of science, though not necessarily hostile to

---

[1] Such as Sir Geoffrey Keynes, Dr. J. D. Bronowski or the late Père Pierre Teilhard de Chardin.

[2] *Nineteen Eighty-Four*, by George Orwell (Secker and Warburg, 1949).

[3] Established 1st November, 1955.

them, has no inevitable connexion with value-judgements of taste, ethics or wisdom. Secondly, the material of scientific study is so difficult and so extensive that only the highly gifted can undertake it and still rejoice to find other outlets for their vitality. This would not be a serious matter if the advanced study of science were confined to such people, but it is not. Present conditions seem to make it necessary that students of the second or even third rank should take science courses, taxing to the utmost their memory and skills, until their execution far outruns their insight. They are in a state of πιστίς – they hold the right beliefs without understanding. No one need feel surprised if they show a compulsiveness in their work, begrudge time taken from it, and look askance at well-meant attempts to add liberalizing supplements to the sixth-form curriculum. It need hardly be added that this attitude can be paralleled in the staff. Though some science masters and mistresses are the finest of humanists, there are inevitably in these days many of the same type as the pupils just described, and they naturally communicate their mood. Thirdly, because of the pull towards science, there is a tendency for such subjects as history to be left to somewhat weaker students. This subtly discredits these studies in the eyes of the science side, and incidentally promises to leave them progressively depleted of adequate apologists in the coming generations. Fourthly, not only in universities but now also in schools the prestige of science creates a tendency to apply 'scientific' methods in fields where their appropriateness is not immediately obvious. This tendency, though not new, has taken some time to penetrate into the classroom. Its result has been in many ways to introduce a salutary astringency into arts studies. It is at the worst a good fault. But it can create aridity at an age when the mind needs vision as well as discipline. Finally, and perhaps most important, the whole fashion of the age is to emphasize the quantitative as opposed to the qualitative aspects of existence. This too is a process which has been going on for some time. It was a quarter of a century ago that Michael Roberts[1] observed:

'The assumption that we can find passive quantitative concepts which will enable us to attain our ends can be justified as a working hypothesis; but the true materialist goes further, and asserts that there *must* be such concepts, that reality is like that.'

But the tendency is growing, and does not make it any easier to teach Vergil or justify his presence in the school curriculum.

[1] *The Modern Mind*, by Michael Roberts (Faber and Faber, 1937).

A school staff is thus no longer supported by a tacit but strong general demand for the production of educated human beings, in at least a section of society. The present demand is for specialized training. Very high degrees of skill are needed. Initiative, too, is desirable, but in carefully delimited fields. In such a context an aspiration to educate the 'whole person' is bound to seem romantic and pitiably imprecise, even to those who themselves profess it. Yet because it is part of the grammar-school tradition, and because, however academically and mechanically expressed, it has formed part of the education of most teachers, the aspiration lingers. The notion of the Christian gentleman conflicts with that of the backroom boy as an educational ideal. Not that they are necessarily incompatible. A moment's reflection will show that they represent two different methods of classification rather than two mutually exclusive items within the same system. But while working one cannot be continually changing one's framework of reference, and in practice they often seem to be opposed. This creates an ambivalence in the teacher's assumptions concerning his own function. It also means that whereas when he is concerned with specialist training which has a perceptible object he is upheld by a strong substratum of common approbation, when teaching poetry or dealing with modes of behaviour he is infected by an unconscious but deadly lack of conviction, or at best has to manufacture his certainties from within. Signs of this unease are seen in the present pattern of grammar-school attitudes to the less tangible elements of its curriculum and general life, which ranges from a rarefied atmosphere of ideals and aestheticism to heartiness and a somewhat ostentatious avoidance of humbug.

Teachers are affected as ordinary human beings by the social influences of their time. They also, as has already been indicated, encounter in children a set of assumptions which may or may not harmonize with their own and which forms part of the complexity of the teaching-situation. Attitudes and expectations are first transmitted to children from their parents, and parents, like teachers, are affected as mere human beings by the general influence. Most of them, moreover – if they do not happen to be teachers themselves – are more vulnerable than teachers, and for a very good reason. Teachers do not always realize to what extent they are, whatever their hardships and difficulties, a protected class. They are set aside for a flatteringly edifying purpose, they are able to be disinterested and they are not only allowed but expected to have high standards. They have the opportunity to work out their ethical and cultural conflicts from first principles without the considerations of expediency which cloud judgement in the factory or the board-room. Many children sense this, and even a good teacher needs to cultivate a strong imaginative awareness of the predicament of the common man if he is not to leave the child with a faint feeling that he inhabits a less genuine world than that of the child's father. The average parent is by definition a common man, a thoughtless and not very adventurous hedonist and materialist. It may be noted, however, that his materialism differs from that of the Victorians in being less optimistic. Arnold refers ironically to the sublime example of Mrs. Gooch who said to her son: 'Ever remember, my dear Dan, that you should look forward to being some day manager of that concern.' Modern materialism is not so aggressive. Its television sets, washing machines, powerful cars and – significantly – its sweets, are so many defences against 'the growing terror Of nothing to think about', so many assurances of significance in a world whose only meaning seems to be spun from its own vitals.

Perhaps the 'average parent' is an abstraction that nowhere exactly exists. In any case, in their capacity as parents people tend to be somewhat less subject to mass influences, somewhat more apt to declare themselves as real and even eccentric individuals. The mother who refuses to let her boy give up his seat to another passenger in the bus or defies the head-master and board of governors by sending him to school in an ornate sweater is demonstrating her obscure feeling that, although she herself is largely at 'Their' mercy, she is not going to allow her child to be pushed around. There are, too, vestiges of the old desire to see one's children do better than one has done oneself. Unfortunately, however, such vitality and individuality as parents possess seems often to exhaust itself in odd by-ways. While some over-drive their children, and many others really care for learning and are eager to be good partners in the tasks of educa-tion, there is an appreciable number of 'new' parents and even some of the 'old' who do not seem to be capable of the long view, and possess little stamina to fortify either themselves or their children in the necessarily arduous ways of serious learning. The modern situation is full of paradoxes. The much-publicized anxiety over the 'eleven-plus' does not seem to be closely linked with high educational ideals, and there are children who find themselves, with a faint sensation of surprise, in the grammar school, without much notion on their own part or their parents' of why they are there. A headmaster and a headmistress have independently quoted a frequent remark made by parents, 'Oh, I thought I'd let him [her] come.' Stories of parental ambition for eleven-year-olds have to be balanced by statistics of premature leaving –

fairly rapidly declining but still serious, especially in certain industrial districts.[1]

There is undoubtedly much confusion and uncertainty. Parents who were pleased by the feeling they experienced of having acquired social and intellectual prestige when their child 'won a scholarship', lose their enthusiasm when the glittering though unspecified distinctions for which they hoped seem to prove inaccessible, when school leads to extra expense in its requirements of dress or equipment, when school work either demands a discipline to which child and family are unaccustomed or conflicts with family habits and pleasures, when the prolonging of school education does not seem likely to lead to a better-paid job or when the earnings of an adolescent would be a welcome addition to the family budget. Children reflect their parents' misgivings. Within the school, moreover, they may meet no clearly defined and accepted pattern and yet find themselves required to conform to standards which have no counterpart in the society they know outside school. Teachers are sometimes dismayed and even overwhelmed by the new problems of learning, manners and conduct with which they are faced and by the absence of an agreed set of criteria to which they can appeal.

Yet there is as much brightness as darkness in the picture. High standards of scholarship are reached in many schools, and are still rising. The grammar school is for many children a place of rich self-fulfilment. Sixth-form numbers show an impressive increase.[2] Most important, if some of the 'new' population fall out, others succeed extremely well and a few represent an educational triumph against apparently quite insuperable odds. In the face of so many contradictions, so much success and so much wastage and frustration, it seems that the time has come to analyse the assumptions and attempt a formulation and assessment of an institution whose fortunes can no longer be left to tradition and intuition alone.

[1] In the grammar and selective technical schools of one large city authority, the numbers reached a peak in the early 1950s, then declined rapidly, but seemed to have 'flattened out' at something over 8 per cent of a school year. Numbers of pupils not completing a five-year course in 1957, 1958 and 1959 are as follows:

1957: 89 (out of 1,101 on 4th-year registers)—8·08 per cent.
1958: 105 (out of 1,121 on 4th-year registers)—9·37 per cent.
1959: 101 (out of 1,163 on 4th-year registers)—8·68 per cent.

[2] According to the Ministry of Education's annual report, in 1958 the number of 17-year-old pupils in grant-aided and recognized schools was 53,200; that is, 8,300 more than in 1956, and representing an increase for boys from 8·7 to 10·9 per cent of the age group and for girls from 7·1 to 8·5 per cent. The majority of these pupils would have been in grant-aided grammar schools.

PART TWO

The Teachers Speak

3

School Subjects and Public Examinations

Subjects and Pupils

GRAMMAR-SCHOOL staffs think in terms of 'hardness of the material' rather than of 'softness of personnel'.[1] For the most part, that is, they see themselves as teachers of subjects. Human, kindly, cultured, deeply concerned for their pupils' welfare – all these they may be, and usually are. They may also have a very strong conviction that character-building is part of their professional duty. But the child in school, however affectionately, sensibly or firmly treated as a person, is *as a pupil* thought of chiefly in relation to his suitability for a certain assignment of learning; not, except under pressure of extreme necessity (as when he is demonstrably 'unmathematical'), as the object to which the curriculum is adjusted.[2] A master puts it thus:

I cannot bring myself to take a 'child-centred' attitude of playing to the gallery by *noticing* which lessons could be made most entertaining.

In the grammar-school world the subject is the constant, the child the variable.

Subjects are not natural and inherent divisions, like day and night, or land and sea.[3] But from a variety of causes the curriculum of the grammar school is highly fragmented, and staffs reflect this fragmentation not only by regarding themselves very much as specialists but also by distinguishing children according to their ability to 'do' certain subjects. Some teachers, indeed, seem to think in terms of highly specific aptitudes, as when a mathematics master says that seven per cent of the pupils will never learn anything in his subject, or a geography mistress confidently asserts that as some people are born without a sense of space, maps are meaningless to them. Teachers of foreign languages (classical and modern), science and

---

[1] The expressions are taken from David Riesman's *The Lonely Crowd*.
[2] For a fuller discussion of the objects of education, see Chapter 14
[3] 'A failure to attempt to understand the unity of all knowledge induces in our special studies themselves either narrowness or apathy.'
Professor John Pilley, Professor of Education in the University of Edinburgh, speaking at the fifth Leeds University Institute of Education conference on *Attitudes and Standards in Grammar School Teaching*, May, 1958.

mathematics are the most conscious of pupils finding serious difficulty in
their subjects, and Latin is considered exceptionally hard to learn. It
seems to be frequently assumed – and, curiously enough, almost irrespec-
tively of the degree of selectivity of the school – that only a proportion,
certainly less than half, of the children in a grammar school will be capable
of ever beginning to learn Latin and that, of these, many will find it
difficult. One highly selective school allows only about a third of its
pupils to start on the subject and apparently expects a minority even of
these to find it very difficult.

Through the eyes of their teachers, boys and girls are seen enjoying
drama and oral activities of many kinds – class discussions, talks and
debates. They respond enthusiastically at first to all aspects of French and
find its speech fascinating; later on, the popularity of oral work in this
subject sharply declines and it tends to cause embarrassment, particularly
to boys with changing voices. Many children like map-making, and, in
the sciences, practical work evokes the greatest enthusiasm. 'In all parts of
the school', says a science master, 'experimental work is most enjoyed by
master and pupils.' In short, most grammar-school children like lessons in
which they can be active, and work that produces observable results.

There is no mistaking the appeal of the human. The children are said to
enjoy social and biographical aspects of history, and to be attracted to
human geography. Human physiology is nearly always found to make a
very strong appeal. Closely related to these human interests is the popularity of studies clearly seen to have relevance or topicality. A history
mistress comments:

I find that response depends much more on presentation and treatment of
subject-matter than on the subject-matter itself; for example, almost any
subject studied in depth will receive a good response (but time does not
always permit). Broadly speaking, so long as an aspect can be given reality
there is every chance that interest and imagination will be captured. That
is probably why the present-day bias in favour of social history, and the
approach through local and family archives rather than the public records, has
made the teaching of history in schools so much more attractive to the majority
of children. I think the importance of original sources, judiciously selected,
cannot be over-emphasized.

Another form of personal appeal, probably even more important, is
the influence of the individual teacher. Children, understandably, like
to know how their own bodies work, or how other people lived
or live. But it is even more enjoyable to see another human being in

the classroom, obviously devoted to a study and wanting to share his discoveries. A geography master describes the situation very simply:

I find that what really interests *me*, interests them.

Intelligent children are found to respond well to most aspects of a subject. They enjoy learning, and their attention is quickly engaged. The ablest of all show an original 'something' that is more than satisfactory response to good teaching. These are the children who not only understand and learn their work, but who recognize mathematical form and beauty, have a natural feeling for the idiom of a foreign language, can abstract essential principles from a mass of detail, or take spontaneous pleasure in tracing logical relationships.

Most children, however, are not like this, and meet with only partial success in their studies. There are certain well-marked areas of difficulty: grammar, in both English and foreign languages; economic, political and constitutional history; climatology; map projection (for the unmathematical); formal proofs and riders in geometry; algebraic symbolism; theoretical work in the sciences. A difficulty in remembering facts is noted in many subjects, and anxiety about this increases in both teachers and pupils as the time of public examinations draws near. A chemistry master writes that there are very few boys who could not study his subject if the difficulties were adjusted to the capabilities of the form, but

probably fifty per cent have no chance of reaching the 'O' level standard of retention of knowledge.

Another, perhaps the chief, weakness is in powers of abstraction and deduction. Often the two weaknesses are associated, in both arts and science subjects. A biology master, for example, names as sources of difficulty in sixth-form work:

evolutionary concepts and the memorizing of anatomical details – two extremes, the first requiring more analytical thinking than most boys have a capacity for; the second requiring concentration on learning apparently unrelated facts.

A French mistress makes a somewhat similar point; after the second year, she says, the duller children, though capable of understanding and dealing with grammatical concepts one at a time, cannot retain sufficient grasp of the whole grammatical structure to use this knowledge instrumentally.

Many children show that they have difficulty in handling language. In English this appears as a weakness in written composition, which is attributed partly to a failure of reasoning, partly to paucity of ideas and limitations of vocabulary. Such limitations also affect the appreciation and understanding of literature. The language of Shakespeare's plays is found remote and strange by middle-school pupils, and imagery is not readily appreciated.[1] These difficulties also hinder the learning of a foreign language. One teacher thinks that formal grammar can usually be learnt, but that the acquisition of a true idiom is beyond the power of most pupils because of their lack of sound knowledge of their own language. They also suffer from a weakness of imagination which makes it hard for them to form a clear mental picture of a scene described or story narrated. Many children have to struggle to acquire an 'active' vocabulary, and poverty of vocabulary and idiom is the main cause of difficulty in English-into-French translation. Translation is, indeed, found to be difficult in both modern and classical languages. It is not only in avowedly linguistic subjects, however, that weakness in written work is noted. It is mentioned also by teachers of history, geography and Scripture, and is seen to consist in an inability to select relevant material, use evidence to justify opinions, trace cause and effect, and – out of all this – produce accurate, well-reasoned writing.

At eleven, children are eager to learn. Three or four years later many of them are no longer eager. Is this an inevitable development of adolescence? Not entirely, according to the teachers. Most, perhaps all, of their pupils, they say, can learn a subject in its early stages, but some are unable to deal with the extent and complexity of later requirements and the speed of more advanced work. There are also children who without insight go through the motions of learning, not perceiving their own limitations. 'They do not realize it is difficult', says a biology mistress, 'because they jog along happily.' Others appear to be capable of passing the point of real difficulty and thereafter learning, without much understanding, sufficient material for reproduction in an examination. This is the position of the children said by a geography mistress to constitute a third of her pupils, who do descriptive work well, and write and speak thoughtfully on human problems, but do not reach G.C.E. standards on 'reasons' without much coaching. There also seem to be in all subjects children who can enjoy and profit from their work and can understand it, but who become overburdened by the load of memorized material required for public examinations. Finally, and most important, teachers of English and foreign languages in particular are well acquainted with

---

[1] A north-country English master speaks of the almost complete inability of his boys – otherwise able and responsible pupils – to understand metaphor.

children who find difficulty not because of any supposed initial lack of aptitude but because of the incompatibility of their social assumptions with the nature of the subject.

Such are the children who achieve at best incomplete success. Beyond them are those who, in one or more subjects, experience really serious difficulty, and who scarcely ever make a satisfactory response. What is the teacher's duty towards them? Is marked failure in a subject or subjects necessarily proof that the child is unfit for grammar-school education? Should he be allowed or encouraged to drop a subject in which he is unsuccessful? Should he be made to undergo the discipline of studying it, even though he does not understand it? Can content or method be so modified that the subject is adjusted to the child, not the child to the subject?

These are not easy questions to answer, for the intelligence of the pupil is not in every case the only or the most important factor, nor is it a matter of 'good' or 'bad' teaching in any simple sense. Many children, their teachers feel, are undertaking study unsupported by any notion of what serious grammar-school work means. A mistress writes:

In about a quarter to a half of these cases [i.e. those children experiencing serious difficulty in a subject] the pupils seem to have been wrongly selected. This may not just be due to lack of intelligence, but often to lack of persistence, to parents who have not themselves had the education to take an interest and help them at home, to the parents' lack of sympathy with a grammar-school education, to the fact that they do not *make* the more indolent child do adequate work because they do not know how much industry is necessary, to lack of concentration.

The estimated number of failures varies considerably: some teachers seem to encounter no more than an occasional one or two, others a much larger number. This variation is connected to some extent with the degree of grammar-school selection, but it by no means shows an exact correspondence – there is not always a higher estimate of failure in the less selective school, nor is the converse true. The estimate itself is an important indication of the flexibility and limits of tolerance of a teacher's concept of grammar-school education. When a master says:

At least a quarter [of the pupils] one finds it's a waste of time teaching from a grammar-school point of view

it may be conjectured that his limits are rather narrowly drawn.

Some teachers – an appreciable minority – consider that children showing serious weakness in their subject should not be in the school. A few add the proviso 'if they are equally weak in all subjects'; others feel that their subject is inseparable from the very notion of grammar-school education, and that lack of success in it therefore implies general unsuitability. On the whole, if such children remain in the school, teachers are against the idea of their dropping the weak subject. (It is probable, however, that this opposition does not apply to the fairly common system of so-called choice – often in reality direction – that exists in the middle school, whereby the weaker pupil is drafted away from mathematics or Latin and into art, domestic science, or woodwork.) There is a strong feeling, consistent with the strain of 'fire and strength' inherent in the grammar-school tradition, that children must tread the hard path and not be encouraged to shirk hardships. Teachers, as of old, attach value to the grind of a subject and credit it with certain character-building qualities. The notion of training is still fairly frequently invoked, as when one master claims that 'modern languages provide almost as good a mental training as classics.' Some people, however, are obviously troubled. As one master puts it:

Many will gain something by being made to persist with their difficulties and overcome them. How much history they will learn is doubtful.

When teachers agree to the suggestion that the syllabus should be adapted to the needs of unsuccessful pupils, or assert emphatically that it is so adapted, they do not always intend to imply that (starting with the datum of a pupil who does not conform to the usual pattern of grammar-school learning) one should construct an entirely different syllabus, and try quite new approaches, in an attempt to meet new needs. They usually have in mind a not very startling adaptation: an abbreviation of the syllabus to the minimum, and a concentration (as far as possible) on the more practical or the more easily memorizable parts of a subject. Yet few show a completely inflexible concept of plans and mode of work, and some speculate somewhat wistfully on the possibilities of alternative, non-examination courses. Most teachers are keenly aware of organizational difficulties, particularly at the present time, and of restrictions imposed by the necessity of conforming to examination requirements. There is, in fact, overwhelming evidence of the extensive influence of public examinations on teaching-attitudes, and this must now be considered.

Public Examinations

Secondary education has passed through its early phases; it can stand alone and already finds the framework which supported it to be a barrier preventing growth.

Teachers are more confident of themselves; they have been increasingly associated with the work of examinations and can no longer be said to be inexperienced. In our view the time has passed when such guidance and direction of their work as teachers can best be given by means of an external examination.

These, in 1943, were the words of the Norwood Report on Curriculum and Examinations in Secondary Schools. In 1951 the Ministry of Education expressed, in a publication entitled *The Road to the Sixth Form*, the following hopes and opinions:

If an able boy or girl is to achieve an education of any depth, he cannot afford to break it off at 16 or so . . . An academic course especially can hardly hope to pay much of an intellectual dividend before the age of 17 or 18 . . .

. . . Pupils who take their main subjects at Advanced level (towards the end of their school career) will not need to take them at Ordinary level . . . It is hoped that subjects will be taken at Ordinary level only by candidates who have reached a reasonable competence in them . . .

Real freedom for the pupil is bound up with a more personal approach to his work, and such an approach should be easier, now that boys and girls of 14 and 15, however able, do not have to concentrate their energies on passing a standardized test of attainment.

It is now possible for a pupil to postpone examination in his main subjects until the end of his career, and this is an opportunity inherent in the new examination system which ought not to be missed . . . It may be categorically stated that no school using the new system in the old way can claim to have accepted the challenge and the opportunities offered to it to base its plans on the interests of its pupils.

In 1950 the School and Higher School Certificates came to an end. No longer would one examination have to prove simultaneously that the less academic pupil had acquired a good general education and that the more academic was ready to move on to pre-university studies in the sixth form. Consequently there was no more need to differentiate grades of success. No longer would boys, and occasionally girls, be hurried on to gain their matriculation exemption at fourteen or even thirteen years of age in order that they might 'get rid of' their Higher School Certificate subjects proportionately early and spend one or two years being groomed for university scholarships. No longer would the non-linguistic pupil toil over meaningless French verbs in order to gain a bare pass in the language group, failure in which would cost him his whole certificate. Instead, the school, freed from the burden of detailed examination requirements, could encourage him to talk colloquial French, read French newspapers and magazines and perhaps study French literature in translation. Similarly, the non-mathematical pupil would play chess, make surveys, construct models, study and discover number patterns and use formulae (that he need neither educe nor memorize) in exploration of the properties of space and number. Both pupils might go on, the one to become a student of physics, the other of history, without having been either frustrated at an important stage of their development or deprived of an essential element of a good general education.

Now that fees were abolished in all secondary schools and family allowances had been introduced, it was hoped that more and more boys and girls would have a continuous school course. This would be unbroken by examinations for seven years; they would then take an examination in a few subjects, some at 'Advanced', some at 'Ordinary' level, designed to test simultaneously both their specialized and their more general studies, and itself not intended to be fully concerned with the whole spread of their school education. The grammar school had attained its majority.

It was also hoped that, as the selection procedure became increasingly reliable, children who entered the secondary grammar school would be more exclusively those suited to the seven-year course terminating in an examination. The children for whom a more general and less academic education was appropriate would go to the secondary modern school, the curriculum of which should be developing in ever more varied and adventurous ways.[1] Until employers had grown fully accustomed to accepting schools' assessments, and as long as some able pupils continued to leave after five years, the examination might be taken in one or more subjects from the age of sixteen, and subjects might be added in successive years. This was a concession, however, and was regarded by advocates of the new examination as an interim measure.

Might not one have expected, then, eight years after the establishment of the General Certificate of Education and fifteen years after the publication of the Norwood Report, to find the grammar school liberated and flourishing, with a staff eager to experiment – a school no longer hampered by the less intelligent pupils of former years, no longer cramped by complicated examination requirements? Surely, a theorist might suppose, such a school, pursuing scholarship no less eagerly but at the same time more able than ever before to consider, test, and apply the principles of general and personal education in a changing world, would be seen to be confident and flexible – exhibiting, within the common framework of

[1] The Norwood Report had envisaged longer courses, and much interesting development in many modern schools.

regard for learning, a great variety of curricula, teaching-methods and organization.

A liberated school? Virtually all pupils are found to be taking the examination at 'O' level in five to nine subjects. A staff eager to experiment? By their direct testimony most of the teachers show that syllabus and teaching are geared to the examination, and a headmaster writes:

> I can say for all subjects that the teaching is bounded by the 'O' level syllabus.

Even the comparatively few who say that the examination has little effect upon their work are far from defying it: they are unaffected merely because the requirements accord so closely with their own inclinations.

How excellent to have an incentive! The examination, says a master, is 'an entirely justified spur and guide to work'. Others, more high-minded, say that it provides a valuable mental and moral discipline. It is particularly good for weaker pupils, in whom the love of learning is not strong enough to provide its own motive power, but who are capable of responding to a goad externally applied. It is also useful for the intelligent, who often show a reprehensible willingness to get by with the minimum of effort, but fortunately can be rendered ambitious by the prospect of examination success. In the words of one master, 'Self-interest can be harnessed.'

Nor are these all the good effects claimed for the examination. We learn that a few initially careless and unpromising children, whom only examination pressure could force into a sufficiently close study of a subject to obtain any idea of its real nature, come to find interest in what they at first undertook only under compulsion, and proceed to advanced work with enthusiasm. Moreover, the examination sets academic standards, and presupposes effort, appropriate to the training of leaders. In practical activities, time limits make quick and accurate work essential *and therefore* produce a lasting improvement in efficiency. Work done in preparation for the examination is also more vigorous and exact than it would otherwise be.

There are even good effects on the teacher. The examination gives direction for the planning of work. It disciplines the teacher (presumably by discouraging irrelevancies) and it encourages him to insist on accuracy of detail. Let us watch an English master responding to this discipline:

> In literature, I have recently begun setting to junior classes questions of the same type as those set in G.C.E. because I have found that many pupils do not pick up the right way of answering these questions if they are introduced as late as the fourth year. As such work demands more understanding of the literature, I tend

to spend more time on a smaller amount of literature, generally, I believe, with more satisfactory results.

Yet, though dominated by the examination, the teachers are by no means unanimous in approving of it – on the contrary, those who think its influence to be bad are appreciably in the majority. Chief among the undesirable effects is the restriction it places on the scope of their work. It imposes, they say, a tight control on the syllabus; for example, by forcing attention on a few books (and those often of inferior quality) in English literature, or by demanding, in geography, over-concentration on the British Isles. It discourages valuable activities and modes of learning because of the need to learn what is examinable; thus, teachers devote too much time to written work in French, too little to field work in biology. Pace, too, is a problem; there is 'one mad rush to get through everything required'. The sensation of haste and pressure creates fear in the minds of weaker pupils and causes them to do themselves less than justice. A geography mistress writes:

I think staff unconsciously discourage weaker pupils through their anxiety to get them through G.C.E. If we *feel* despairing about them they pick up an atmosphere of despair. Discouragement in middle and upper forms shows readily in written work. Children who have not lost confidence will write exhaustively on something which interests them; even though they do not write very much or very well, they like to write all they know about it. In the 3rd and 4th forms, some B-formers begin to write the least possible amount, although they have appeared interested in the lesson . . . Their best isn't good enough, so what is the use of trying?

Most important, the total effect is to drain the life from teaching and learning. 'It turns the subject', says a history teacher, 'into a fact-grind in which the real educational value tends to disappear.'

Perhaps the following comment by a mathematics master is remarkable only in being unusually frank:

I cannot but think that I could employ my time, and that of my pupils, much better. This is especially the case, since I know what I want of my classes, but I don't know what the examiners want . . . However, the 'O' level spurs on some lazy characters and allows me to bully other sluggards into some kind of activity. And, of course, it's much easier to teach 'O' level work than to make out a satisfactory course of your own.

It is quite clear that the principle of a merely qualifying examination has never been acknowledged. Most of the teachers questioned would like the introduction of graded marks at 'O' level; some think a change unnecessary only because they are concerned with an examining body which in effect already gives grades. A very few oppose grades 'from sheer egalitarian prejudice' or because 'they intensify competition and anxiety'. Graded marks are desired by the teacher because they would encourage the clever pupil to work harder than he now works for an examination he knows he can pass comfortably; give a deserved reward to the able or more industrious; and be a useful guide to a prospective employer, or to a pupil in his choice of advanced studies.

Since they make such a determined attempt to assimilate the General Certificate of Education at 'O' level to the old School Certificate, teachers might perhaps have been expected to favour the completion of the process by a return to a lower pass mark. On this, however, opinions are divided. Those who oppose such a measure fear that it would lower the standard of acceptable work, and so weaken the prestige of grammar-school education. 'Any child fit to be in a grammar school', they say, 'ought to be able to pass in my subject at "O" level.' (The implied argument is of course tautological.) They also fear that a lower pass mark would encourage the lazy child to be even lazier. Those who favour a lower mark – which, they suggest, should be about 40 per cent – do so on the grounds that it would encourage the limited but hard-working boy or girl and would enable the G.C.E. to be properly used as a leaving certificate.

In short, few teachers ever accepted the change of policy associated with the General Certificate of Education: few understand or accept it now. Most felt at home with the School Certificate and still feel lost without it. The following testimonies can stand for many:

I would like to see the old graded system restored. I think its removal was a political move, part of the 'levelling down' policy.

I saw and can see nothing wrong with the old School Certificate that minor adjustment would not have put right.

Since, however, the old certificate was in their view arbitrarily and inexplicably abolished, teachers feel that they must make do with its successor. They are for the most part opposed to the idea of an easier examination for weaker pupils. Such an examination would debase the currency of the grammar school, for which the staffs feel themselves to be fighting a hard if not a losing battle, and would 'grade' the pupils in their own and one another's eyes far more clearly and more detrimentally than would any common examination. It is better to regard the 'O' level examination as an institution: capable of improvement in detail, and at present insufficiently competitive, but dealing out success and failure with rough justice and relieving the teacher of too much responsibility in the initiation of his syllabus.

At 'O' level the G.C.E. is a known tyranny and accepted, though often with regret. What of the sixth form? Since the examination at 'A' level is closely associated with university entrance requirements, we may expect that it will largely determine syllabuses for specialist courses. But here, surely, there will be less domination. A sixth-form syllabus, we may reason, is so extensive and lends itself to so many different kinds of treatment that here if anywhere teachers will be themselves, using the examination programme chiefly as a stimulus for the sharing of their own scholarship in their own way.

So we may reason. The reality is different. Sixth-form masters and mistresses are as anxious to train their pupils and to cultivate examination 'form' as any primary-school teacher obsessed by the 'eleven-plus', and feel equally entitled to demand a predictable examination.[1] It is evidently common practice to make a close study of past papers and, in varying degrees, to make direct use of them in teaching. Indicative of an exceptionally restrained use is the following:

I ignore past examination questions till late in the year. Their only value for 'Advanced' level Latin is to show pupils the form of the examination. The standard is reached quite independently of reference to old papers. No doubt it is a moral incentive to tackle old unseen translation papers and prose compositions successfully.

Many teachers would see nothing excessive in this comment from a physics master:

I use these, as well as books of graded exercises, continually. They do very many of these questions – about six a week – which I correct, and where necessary give further explanation to the class as a whole. They enable me to judge whether my own teaching has been satisfactory, and to find out particular weaknesses of individual pupils. They are useful in enabling me to establish a standard, both for myself and for my pupils. I find that even after many years of sixth-form teaching, I still am not sure whether a particular question will appear easy or hard, and find it difficult therefore to make up questions of the right standard.

Not, then, the syllabus alone but even the very questions set are brought frequently before the minds of sixth-form students and largely determine both the content and the form of many teachers' work. The following quotations give some idea of the range of practice:

[1] When, some years ago, a liberal-minded examiner introduced questions on contemporary developments in art and science into a paper on nineteenth-century history, he was met with cries of 'Unfair', even though the paper contained a wide choice of questions.

The questions always demand some basic knowledge and appreciation,

$$\text{e.g. Shakespeare} \begin{cases} \text{one on plot} \\ \text{one on character} \end{cases}$$

$$\text{Poetry} \begin{cases} \text{one on style} \\ \text{one on subject matter} \end{cases}$$

though the wording of a question may obscure this fact. Consequently, previous questions are useful in ensuring that candidates realize the scope of questions they may meet, though there is little value in answering any one specific question and it is clearly common sense to frame one's own. Fortunately, model answers would serve no purpose.

(ENGLISH MISTRESS)

I direct the study of the set books almost entirely in accordance with the questions which have been asked on them.

(ENGLISH MASTER)

(a) Questions are set each fortnight selected from past examination papers, so that even at the beginning of the first year when the work is new the girls become familiar with examination phraseology.

(b) Later in the year, and during the second year, questions are selected for revision purposes, and now that the factual content is more easily obtained, methods of answering can be discussed.

(c) Mapwork: Previous ordnance survey maps and the questions set on them are invaluable since, apart from work actually in the field, the only method of learning here is practice and more practice.

(GEOGRAPHY MISTRESS)

I have examination questions over several years arranged under headings and I give the girls the questions whenever the work done is relevant. As they only write an essay once a fortnight they work only a fraction of the questions given them, but they know these questions may come in terminal examinations – and I know they ponder over them!

(DIVINITY MISTRESS)

I use the past papers . . . to provide essay questions in literature. A skilful (!) analysis of past papers . . . often suggests a topic that has not occurred for some time and is due for revival in the coming examination. A study of past papers too gives the teacher lines on which to work in his own preparation of the text.

(FRENCH MASTER)

In mathematics, where good examples of a varied nature are required, I make great use of papers set in past years, using them for regular tests. (As you know, most textbooks also quote frequently from examination papers in mathematics.) I do not think that mathematics suffers from the dangers of this practice as do some other subjects.

(MATHEMATICS MASTER)

I make full use of examination questions – they are so searchingly set and they certainly pick out the physicist.

(PHYSICS MASTER)

Only used in the upper sixth (that is, 2nd year after 'O' level) and in the last two or three months many years' papers are worked. This is a 'sop' to the need for passing an examination rather than a desirable facet of the teaching. It seems a very valuable aid and almost foolproof method – but really not easily defensible on wide educational grounds.

(MATHEMATICS MASTER)

From many conferences and discussion groups of grammar-school teachers and from conversations with teachers in many different parts of the country, as well as from the results of this particular inquiry, it is evident that the policy stated in *The Road to the Sixth Form* has found little direct or lasting expression in the maintained grammar school. Recommendations that the course should normally be a seven-year course, and that either all subjects should be examined simultaneously or that, failing this, 'Ordinary' level subjects should usually not be those that were being taken at 'Advanced' level; that courses leading to external examinations should be by no means the only serious and exacting courses pursued in school; that only those pupils who, in the opinion of the school, were clearly at 'pass' standard in a subject should be examined in it; and that no one should be entered for public examination under the age of sixteen; all have borne little fruit. It is significant that at the very outset protests arose, chiefly from boys' schools, against the age-limit: protests which showed how very far teachers were from entertaining any idea of freedom from examination 'pressure' or from accepting the idea of a continuous course (in which, be it noted, the existence of an age-limit need not have precluded the possibility of a young pupil's proceeding to advanced study).

Nevertheless, it was not only in some highly selective and privileged direct-grant schools, which could afford to some extent to dispense with yearly assurances of academic success – nor in some independent schools, many of whose clientèle retained the idea that education till the age of eighteen was desirable for its own sake – that an effort was made to carry out the intention of the examination. Some maintained schools, already struggling to uphold sufficient continuity of tradition amid all the changes enumerated in Chapter 1, made a brave attempt to give the new system a genuine trial. They were, however, a minority – though not limited to any one district – and for the proposed system to have any hope of success it would probably have been essential to achieve virtually unanimous agreement among the schools. The lack of such agreement, and indeed of any widespread conviction about the possible merits of the new scheme, predestined it to failure, If some headmasters or head-mistresses scrupulously refrained from entering candidates whom they could not describe as being certain, in their opinion, to reach the stated 'pass' level, and their less scrupulous fellows found no difficulty in an easier interpretation of the guarantee they were asked to give, the first class of school heads felt – and were often told by parents in no uncertain terms – that they had unjustly penalized pupils who 'might have stood a chance'. If they also observed the recommendation not to enter pupils at 'O' level in their 'best' subjects (i.e. those likely to be taken at 'A' level) and if other heads, eager for school honours, disregarded this recom-mendation and entered candidates in their 'best' subjects, there was a chance of penalizing the restricted candidates, since the familiar procedure of scaling the marks might tend to raise the pass standard.[1]

Certain universities made an attempt to write into their regulations something of the spirit of the new examination by requiring as their minimum condition of entrance two 'A' level passes together with appropriate assurance of a general education. But the intention was defeated by their own faculty and departmental requirements, and by those of other universities. Three 'A' level subjects,[2] still in a limited number of combinations, is for nearly all pupils the very least that can ensure uni-versity entrance. Training colleges, too, are increasingly looking for this qualification.

As for the 'O' level, even those schools which at first tried to use it in the manner described have for the most part abandoned the attempt, largely because of the unwillingness of parents to commit their children to a seven-year school course without a recognizable interim guarantee of achievement. Some schools still try to limit the number of 'O' level entries. Most, however, enter their pupils, as in the old School Certificate days, for seven, eight and even nine subjects. All except the highly selective schools have at least a sprinkling of pupils who leave with only

[1] In fact this danger was largely illusory. A far more likely danger, if modern schools begin to take the examination in large numbers, is that of appreciably lowering the pass standard. Of course impressive numbers of modern-school pupils will pass, if passes continue to be awarded on a percentage basis.

[2] Thus, the matriculation requirements of the Northern Universities Joint Matriculation Board can be met by a combination of 'O' and 'A' level passes that include only two at 'A' level. But at Birmingham, a representative university, the Faculty of Arts demands at least three 'A' level subjects passed at one and the same examination, and the Faculty of Science, making the same demand, is even more specific in its details of subjects necessary for entrance to particular departments.

two or three 'passes' on their certificate – pupils who in the old days would have gained a School Certificate with perhaps two 'credits' and four 'passes'. 'A certificate with only three passes is not worth the paper it is written on,' says a master answering this inquiry. That is true, if it is to be a *general* certificate of education – but, in one sense, never was a certificate more ironically named.

Whether it was wise to create the new examination in its existing form may still be discussed; what is certain is that it has been forced, through educational conservatism, into a use for which it was never intended. It may also be noted that now that the modern schools have entered the field, most of them with even less appreciation of its original design, the situation is likely to become more confused than ever. This G.C.E., intended to be more specialized in function than the old School and Higher School Certificates and in no way to be a leaving certificate (indeed, one of its aims was to remove that unintended function which had attached itself to the School Certificate), has become a ladder of trapezoid shape, with one end in the academic empyrean, while on its wide bottom rung clusters a larger and more variegated throng than any former system has seen.[1]

It may be that public examinations restrict curricular development, stifle spontaneity, and set up inhibiting anxieties in teacher and taught. It may be that they are the best means yet available for creating a necessary and salutary tension conducive to concentrated work, providing both a reward for effort and an intelligible sign of achievement to outside parties, giving useful guidance in the construction of syllabuses, and releasing the pupil from the caprice of the teacher. Both arguments, forcefully expressed, were met in the course of this inquiry. If the teachers and schools concerned are at all representative, it is at least clear that the General Certificate Examination makes up an important part of the assumptions of the grammar school. Teachers assume, whether with approval or with disapproval, that the examination is 'given'; that it is, at any rate from the end of the third year, the generating force of the curriculum; and that it is the goal and justification of most school effort.

'We do hug our chains, don't we?' said a head of department in 1951. Why did grammar-school staffs not leap to lose them? One sees now that it would have been astonishing if they had. The curriculum was for the most part examination-centred in the days of the old certificates, which, with their system of 'groups' and their clearly stated grades of pass, had

[1] Larger and more variegated than ever since the ninth examining body – the Associated Examining Board – came into being.

constructed a fine complicated hierarchy of achievement and corresponding endeavour. To have abandoned these securities would have been possible only if most grammar-school staffs had been passionately convinced educational theorists: or, to put it another way, if the recommendations and legislation of the '40s – though derived partly from consultation with teachers' representatives – had been following, rather than trying to lead, ordinary professional opinion. It should be observed, incidentally, that there has been a tendency in the past for those who represented the grammar schools at the highest level to be drawn from very old-established or privileged schools. Perhaps this was inevitable, yet one of its consequences was to reinforce a half-defined feeling that the system was being manipulated by legislators and administrators who had no first-hand knowledge of the conditions and problems of the average secondary grammar school.

Moreover, as we have seen, the change came at a time that was unpropitious – when the school population was beginning to present problems that left teachers with little room for theorizing, and when the social climate, though inclined enough to applied science or to money-making, was anything but favourable to intangible educational 'goods'. Yet, however understandable, this refusal to slacken the hold of the examination has been unfortunate, not least in its effect on other schools. Modern schools, being (under the original plan) rationally excluded from an examination that most pupils were not expected to reach till the seventh year, soon found themselves forced to deny to their abler pupils the right to take a school-leaving examination which boys and girls of very similar abilities on the other side of the fence were taking. The inevitable next step was to introduce 'O' level courses into many modern schools, reversing the promising earlier trend of some of the schools towards curricular adventurousness and achievement. Another consequence was to make comprehensive schools seem to many people the only certain way of abolishing unfair privilege in secondary education.

One thing, however, remains to be said, and said with emphasis. If we regret that this oldest form of State secondary school would not or could not take the lead in boldly devising a curriculum that (until the pre-university stage) should be free from the dictation of an external and impersonal examining body, this constitutes no argument against the grammar school as an institution. Quite the contrary. Comprehensive, bilateral, technical – in fact, all other kinds of secondary schools – are even more examination-conscious. Does an apologist for the comprehensive school[1] wish to prove that academic standards are maintained? He quotes its examination successes. Does a modern school seek to demonstrate that its pupils are not 'inferior'? It publishes its 'O' level results. Regrettably or not, the examination is now riveted on the whole secondary system for many years to come. The grammar school, which is often sophisticated enough to preserve considerable freedom of manœuvre within its bonds, may yet in the end be the school to deliver itself from them.

---

[1] *cf.* the leading article in *The Times Educational Supplement*, 11th September, 1959: 'If the comprehensive school should show any laxness in the gaining of certificates it will be hooted down.'

4

Estimate of the Sixth Form

G ENUINE original thought, say grammar-school staffs, is rare in the sixth form as elsewhere in life. A true thinker is born, not made: the teacher cannot give originality. But independent, as distinct from original, thought can be trained. Not that independence is necessarily considered to be desirable. A history master, for instance, says:

> I don't really expect them to 'think for themselves' in my work. The motivation is enormously varied and it isn't my business to bother with it much.

Second thoughts, however, modify this opinion; going on to consider whether any change is discernible in a boy in consequence of his being a sixth-former, he adds:

> The only marked variation I can think of is when a boy has, as a result of some maturity of his social consciousness, 'discovered' something revelatory in my subject and begun to 'think for himself' in the sense, perhaps, intended by the question.

Sixth-formers who can think independently are generally judged to be about equal in number to those who have little originality but can for the most part learn and follow instructions carefully and accurately.[1] The power to think for oneself does not come automatically to everyone: careful training is therefore necessary. But at the same time it has to wait upon maturity – maturity that may not manifest itself till the university stage, or even later.

The sixth form is the crown of the grammar school, almost its justification. From the sixth will come the scholars and the administrators. Here the intelligent minority will be trained to take responsibility. Here the thinkers are at home. Such, outside the profession, is the common stereotype. It is consequently somewhat disquieting to meet among teachers the frequently expressed opinion that grammar-school work at the senior stage is not always conducive to the development of

---

[1] Since several teachers make such a careful distinction between original and independent thought, the two categories are slightly blurred.

independent thinking. The student, says one biology teacher, is pre-occupied less with thinking than with learning the mass of facts required for the examination. Before the sixth-form stage is reached, we hear, work at 'O' level in other subjects has meant an emphasis on routine methods and pedestrian learning that is a poor preparation for the kind of thinking desirable in the sixth. The pressure to achieve 'A' level for entrance to a training college forces many students who are only capable of steady undistinguished work into courses unsuitable for them. Moreover, in some schools a too strong drive for a big sixth is bringing many mediocre minds into sixth-form work.

Does the sixth form dramatically change a pupil? Some say not. There is little alteration, they think, if we make adequate allowance for growth. A history master says that in twenty-six years' experience he has never known a good fifth-former to become a poor sixth-former, though the growth of a very few has been a little below expectations. The change from scatterbrain to serious worker, says a geography mistress, usually occurs earlier, in the fourth or fifth year. Another mistress says that, although on rare occasions academic sixth-form work is found to give somewhat unexpected delight to a girl who has matured slowly, this latent zest could usually have been inferred from her attitude if not from her performance in earlier years. One master writes:

Whenever I am surprised by a sudden favourable development in the sixth form, I attribute my surprise not to a change in the pupil but to my former ignorance of him.

Other teachers, however, – the large majority – see a marked change in many boys and girls. Sometimes it is noticeable in attitude, sometimes in performance. It is particularly interesting to find that performance at 'O' level is considered by many to be a poor prediction for sixth-form work. A geography mistress reports that some pupils with a poor pass or even a failure at 'O' level have been known to achieve excellent results at 'A' level, and another in a different school comments that there is in this subject no connexion between a high mark at 'O' level and the ability to do advanced work. A Latin master says that, in the sixth, performance is much more related to intelligence than it was previously. Mere hard work, that might have sufficed for 'O' level, is now no longer adequate.

There is no marked difference of opinion between the teachers of boys and of girls, though there seems to be some slight feeling in co-educational schools that girls change less noticeably than boys. Opinions are divided on whether the intelligent pupil's performance is the more or the less likely to change. A geography master asserts that, although performance and attitude in general remain fairly consistent, a few pupils, usually the most intelligent, show marked improvement at the beginning of the second year, as they begin to realize the prospects opening out before them. But a mathematics master says that all who do really well have shown their ability early in their school career, and a physics master, saying that the very good pupil remains very good, adds that the potential State scholar can usually be picked out in the lower school.

Many teachers observe the failure of some boys and girls to make expected progress in the sixth form. A few record actual deterioration of attitude or performance or both, and this is attributed to the influence of the home. A mistress writes of those who become 'so emotionally disturbed in the sixth form that it affects their ability to work – often those with homes where the parents are difficult (in the eyes of their children) and bring pressure to bear on a girl to leave school.' A master (perhaps significantly, in the same district though not in the same school) says that lack of home co-operation causes loss of interest in school work at about fifteen, and a desire to leave school. It is implied by more than one master that if a boy who has absorbed the influences of an unco-operative home enters the sixth form, he is unlikely to stay the course.

Most of the pupils who do not succeed fully in sixth-form work are, however, thought to be those who have 'shot their bolt' by the time they reach 'O' level and are unlikely to make much further progress in scholarship. As a mistress writes:

A hard-working 'D' can be drilled up to 70 per cent at 'O' level . . . Yet this same girl may be quite incapable of writing a logical paragraph, and will almost certainly not be able to apply her knowledge to map interpretation at an advanced level.

It is not always possible to see in advance which pupils are merely industrious and which have a genuine spark. Moreover, some pupils are said to be exhausted and to suffer a reaction from the factual grind of 'O' level work, while others are said to have been trained by it in habits opposed to scholarly thought.

Notwithstanding the prominence given to those pupils who fail to make good progress in work after the fifth form (though, as is pointed out, they may nevertheless reach 'A' level), there is much evidence of encouraging developments in attitude, in performance or in both. Often the teachers observe an initial period of adjustment to new fields of study, new methods of work, and a new status in the school: this may include the emergence of a changed attitude to the staff – an attitude which eventually settles down to a friendly regard. The transition may bring, temporarily, apparent recession in work. For example, girls who have hitherto competently translated English sentences into Latin may take a year to begin to write acceptable Latin prose.[1] When adjustment has taken place, progress begins to show. 'Character' develops (or counts for more). A mathematics master writes:

Many boys from 'B' and 'C' forms do well in the sixth – boys of character who suddenly see what they want and go for it.

Another from the same school comments:

In general each boy has developed so much and seems so much more interested that it is hard to believe that he was so recently in the fifth form.

A change of attitude develops through maturity and confidence, and specialism in preferred subjects. A boy sees the goal ahead, and the atmosphere is congenial to the independent. Some girls with low 'O' level marks show themselves capable of responding to work which requires maturer judgement; and occasionally a different type of work will stimulate a girl's interest and cause her attitude to change. Maturity is associated with new responsibilities. 'Age and responsibility often redeem the previously unamenable', and the improved attitude is shown in willingness to help and to take responsibility in chosen work. A new attitude of co-operativeness sometimes develops. Fairly often, a master observes, a boy who – usually because of an unhelpful home background – has been unsettled earlier, at least comes to realize that the school is trying to help him; at this point he rapidly matures and may do much better academically than had been expected.

New and widening interests are apparent at the sixth-form stage. These may indeed cause difficulties, for, as a master points out, many boys are committed to a specialized course from the age of thirteen. For the most part, however, the change of interest results in an increased vitality and concentration. It is often stimulated by the choice and nearer prospect of a career. It manifests itself in what several masters and mistresses call 'seriousness', a quality recognized with delight by the enthusiastic teacher. There is, in fact, a strong impression that many pupils, through immaturity or casualness or because pre-sixth-form work is not

[1] See The Road to the Sixth Form, page 12:
'. . . pupils . . . in the fifth form . . . mastering the curious knack of translating somewhat disjointed sentences into Latin; when they come into the sixth form, they find it anything but easy to master the very much more difficult work.' (H.M.S.O., 1951.)

in the right key for them, do not begin to show their real mettle until they reach the sixth, when, as a mistress puts it:

They develop well and rapidly and show resources hitherto unnoticed.

Several causes are suggested for this rapid acceleration. Some contributors think chiefly of the smaller sets and different teaching methods which allow more freedom of discussion and more individual attention. The timid, it is said, gain confidence; the impressionable are not distracted by the presence of casual companions; and individualism is valued. Others consider that this is a stage at which the fruits of long conscientious effort begin at last to be seen. There are several testimonies to the 'B'-former whose hard and patient efforts produce results that 'exceed the rosiest expectations'. Such pupils are, however, comparatively rare. The teachers think more frequently of those who, feeling the atmosphere to be helpful, and glowing with interest in their chosen subjects, find scope for originality and scholarship. Particular progress is noted in those who are at last freed from the burden of failures in uncongenial studies, such as the boy, mentioned by one headmaster, who had held a lowly position throughout the school because of his inability to tackle arts subjects but who, changing his attitude on reaching the sixth and being allowed to specialize in mathematics and science, 'forged ahead and won a university scholarship'.

But the view begins to be too cheerful. Before we proceed to congratulate ourselves that things are substantially well with the sixth form, let us take a look at some of the effects of the post-war inflation of science studies.

At once we have stepped through the looking-glass. A science master says:

I have had pupils . . . whose only qualifications for studying in the Science Sixth have been failures in all science subjects and in mathematics at 'O' level.

He is immediately countered by an English master:

I believe that Arts Sixths may suffer from the panic demand for science pupils. The two second-year sixth English students this year both failed English at 'O' level, while the more successful students have gone over to science even though their performance on that side is poorish.

Teachers of the arts, and of 'mixed' subjects like geography, assume nowadays that they will receive the weak students or the careful plodders. If by chance they find themselves with a brilliant pupil, this may very occasionally be the gifted eccentric who flies in the face of fashion and good sense to choose the study of his preference. He is more likely, however, to be one whose gifts are altogether too specialized or who has developed too late to be seized in time for the science side. 'Best scientists make the best geographers,' says a regretful contributor, 'but science students usually drop geography after "O" level.' There are casual students of English – often, it is said, those without much background – who have intelligence but not a real scholarly love of the work. Others are not even very intelligent. Many English students, in fact, subsist on a thin cultural soil, particularly in music and art, and suffer from the indulgence of poor reading habits when they were younger. This poverty, especially if added to intellectual limitations, is particularly noticeable when they study sophisticated writers such as Pope and Dryden. No wonder that, on the rare occasions when a former careless indifference changes to real interest, the pupil is handicapped by his lack of verbal resources. It is a crazy educational world – a world in which an absence of sensitivity and literary awareness has become the usual and accepted preliminary to the study of English.

This is the biggest problem, the present unbalance and irrationality in sixth-form studies. Other problems, minor in comparison, are concerned with general attitudes and capacities. Some students, it is felt, are too casual, and are unwilling to make the effort requisite for ultimate success. On the average, because of the increase in sixth-form numbers, sixth-form pupils today are neither so well equipped nor such hard workers as their predecessors. Although the best students today may well be better than those of former years, there are many who do not pull their weight.

Yet, despite their awareness of obstacles and limitations, most of the teachers speak with unmistakable zest and warmth of their sixth-form pupils. Their very language becomes heightened: the verb 'blossom' is used by both men and women in attempting to describe the change seen after entry to the sixth form. There is, indeed, abundant evidence that sixth-form work is the joy and reward of the grammar-school teacher. As a headmaster said in conversation:

We are all, at heart, university lecturers in our chosen subjects.

This last statement raises a question: what would be the satisfactions of the 'true' grammar-school teacher if comprehensive junior high schools, without senior work, became the fashion? Other matters, too, invite reflection: the teachers' assumption of entities such as 'character'; their fixed notions of subjects, with attendant *mores* and disciplines; their undefined yet powerful concept of 'background'; most important, perhaps, their usual acceptance of the necessity of a sharp break between fifth-and sixth-form work. For the present, the testimony of a master with sixteen years' experience may give both encouragement and food for thought:

I am very pleased with the attitude of boys in the sixth form . . . They find it stimulating to work out problems in mathematics (applied) on their own and soon acquire the ability to think for themselves and to this end I encourage work on their own and cut down formal teaching to the minimum. It does lead me to believe that in the earlier years – the first, second and third – we should reduce the content of the syllabus to allow more time for individual work and less talking by the teacher, and that we should then be able to cover more ground in the fourth or fifth years when the boys had learnt to think for themselves and that they would be more interested.

Here is the voice of a teacher mature and confident enough to be critical of himself and of the system. Surely, if junior work ceases to feel the impact of such people, the result will be a maimed and disharmonious course.

5

Social Observations and Assumptions

In my day, it was a privilege to attend a grammar school. Today, the children seem to regard it as our privilege to teach them . . . Inability to take part in school activities or to play games for a school team because of other commitments was unheard of at my school.

(MASTER)

Most children leave home behind on entering the school. The parents provide facilities for homework and make as few demands on a girl's time as possible: 'reverence' is far more common than indifference. But a home where there are books and intelligent, lively conversation makes an enormous difference to a child's alertness, and to her well-being. She is not living in two worlds – the one where the mind matters, and the world of mass-thinking. School is no longer the main interest in a girl's life. She has a panorama of interest, she is conscious of her own importance in society, she expects entertainment as well as instruction.

On the other hand, the classroom is more of a microcosm than it was before. It is no longer a narrow, ideal world from which the child will proceed to a world where the values are quite different – the same problems are wrestled with . . . I think it good. The child, younger for her age than previous generations in her ability to read serious literature, is often far older in her readiness to discuss serious adult problems. The ivory towers have gone.

(MISTRESS)

These grammar-school children – the brilliant few, as always, a joy to teach; the many who like activity, understand the personal, evade drudgery, are puzzled by symbolism and cannot readily grasp abstractions; those who begin eagerly but whose interests flag in the middle school; the perplexing minority that shows neither comprehension nor enjoyment – what, in the eyes of their teachers, are they really like? Are they, in general, more or less intelligent than their predecessors, and do they show a comparable interest in work and power to concentrate? What kinds of homes do they come from, and what are the family and neighbourhood assumptions? Is there a discernible difference between the average 'post-war' and 'pre-war' child?

As we grow older, the past becomes golden. But this is hardly sufficient explanation of teachers' evident feeling that the task of the grammar school today is harder and more complex than it was before the war. The average intelligence of pupils (if that could be isolated) has perhaps not altered much, but many experienced people sense a wider spread in the abilities of the children they teach.[1] Whether this is associated with real differences of intelligence or with social factors, the effect on teachers is the same: to make them aware of an increased number of children who find difficulty in learning, and thus to give them the impression of a less compact and less manageable group. Individual opinions, of course, vary. One mistress, teaching in a school whose development and expansion have coincided with the period under consideration, thinks that she has seen a steady rise in intelligence; another says that although her intelligent pupils are more numerous, the best are no better than in former days; a third remarks that twenty years ago the weaker pupils worked harder. A master says that many pupils of today, though more intelligent, are more slipshod; another thinks that there is a wider range of intelligence; a mistress teaching in a co-educational school says that her present pupils are less ready to 'learn', but more ready to think: this she considers a change for the better. The feeling of many teachers is, however, expressed in the following statement:

Twenty years ago the unco-operative child was a phenomenon, and her problems were soon solved . . . Reading was the chief home recreation – intelligence seemed higher and probably was – there was more initiative, resource and imagination. The hard core of intelligent, willing and lively girls still exists, but one must admit that the surrounding pulp often hides or smothers it, so that contact between staff and willing pupil is difficult to sustain . . . Twenty (or more) years ago one entered a classroom more certain of co-operation, and on more friendly terms, than one does today, especially in the middle school.

'Home background' is a term frequently used but seldom defined in educational discussion. When teachers differ in their judgement that the background of the average pupil is better or worse than it formerly was the difference is generally in their criteria. Where improvement in the home is observed, it is most frequently in material conditions: many teachers testify to the decrease in anxiety that has accompanied the advent of almost full employment, and the marked improvement in the furnishing and general comfort of the home. Boys and girls are also said to have better health and physique, and to be tidier and better dressed.

[1] Theoretically, even allowing or errors in selection procedure, the range of ability in most grammar schools should now be narrower than it was before 1944. That teachers often feel the contrary is a sign that attitudes and assumptions, as well as measurable ability, are important conditions of successful learning in the grammar school.

Occasionally this progress in physical conditions is associated with a good development in the family attitude towards education. Now that there is less financial strain, there is sometimes more willingness to allow boys and girls of only moderate ability, as well as those who are highly gifted, to go as far as they can at school; at the same time they are often encouraged to grow up earlier, and this presents new problems. In places, the effects of a second generation of grammar-school education are beginning to be felt: a master says that in the homes of many keen bright boys the standard of education is now higher. Others say that there is less interest and co-operation. A balanced view is given by a master who thinks that there is a growing number of homes indifferent to education, offset by a growing number eager to help and co-operate: hence, he says, the differences between homes are accentuated.

Many teachers assert that the average home is now less conducive to grammar-school education:

There were fewer grammar schools in this district twenty years ago, so that pupils came from the ambitious middle classes who were anxious that their boys should enter one of the professions – banking, accountancy, teaching, legal. Their parents were prepared to pay the fees demanded and took a keen interest in the education of their sons. They co-operated with the school in ensuring that home-work was done and not shelved in the interests of pleasure. They gave help and encouragement . . .

Boys of weaker intelligence and ability do not display the same qualities of perseverance as did those of their category twenty years ago. They are weaker in concentration, and their attitude to work and their conduct are less satisfactory. I would sum up by saying that whereas intelligence has been constant throughout the past twenty years, more drive and persuasion are necessary to get boys to give of their best today.

There is said to be an increase in the representation of families indifferent to education; more children are unstable as a result of unhappy or broken homes, many mothers are at work, there is a less keen social conscience, and families, including the children, are exposed to more distractions. Many children now come from families with no educational tradition. It is not so important that the parents, being themselves uneducated, are unable to regard their children's work with informed sympathy – though this is true. What matters more is that they lack the stamina demanded by an advanced education. There are people who are delighted at the result of the 'eleven-plus' but later become indifferent: they either do not understand the implications of the grammar school or, if they begin to understand, do not care for them.

The very few teachers who see an improved interest in work say that this is found almost entirely in the form of wider rather than deeper interests. One English mistress, however, considers that the interest of both boys and girls is more genuine nowadays; they are less willing to try to acquire technical proficiency in writing, but more ready to read widely. Of those who see a deterioration, many agree that interest is initially keen, but that the children lack staying power. Typical remarks from men and women working in different schools are:

I have seen a gradual but definite slackening of interest.

They lose interest when the work becomes harder, and stop trying.

Work is more superficial and spasmodic.

After the third year, there is a deterioration in those below the 'A' stream.

Effort is less sustained.

Their attitude towards the work they present is 'Take it or leave it'.

The decline of interest is usually attributed either to parents' shortsightedness, combined with the comparatively easy availability of well-paid employment, or to an age of ample State provision and a contemporary mood not conducive to strenuous effort and the pursuit of distant goals. It is, however, pointed out that ten years ago interest in work was sometimes less than it is today. Some contributors also think that potential, as distinct from actual, interest is as great as ever, and one says plainly:

As always, it can be stimulated if the teacher tries hard enough and has enough skill.

Most of the teachers agree that concentration, if no worse or even slightly better than it was in 1948, when many children were still unsettled by war conditions, is much less good than it was in 1938. Some say that not power but willingness to concentrate is often lacking. One contributor writes:

Many boys do not see the point of concentrating on certain subjects, and the teacher ought to make a much more positive effort to cope with this problem.

Others consider that it is no part of grammar-school teachers' duty to make their work interesting. It is felt that pupils ought to come to school prepared to be interested, or to persevere with uninteresting work: in any case, to concentrate. The 'child-centred' primary school, according to this view, has betrayed its trust, and in consequence hands over children whose will to work has already been sapped:

In the '30s I did not have to teach the parts of speech in Form I; the girls came in having been taught that and a little revision was all that was necessary. I do not mind doing that bit of teaching but I realize that I have to do it because that kind of teaching is no longer a part of the junior school; the new set-up does not train children to get down to learning; they expect everything to be easy and to catch their interest. I can tell this from the unsatisfactory learning by heart I always get in Form I until the girls learn, eventually, that they must be word perfect.

This kind of regrettable softness is fostered, needless to say, by educational theorists!

Again and again teachers look back at the vanishing or vanished world of middle-class attitudes:

Once education was free, and the new examinations came in, standards of work, interest in dress and school, homework, etc., went steadily down. I try to believe that this is not so but know it is so when I see with my own eyes. We seem to have lost the boys who were not bright but who tried hard, plodded away, and were a credit to the school in their behaviour. They were often the salt of the school when it came to character, the boys one remembers long after they have left. As I look at grammar schools today the word that constantly comes into my mind is 'loutishness'.

The new generation has a different set of assumptions:

A number of boys have no real desire to be in a grammar school. They have passed the 11-plus and that is their final effort . . . In sexual interest the boys seem to be more precocious each year. Whereas eight years ago, girl friends were sought at about the fifth-form level, now it is not unusual to hear of such relationships two or even three years earlier. From the scraps of information one gleans, the reading matter which is hastily hidden at one's approach, and so on, it appears that cheap, trashy magazines with an emphasis on sex are completely ousting more sober reading matter.

The change, however, is not all for the worse:

I do not think homes were necessarily more co-operative, but I do think that more girls came from homes in which books were read and ideas discussed . . . I think we picked up much by the wayside that now seems to require formal teaching (e.g. how to memorize, how to take notes). On the other hand I find children today, generally speaking, more poised and assured, and more self-reliant about managing their own affairs, though less so in matters of work.

The tacit contract that formerly existed between the school and its pupils (or their parents) – that the children should be prepared to take the school on trust to some extent, to accept drudgery in the interests of later achievement, and even to believe that there might be some intrinsic virtue in toiling at a disagreeable task and being modest, well disciplined and loyal – can no longer be assumed to exist. Where the old standards are still considered to be valid, they have usually to be made explicit. Members of staff regard the development with mixed feelings. A few consider it to be for the better. A mistress writes:

More girls stay on in the sixth, and more enter the professions; there is certainly more vigour and enthusiasm in the school than there was then. I remember being appalled at the general apathy in earlier days, which may have meant the school was quieter, but was deadly to teach.

Moreover, if the grammar school has lost its fee-payers, it is beginning to recruit, at both ends of the social scale, children from classes not hitherto strongly represented:

It is socially an achievement to get into a grammar school. Very rarely do working-class people turn down a place for their child, although they don't really know what is involved. Thus some lack sticking power, especially beyond the age of 15, while others' achievement is amazingly good. At the other end of the scale for the upper middle classes the grammar school has become much more respectable, partly owing to the high fees of independent schools. When I went to a grammar school sixteen years ago it was considered rather a 'come-down' for a clergyman's daughter.

Many teachers refuse to be *laudatores temporis acti*, disclaiming with humorous good sense the role of judge. 'I tell them that they are not as good as their predecessors in these respects,' says one master, 'but basically I feel they have not changed.' Another speaks for the younger professional generation:

Ten years ago I was a member of a grammar-school sixth form. We should have been more intelligent – a small percentage intake over a wide area – but I don't remember it. Most of my sixth-formers seem more interested in their work and better concentrators than I was.

In the unstable world of today, assumptions vary greatly from school to school. Some members of staff are more flexible than others; but we should remember that the difficulty of their task is not uniform. In a school that is the object of much striving, and whose pupils come from families that know the traditions, teachers can afford to be tolerant. In another kind of school, a staff may feel itself obliged to fight for almost everything that means education in the sense in which its members have understood the word. On the whole the evidence of the teachers is that, while as before they have a small minority of the brilliant (though this may hardly exist in certain schools) and a fair number of intelligent pupils possessing the old recognizable attitudes, they have lost many of the steady co-operative children. These steady children in the past more than compensated for their lack of intellectual distinction by the unquestioning support they gave to the principles of the school. In their place is a new generation, sometimes lively and curious, sometimes casual or apathetic, that comes with little traditional respect for education or teachers, has no regard for the virtues of perseverance and hard work, and sees no point in putting school loyalties before the many exciting claims that compete for the attention of the adolescent. This is a strain on the teacher. Perhaps we do not always realize that it is also a strain on the child. Bright, brash and suspicious, he waits in the wings, his cue not yet spoken.

6

Conceptions of Grammar-School Function (1)

Boys and girls in every generation normally wish to establish their
independence, and to have some freedom to work out a new
pattern of life and to try to improve on the achievements of their
elders. We sometimes find these desires hard to tolerate. To complain of
young people's foolhardiness, frivolity, extravagance, selfishness, lack of
courtesy, and disrespect for authority is nearly as old as humanity. But
when a university vice-chancellor, speaking in no hypercritical spirit,
says that it is almost impossible for a middle-aged person today to enter
into the mind and mood of a young man or woman of student age, or a
psychiatrist declares that the teen-age culture of our time (of which, he
says, the violence and sartorial extravagance of so-called Teddy boys are
but one extreme variation) amounts to a true sub-culture virtually inaccessible to the older generation, they speak for a considerable number of
experienced and moderate observers who have come to believe that we
are witnessing a more complete break – not always marked by conscious
hostility – between the generations than has ever been known before.
That this division is accentuated by publicity, and by commercial cultivation and exploitation of the tastes of the teen-ager, they are willing to
admit: but they feel that the phenomenon itself has deeper roots. They
see these adolescents as people trying to master a mode of life which
is changing too rapidly for easy adjustment after the years of youth.
In such circumstances, however they achieve their learning, it will be
only to a limited extent through either the example or the precept of
adults.

The role of the teacher, as well as that of the parent, must in such an age
be especially difficult. Schoolmasters and schoolmistresses have seldom led
the young towards rebellion or innovation. Socrates was a gadfly who
unsettled Athenian youth; but teachers, for the most part, when they
attempt to teach anything beyond strictly limited skills, regard themselves
as transmitters of tradition, even though the material of their teaching
may contain seeds of revolution. This is particularly true of teachers in
the State grammar schools, which have indeed made certain concessions

to changed conditions, but in the brief period of their history have been chiefly concerned to establish themselves as worthy supplements or alternatives to an old and respected form of education. It was therefore thought advisable in connexion with this survey to invite teachers to say what they thought should be the attitude of the school towards five specific matters in which its assumptions might be found to conflict with those of family or society, or in which the school might be called upon to assume novel responsibilities.

Dress is a significant part of any society, expressing and also partly conditioning its culture. When Thomas Hardy referred to 'the regularly interchanging fustian folds' of Gabriel Oak's clothing as he walked along the road, he knew that he was indicating to the reader, at one economical stroke, a host of associations of class, setting, perhaps even philosophy of life, which would need no further elaboration. The most extreme and explicit signal of such social assumptions is uniform. From the habit of a nun to the full dress of an admiral, it emphasizes the conservatism and exclusiveness of a human group and the strictness of the code by which it is governed. The primary function of uniform is never practical, always symbolic. Eating-customs also are of immense importance, and the vast communal meals which have become a feature of modern English schools will be seen by historians to have had much more than an accidental effect on education. Again, the status of schoolboy and schoolgirl is no longer as strictly defined as it was formerly. The grammar-school popula-tion is increasingly drawn from social groups in which it has long been customary for boys and girls in their teens to begin earning, and there is at present an abundance of available employment, from newspaper delivery to serving in a multiple store at week-ends, or even baby-sitting, to tempt the adolescent and relieve the strain on parents' pockets. The fairly common practice of part-time employment, besides encroaching upon time for study and recreation, is also bound to be to some extent incompatible with older grammar-school ideals of service. At the same time, social organizations such as youth clubs make claims upon boys' and girls' leisure. These, though at least partly educational in intention, offer a range of interests, activities and companionship often much less compatible with grammar-school assumptions than those of the more traditional scouts and guides. Finally, the social codes affecting the mutual relationship of the sexes are neither as strong nor as clearly defined as they were in earlier days, and the encouragement of earlier social maturity, which has already been noted in the groups from which much of the grammar-school population is now drawn, affects not only wage-earning but also boy-and-girl friendships and the age of marriage.[1] In particular it profoundly affects the attitude of both parent and child towards the higher education of girls.

The same social groups exhibit a great variety of tradition. Some of them know and tolerate a frankness and a laxity of sexual behaviour almost unheard of among the middle-class and thrifty working-class families that supplied most of the secondary-school children of former times: others often show a rigid prudery, especially where there is a strong nonconformist heritage. (They are sometimes firmly, even fanatically, resistant to a school's programme of sex education.) Further complications are the social filtering down of supposedly advanced notions of love and marriage, a knowledge of the precocity and 'dating' that find their fullest expression in American culture, and the ultra-romantic or brutal treatment of sex in films, television, the Press and the paper-backs. All this presents problems for the school, in both the extent and the mode of its concern. Nor is it possible to draw much on past experience. Not only are parents and schools alike facing a radically changed social situation: the grammar school is also ill-equipped by its history to deal with these matters. Though there are co-educational schools of excellent reputation and of long standing, most grammar schools, and usually those with the greatest prestige, have been for boys or girls only. Taking their cue from the public schools, they have developed a markedly masculine or feminine tone, and have tended until recent years to act as though, for educational purposes, the other sex could be assumed not to exist. As for the deliberate initiation of the boy or girl into socially desirable sex roles – that would have been regarded by the grammar school of the past as entirely the responsibility of the parents. Resting on the tacitly-agreed identity of assumptions of school and home, the school would have thought it improper to encroach on the province of the family, just as it would have resented the direct interference of parents in educational matters. But the war and the social revolution have removed former securities, have brought to adolescents confusion as well as emancipation, and have forced upon teachers and parents the necessity of reconsidering their relationship and their respective functions.

Teachers who are in favour of school uniform (the majority) range from those who believe that a child ought to be proud of a uniform

[1] The Report *15 to 18* of the Central Advisory Council for Education (England) issued in 1959 (the Crowther Report) states (Section 662 (*d*)):

'The early age of marriage points to a radically different concept of how girls of this age should be treated and educated. Over 4 per cent of the girls with whom this report is concerned are married women.'

merely because it represents the school to those who emphasize that the older boys and girls in particular must not be made to look or feel ridiculous. Details vary: some masters insist that the school cap must be retained and worn, whatever else is modified, others that the cap is the one part of the uniform that should not be compulsory; some mistresses say that girls' uniform should be kept up to date, others consider that, since fashions change so quickly, it should not attempt to be fashionable. Some teachers think that uniform regulations should be rigidly enforced, others that 'a fussy insistence on absolute uniformity is a waste of staff energy'. Reasons given for having a uniform are that it hides differences in parental income and taste, encourages neatness and pride in appearance, enables pupils to be easily identified (this is held to be useful both on school visits and as a means of checking on out-of-school conduct), aids discipline (presumably by emphasizing uniformity of behaviour), encourages concentration by distracting attention from appearance, symbolizes the school tradition and thus fosters pride in belonging to the school community. An ingenious argument advanced more than once is that uniform actually helps the development of individuality by forcing boys and girls to express themselves in more fundamental ways than, as one master says, 'through the medium of their outer tegument'. The mistress who asserts that 'it helps the girl through a difficult period physically and artistically' is presumably voicing an opinion which has also been heard occasionally in teachers' discussion groups – that a young girl's developing figure is difficult to clothe becomingly and can be a source of embarrassment to her. It is also not unconnected with the judgement of a mistress in a co-educational school:

> It is a means of encouraging pride in school, of ironing out social differences, of keeping *girls* young for as long as possible.

Some teachers, on the other hand, are either doubtful of the value of uniform or opposed to it. A master of thirty years' experience writes:

> In a boys' school, uniform is irrelevant to tone and discipline. I have been in good schools with and without uniform and in mediocre to bad schools with and without uniform. I have seen uniform introduced to improve tone and discipline and of course it did nothing of the sort. Probably some kind of distinguishing mark is helpful and with more men not wearing hats the wearing of a blazer may well be a good distinguishing characteristic.

A very interesting comment comes from a master in another school, who is in favour of uniform for the lower school:

Beyond sixteen, I feel that boys at school are having their independence and maturity as adults retarded in the interests of ultimately a fuller development of personality, and therefore they should be aided rather than thwarted in at least appearing as grown-up as their contemporaries who have gone out into the world. I therefore feel that they should be *forbidden* to appear in guises which are discordant with 'the dignity of the school' rather than *made* to wear a school-classified uniform.

A master in a third school states the modern problem:

Among younger boys, who appear to have an aversion to being tidy or clean, a uniform is a help in developing a pride in their appearance and in their membership of the school. In this respect wearing of uniform by seniors is a good example. On the other hand, where boys live in streets where the great majority of their neighbours are out at work, wearing a uniform tends to increase the differentiation and leads to the isolation of the older boy from the life of his community.

Teachers of girls, even when they dislike uniform, can seldom bring themselves decidedly to advocate its abolition, though several say that it should either be strictly enforced or abolished, and some think that it should be discontinued, or made optional, for the sixth form. A drawback of uniform is indicated by the mistress who writes:

I do not know. I can see advantages in a uniform, but the use of it means that the pupil receives little guidance from school on the appropriate choice of clothes, unless this is done through needlework lessons.

It is evident that the fairly strong attachment to uniform is emotional, and that most of the practical advantages claimed for it, such as neatness or ease of identification, are rationalizations that would soon lose their force if there were not more fundamental causes of the supporters' advocacy. These are clearly indicated in two replies, the first from a man, the second from a woman:

Still rather important. Grammar-school work is of an academic type and it does not go well with acceptance of everyday standards of outside interest. Pride in belonging is not bad if it is belonging to something good.

Encourage a pride in neat and well-cared-for clothes, but use uniform also as a symbol, a reminder that each wearer of it is a member of a very special community.

Grammar-school uniform, in fact, like all uniform, is symbolic of an exclusive group, the exclusiveness here consisting in the combination of 'academic' education with certain social assumptions. Occasionally a reply betrays some fear that it may be threatened:

Every boy should wear the school regulation dress and should be proud to do so. Any departure should be checked, for it is only those who resist discipline who do not conform, and they rarely do themselves or the school credit.

Table manners and all social graces are not stressed enough at present.

But one is tempted to ask the question that perplexed Dogberry, 'How if 'a will not stand?' What is the use of appealing to an authority – authority represented either by a uniform or by a form of words – if the person against whom it is invoked does not know the rules of the game and will not play?

There is considerable feeling that table manners are unsatisfactory, as is illustrated by the following remarks:

Essential to have some control of children at meal-times, if the evidence of this boys'-only school is considered, not only for their own health and safety but also so that it is possible for grown-ups to eat in their presence without being injured, deafened or nauseated. I just like to see reasonably good manners.

We should expect them to be good, but lack of training at home is all too frequently revealed.

It is quite obvious that comparatively few parents train their children to behave properly at meals.

The subject clearly causes irritation. A master says:

The fact that this question can be asked illustrates well the fact that teachers have become more and more general nursemaids, doing all kinds of jobs which must detract from our efficiency as teachers.

Some teachers assert emphatically that table manners are not the school's affair, either because the school, they think, should not interfere in what is a family responsibility or because to acknowledge any concern in this matter is to imperil still further the already weakened academic dignity of the profession. Typical comments are:

I find my day's work hard enough without giving instruction in this.

If this means etiquette, then I do not think the school should interfere. As a parent, I resent any attempt to impose a system of etiquette on my own children.

Table manners should have been inculcated at home and before school age. Such requirements are a mere irritation to the conscientious teacher and undermine the professional approach to education.

Most teachers, nevertheless, while protesting that good table manners are properly the concern of parents and should be taught by them, accept grimly, defiantly or with resignation, a responsibility of their own. 'If the parents will not or cannot teach table manners,' says a mistress, 'then I shall. A girl must have some social graces, and is usually very grateful for help as long as it is offered tactfully.' A master says:

As I see it, one of the grammar school's aims is to develop a cultured manner. This includes speech, bearing, taste in clothes and table manners.

They are agreed, however, that school dinners are not a very good medium for the communication of politeness. A master declares that he cannot think of any other aspect of school life during the last fifteen years that has led to such a deterioration of manners:

Mass 'anything' produces bad manners and mass feeding is no exception.

A mistress says:

A thorn in the flesh. Of course – they should be dealt with while school dinner are with us, but how, with such large numbers, without taking up valuable times needed for other things?

Still, they try to think of the matter constructively. Some are for authoritarian handling: 'Good table manners should be enforced despite difficulties of supervision.' A headmaster thinks that the school should be interested in a satisfactory minimum standard until the boys are about fifteen; then a few refinements may be suggested to those boys who can obviously get little help from their homes. A mistress proposes specific lessons with cutlery, etc., in the first year, while the girls are young enough not to mind. The form mistress, she adds, can take these in a semi-humorous way. One of the few explicit suggestions that instruction in table manners can be the expression of a deeper educational purpose is as follows:

The greatest service that the grammar school, or any school for that matter, can give here is to provide such accommodation and organization as may make a meal a dignified and agreeable social occasion. I see no distinction between table manners and common courtesy, which we should surely encourage in any school, and the girl who has learned to attend to her neighbours and not monopolize either food or conversation knows more about civilization than the one who merely knows how to hold her knife correctly.

Most of the teachers who favour part-time money-earning stipulate that the time given to paid work should be strictly limited, and some would restrict the practice to holidays. Reasons given for supporting the practice are that it teaches the value of money, encourages independence, and enables the grammar-school child to compete socially with his money-earning friends. Some teachers tolerate it without enthusiasm, though one cynic says:

It occurs to me that a boy might be as well employed serving in a shop on Saturday mornings as playing rugger even for the school.

These teachers, again, insist that such work should be limited, usually to holidays, and some utter a warning against what they consider to be unhealthy indoor jobs, such as serving in Woolworth's or acting as usherette in a cinema.

Many teachers feel that, with rare exceptions, money-earning is undesirable. One master makes an extended comment which reveals many of the social assumptions of his pupils and, indeed, of himself:

Fundamentally I am opposed to it, but I do see that for some boys it is necessary to either supplement the family income or provide themselves with reasonable pocket money. Unfortunately, there are far too many today who are using it simply as a means to the acquisition of luxury articles, which in their turn require the expenditure of greater sums of money. For instance, I was astonished to find the other day that, out of twenty-odd boys in the upper sixth, only three did not possess a record player. Again, early morning paper rounds do certainly bring many boys to school tired. The sixth form is a different matter. I think it a good idea that those who are going to take up academic pursuits should have had some experience of manual work, and should have had to mix with manual workers.

Virtually all objections to part-time money-earning come to the same – that it distracts attention, sometimes seriously, from studies. Looking below the surface of apparently rational support or opposition, one can perhaps again see deeper influences at work. The 'liberal' notion that money-earning is hardly compatible with the disinterested pursuit of wisdom here competes with those of 'self-help' and 'sturdy independence', and also with the feeling that if we prolong the pupillage of boys and girls we must compensate by allowing them to participate as far as they can in 'real' life.

A small minority of teachers is indeterminate in its attitude to youth clubs. One master says that they are doing a job that no grammar school can do, but have little to offer the average grammar-school pupil. Except for this group, the teachers are almost equally divided into those who express modified approval and those who firmly oppose membership of youth clubs. Of those who approve, many say that school activities come first, and they would limit attendance to holidays or Saturdays. Some draw a distinction between church youth clubs and others, the church clubs being usually much preferred. It is strongly felt that 'a club with the wrong attitude can do untold harm'. Some support youth clubs as a means of supplying normal and democratic social experience which the inevitable concentration of the school tends to restrict. Here, it is felt, is an alternative or better training ground for leadership:

A place where a boy can find different opportunities to express himself and to exercise responsibility and powers of leadership. It is sensible for the school to establish friendly relations with club leaders and so prevent difficulties arising about homework, etc.

Grammar-school girls mix here with pupils from other schools and learn often the valuable lesson of self-government in a democracy.

There is some feeling that grammar-school boys and girls give more than they gain in membership and that this is part of their social obligation, but that it must not be abused.

Youth clubs are unnecessary for grammar-school girls in that they provide amenities already offered by the school and by experts, and impinge on valuable time. But it is recognized that they provide contact with the opposite sex in the best surroundings and that the clubs themselves benefit from membership of girls with the gift and experience in leadership. There is here a danger of exploitation with which the writer has come into contact, particularly in small village clubs.

It is difficult to lay down rules on this subject. A strict determination to prevent the boys from joining outside clubs prevents them from using their 'grammar-school ability' for the good of the community as a whole and may even sour their religious convictions. At the same time they need encouragement to choose their companions wisely.

The suggestion that youth clubs are for the working classes occasionally becomes explicit:

A good thing on the whole – especially for girls mainly of the working-class type we get.

Of those who are opposed to membership of youth clubs, a few think them decidedly harmful in their influence:

I do not like to say this but I have not found that they have had a good influence on grammar-school boys.

I have helped with a number of youth clubs. A grammar-school girl is a godsend – but nevertheless it is no place for her.

The following remarks, however, embody the chief arguments: that school and home between them should provide all the cultural and social amenities that the youth club can offer; that club activities dissipate the energy and weaken the concentration proper to grammar-school work; and that grammar-school pupils are actually impeded in their development by associating with those who are markedly less intelligent than themselves:

These are entirely unsuitable for grammar-school boys, who have so much to do at school both in work and play. Where youth clubs are encouraged there is a falling-off of interest in school societies and often an increase in the unfortunate habits of smoking, etc.

Most boys should have enough interest in school clubs and youth clubs would only take away from homework time. I doubt if there is much value in meeting children from another intellectual class, such as are found in youth clubs. It would be so easy to drop to their level of activity.

Youth clubs should not interest the grammar-school girl, who is amply provided for at school and at home in social and cultural development.

Girls who do go to youth clubs think of them as a 'right' and by contrast that preparation is an imposition; they overtire themselves in the evening and 'rest' in class the next day.

Homework should take precedence over acting as officials in youth clubs, which in any case are intended for the underprivileged.

With regard to friendships with the opposite sex, teachers can be classified as those who (a) think them no concern of the school; (b) view them as somewhat alarming; (c) consider them to be a potential threat to school work; (d) express a passive tolerance; (e) think that the school should provide opportunities for boys and girls to meet, or (f) favour positive education in such relationships. A master who thinks that they are not the school's concern says:

As long as there is no interference with work these are matters for the parents. If the school usurps the parents' functions it will fail, at least partially, in attaining its own proper aims.

Remarks suggesting some timidity are: 'within reason', 'all right in small doses', 'should be discouraged until sixth form; I think girls are much better in a separate school', 'sex – ignored as much as possible'. Some teachers who see a potential threat to school work are nevertheless on the whole sympathetic. Typical remarks are: 'To be encouraged, but need careful watching to see that work is not interfered with'; 'favourably – provided school work comes first'. Occasionally, however, there is a feeling that boy/girl friendships are incompatible with real academic work.

Friends of the opposite sex should not be encouraged, but such friendships should not be forbidden – after all, to learn to understand the opposite sex is part of one's education, but the longer a person remains free from the encumbrances that such friendships often entail, the greater are one's academic achievements.

The attitude that has been described as passive tolerance is represented by the following remark:

They are natural. No notice should be taken of normally developing friendships, which are basically harmless, and should produce a healthy attitude.

A master, one of the teachers who thinks that the school should provide social opportunities for boys and girls, says:

I was educated and have taught in mixed schools and feel that the more they are allowed to mix the better is the natural relationship. Idling on street corners I do not like, but suppression is hardly likely to help.Where schools are one sex, mixed matches (chess, tennis, etc.), debates, lectures and dances would be useful.

A master teaching in a co-educational school sees the matter this way:

A school has a great advantage and performs a useful social function when it can arrange for boys and girls to meet in normal school activities and social occasions. Hence the great advantage which a co-educational school has over single-sex schools, where joint functions tend to have an unnatural, staged effect. I feel however that schools should discourage 'courting couples', partly because of the distraction from a course of study which by its nature will postpone the wedding day, and partly because I feel that, even for intelligent youngsters, school age is far too young to become committed. On the other hand I like to see frank and friendly relations betweeen boys and girls.

A few who favour a more positive lead think of this almost entirely in terms of manners. A mistress, for example, says:

Such friendships should be accepted as natural, but one should expect good behaviour in the streets: a girl who looks sheepishly in the opposite direction when met with boy-friend should be gently reproved and asked next time to introduce him.

It may be observed that, while few teachers will admit to any views that might be considered 'stuffy', there is a fairly strong undercurrent of feeling that, with reference to school life and work, friendships with the opposite sex are at best unavoidable distractions. This is seen in the suggestion of conscious broadmindedness that accompanies such a remark as 'Inevitable – so why not accept it?' When a constructive approach is advocated, it is almost always thought of in connexion with either special lessons for 'sex education' or the social or extra-curricular activities of the school. There is not the slightest suggestion that the grammar-school curriculum itself should be to any appreciable degree oriented towards preparing boys and girls either for their relationships with each other or for their social roles. It appears to be assumed without question that such preparation is not an essential function of the school, though it may well receive some incidental attention.

All the matters here considered – uniform, table manners, money-earning, youth clubs, sex relationships – are comprehended in one supremely important topic, the attitude of parents and school to each other. The teaching profession's stereotype of the old-style grammar-school parents is of people who handed their children over to the school for so many hours a day, provided them with uniform and books, accepted the school's conditions of work and behaviour and kept out of the way except on recognized school occasions. The school not only taught and disciplined its pupils on the school premises: it also enjoined on them appropriate behaviour whenever and wherever they wore school uniform – chiefly, that is, in their journeys to and from school. Parents, according to this stereotype, accepted the school's right to say: 'Wear your school hat,' 'Wear your gloves,' 'Change your shoes,' 'Give up your seat on the bus,' 'Don't eat sweets in the street,' 'Don't talk loudly in public.' They, in turn, on receiving their children back, resumed their responsibility to feed, clothe, control and advise them, to provide them with leisure interests and activities and supervise their social relationships. New-style parents, also in stereotype, assert themselves both too much and too little. They no longer take the school on trust. They are not fully co-operative about uniform. They meet the school's curricular and homework demands with either apathy or hostility. On the other hand, they take it for granted that the school (or the State) will provide books, milk, medical attention and (at a reduced rate) meals, and themselves accept little responsibility for disciplining their children, giving them social training or providing for their leisure. It may be added that both stereotypes exist together in the minds of most grammar-school teachers.

Those teachers who advocate a close connexion between school and parents do so chiefly on the grounds that many parents nowadays are bewildered and need careful introduction to the methods and aims of the school. A mistress says:

> This is particularly important for those parents who have had little education themselves, if we are to gain their co-operation.

A master states the reason more fully:

> It's very important for parents to know what is expected from a boy in a grammar school (especially if they haven't been to a grammar school). Boys at school probably have to work harder than at any other time in their life and it's vital that parents understand this and help to make it possible . . . An understanding home is a 'must' for a grammar-school boy.

Certain local variations are pointed out: for instance, that in a country district less organized contact is necessary, since within a small society parents and staff frequently meet each other in ordinary daily transactions. In contrast, the difficulty is mentioned of giving sufficient time and attention to this matter in a large city school, where a boy may be taught by as many as ten masters.

A number of teachers, while advocating contact, would like it to be strictly controlled. Some would limit it to the school's public occasions; speech days, sports days, and dramatic performances are frequently mentioned. Some advocate 'open days'. Others think that there should be direct access to certain people, usually the head master or mistress and either form or subject masters and mistresses. Sometimes this seems to be envisaged as a very formal relationship:

> Direct contact with headmaster is most desirable. The headmaster will in most cases consult the subject master at a convenient time.

A very different attitude is expressed in the remark:

> The headmaster and senior mistress are readily accessible to parents visiting the school – often a great nuisance but, in my opinion, absolutely necessary.

It is commonly felt, however, that a certain amount of distance is desirable for both sides:

> I do not think that, from the point of view of the subject master, much more than that [contact with head, housemaster] is necessary. Boys will often become suspicious if a master knows their parents too well.

> I think parents should have access to teachers when they wish, but be able to leave well alone after that.

Headteacher/parent: We do not tell the physician what to prescribe for us, nor tell the builder how to construct our houses.

A somewhat similar caution shows itself in some of the teachers who favour regular organized parents' meetings; but most of them, while saying that such meetings should occur at decisive points in a pupil's career, also think it advisable to supplement them by the activities of a parent-teacher association or by less formal contacts.

A good many teachers advocate a parent-teacher association. A few are against such an organization, for reasons indicated in the remarks of a master and a mistress:

In my experience, both as a teacher and as a parent, P.T.A.s become social clubs in which intrigue is rife.

Not a parents' association which all too often becomes a kind of social club divorced from the needs of the girls.

Those who favour an association are also often conscious of drawbacks or dangers; it is frequently stated that parents must not interfere in the organization and discipline of the school, and there is some feeling that meetings should not take place too often. But one master, representative of several teachers, says:

Parents need as much educating as boys, if not in the same way. A live, intelligently run and seriously minded parents' association makes the teacher's work easier.

Apart from the very few who would have as little contact as possible, the teachers almost unanimously agree that, whatever form of connexion they favour, they can hardly ever reach the parents whom it would be most beneficial to meet – the unsatisfactory parents of unsuccessful or difficult children. Remarks such as the following abound: 'How to contact the indifferent parent I have no idea.' 'The tragedy is that there is very little possibility of voluntary and therefore friendly contact with "problem" parents whose children are usually the school's "problem" children.' Whatever activities and information the school provides are felt to be generally offered to those who least need them, and few teachers have any idea how this problem may be solved. A few advocate persistent efforts by the staff, including visits to pupils' homes, but they are not representative of the majority.

Many assumptions are thus seen to be implicit in teachers' attitudes to pupils and parents. Almost every teacher, of course, represents a unique deviation, but the imaginary norm of the grammar-school world appears on this evidence to be somewhat as follows:

'The grammar school is a minority society, the relative exclusiveness of which is usually and appropriately symbolized by a uniform. Its essential distinguishing characteristic is close and serious concentration on intellectual activity. Such concentration is not compatible with much leisure, and the frequent companionship of young people who have more free time may be distracting; it is therefore wiser to avoid youth clubs or to give them only a little attention. Devotion to study implies some postponement of social maturity, in respect of both money-earning and relations with the opposite sex. Though boy-and-girl friendships may exist, they must not interfere with or intrude upon study. Membership of a grammar school is also associated with a certain refinement of manners and restraint of demeanour: these were originally a class distinction, but are now accessible to all; though a mark of grammar-school education, they are chiefly the concern of the home. Parents should be entirely responsible for their children out of school time; their responsibility includes teaching their children acceptable manners and providing for their leisure interests. They must be interested in school and support school functions. They should not need much personal succour from school, however; they should observe (and make their children observe) its demands and regulations, and should trust its educational methods and provisions. As for teachers, their primary function is to promote study. They should not have to dissipate their energy by giving much attention to domestic matters, though they may and should reinforce ethical and polite standards which are simultaneously being inculcated by the home.'

An educational structure built on such assumptions suffers strains when, as is quite evident from the statements received, actuality so frequently fails to correspond with the imaginary norm. What then should be the main function of a grammar school today? Teachers think of the individual's development chiefly in terms of intellectual perception, skills and knowledge; of preparation for a higher stage of education or for particular employment; of the maintenance of moral and cultural standards in both their individual and their social aspects; and of the training of character. Taken together, these opinions make up a very complex notion of a 'true' grammar-school education.

Of those who associate this education with the fostering of personal powers – a large proportion – many take as their ideal the full development of the individual. Some of them refer to 'balanced individuals' or 'integrated personalities', but it is also apparent that individuality *per se* (with or without 'balance') tends to be regarded as desirable. One master, indeed, says that the function of the grammar school is to produce tolerant eccentrics. Closely connected with this individualism is an emphasis on clear and independent thinking, which is also associated by some with the development of precise expression in speech and writing. The acquisition of powers of criticism and judgement is felt to be important. The practice of intellectual discipline is widely praised and is thought of variously as finding pleasure in intellectual activity, perfecting intellectual tools, and acquiring sound scholarship. The notion of the disciplinary value of particular subjects still prevails, as when a mistress strongly advocates the teaching of Latin, *as a mental discipline*, to all. In this category, however, the most frequently expressed ideal is that of an all-round education. Such an education is generally felt to be disinterested and self-justifying, and indeed the word 'liberal' is often used. The following remarks typify this individualist-liberal estimate:

The concentration of pupil-ability and highly specialized staff is the most effective method of developing, through specialist studies, the mental capacities of boys selected for their intelligence. This is an essential function of a school such as this.

To sharpen and exercise in every possible way the mental faculties of the best brains.

It should not aim at providing a training for a future career, other than preparing the 'field'.

The last-quoted remark emphasizes the ideally self-sufficient nature of a grammar-school education. Many teachers, on the other hand, think of such an education chiefly as preparatory. Where the preparation is for universities or for other institutions of advanced education, it is partially reconcilable with the preceding notion of disinterestedness. But some of the contributors think it an important function of the grammar school to prepare pupils openly and deliberately for a career. A master puts it explicitly: 'A well-paid job which he will enjoy doing.' It is in any case fairly generally recognized that only a section, usually a minority, of the school's population will go to a university. Several teachers are conscious of some incompatibility of aims, which is aggravated by the pressures of the times:

To develop the capacity to think clearly, objectively and independently, and not to accept at its face value every facile slogan of the day. To develop taste and judgement and prepare pupils to make an intelligent use of leisure, viz. in activities that are stimulating to the mind and soul.

Today education is becoming more and more vocational in a technological age, but if in the process the ideals of character-training and of cultural development of the mind are neglected, grammar-school education will be the poorer.

Twenty years ago the warning against a materialistic trend in grammar-school education was necessary; now it is urgent.

(MASTER)

Twenty or even ten years ago, grammar-school pupils aimed more at the professions; today there is a more material approach to life, which does not entirely fit the traditional ideas of a grammar school's function.

(MISTRESS)

Preparation for the professions, however, could never have been entirely compatible with disinterested study. Certainly today, when university work itself is often regarded as training for a specific occupation, the ideal seems to recede. A competitive employment market, the strength of materialism and 'conspicuous consumption', and the obvious interim goals – already mentioned – of university entrance and public examination results, combine to make it difficult for teachers to be actuated purely by a love of learning and consideration of the personal aptitudes of the pupil, even when their emphasis is still mainly on his individual needs.

Not all teachers, however, would place the chief emphasis on the individual. Some regard the social function of the grammar school as complementary to the individualist, others as taking precedence over it. Again, the social purpose of the school can be thought of either as that of developing the individual's social awareness and responsibilities, or as the mechanical provision, through 'manpower', of the needs of the State. Finally, each social purpose can be stated with approval as an ideal to be sought, or stated with disapproval but nevertheless recognized as a *de facto* function. All these views find expression in the answers received.

Some teachers openly regard it as one of the chief functions of the grammar school to meet the needs of the time. A fairly external type of motivation is implied in the following comment:

To build up a large virile sixth form and thereby supply[1] the universities, the services, the Civil Service, the professions, industry and commerce with their future leaders.

It should also be noted that as compared with twenty years ago there is a far greater need today for large numbers of chemists, physicists and mathematicians and these can only be produced by efficient grammar schools.

A more personal function is suggested by a young master:

The main function of any school is to produce men and women who can become full members of the society of which they are part, i.e. can contribute to the society, economically and/or culturally, according to their individual capabilities.

[1] The writer first used the word 'feed'.

In a society such as ours this means that the boy or girl should be trained to think for himself, while having due respect for authority and legislation. For a man to be a full member of society his education should cover all aspects of culture and learning. This, of course, represents an ideal to be aimed at, rather than a realistic view of what actually takes place. Nevertheless, the grammar school provides for a certain type of mind ('academic', if you like) the sort of education which will enable it to contribute to society in the fullest possible way (to mutual advantage). I should say that the present scientific bias of our society should be reflected in our grammar schools (in moderation) and this represents the main difference between today and twenty years ago.

The development of a sense of citizenship, social responsibility and an interest in contemporary social problems is repeatedly stated as a worthy aim. The statement sometimes implies a criticism, as when a master says:

Too often grammar schools produce men (and women) capable of obtaining the necessary qualifications for their future career, but with an inadequate sense of citizenship and their function in a democratic society. This sounds very ambitious; so it should be.

The old grammar-school virtues of social loyalty and service continue to be stressed:

The all-round education of the 15 to 20 per cent of the population who are suitable for an intellectual discipline. This could have been said twenty years ago, but as, even as recently as that, poverty at home prevented a substantial proportion of those who had this grade of ability from going on with their education beyond fifteen to sixteen, the function of the grammar school today is to see that its form of education is broad enough to serve all the community's needs. Many vital functions in society are at present served by those who did not have a university or even a higher education at school, e.g. trade-union leadership. Interest in social problems and the cultivation of a willingness to serve are more important in grammar-school education than ever before.

The general notions of leadership and responsibility need some analysis if they are to be useful. Few think of 'training for responsibility' solely in terms of preparation for a career: nevertheless, it is not at all uncommon for teachers to feel that the cultivation of a desirable moral quality is in some way associated with the gaining of a responsible – *i.e. important and well-paid* – post. Perhaps the commonest attitude is a temperate acceptance of the fact that, as oligarchy more and more gives way to bureaucracy, many of the more intelligent will find their way into positions of considerable power and influence, and that, this being so, it is desirable for them to be civilized, well-informed and responsible. 'The main purpose', says a young master, 'is to produce a sound, well trained, literate and thoughtful governing class. The officers of the fighting and civil services must come from the grammar and public schools, and I take it that the grammar schools will progressively have the larger share.'

The following statements by two teachers of nearly thirty years' experience adequately represent between them the general range of views on leadership:

> The answer will not differ greatly [from that of twenty years ago]. The main function will be to equip boys and girls for the professions; in a wider sense, to train their minds and equip them with information and the means of discovering it in order that by their clear and constructive thinking they may take the lead in society and give willing and enlightened service. The forms of training change as society changes – a girl may now be a personnel manager or lawyer or doctor – but the aim is not different. It is wider in that a number of 'ancillary services' once considered menial are now recognized as worthy of the fullest general education the school can give – nursing, for instance; but the aim is to impart a *depth* of knowledge.
>
> The many excellent responsibilities undertaken by senior boys and girls in grammar schools are important, too, but they exist as by-products of the fellowship in learning for which the school exists.

> To produce pupils possessing a wide general education, a sense of responsibility and the initiative to accept leading positions in the life of the whole community.
>
> Since the grammar-school entry is selected, we must expect it to produce leaders in all spheres of social, cultural, civic, religious and scientific activity. At whatever stage they leave school – at fifteen, as early leavers; at sixteen, at the end of the basic grammar-school course, or later – we should expect them to develop further than the majority of their contemporaries, and to be prepared to accept responsibility sooner. At whatever level they enter the world outside school they should possess a body of knowledge which will enable them to make further progress, but their contribution to society as a whole will perhaps depend more on moral qualities – on a sense of responsibility, determination, ambition, an inquisitive mind . . . than on the amount of information absorbed during their school careers.

Here can be seen the fundamental grammar-school agreement on the association of certain moral qualities with strenuous learning; here, too, the general irresolution as to whether the school is primarily concerned with learning, the moral qualities being consequential, or whether the learning is important chiefly as providing the peculiar atmosphere of discipline and dedication in which certain virtues may flourish.

Whatever the precise emphasis, there is no doubt that many teachers believe an essential function of the grammar school to be the fostering and development of particular human qualities. Sometimes this is seen as a relatively external matter; the setting of high, and usually Christian, standards. The main function of the grammar school today, says a master, should be to produce a generation of pupils who have a clear conception of the correct set of Christian standards and values and who have been trained to think for themselves and to express their views clearly and precisely. Sometimes it is thought of as more intimately concerned with the formation of character:

Primarily the grammar school should provide an academic training to enable its best pupils to fit themselves for professional careers by way of the university.

It must also endeavour to train character and develop personality, to foster intellectual and spiritual humility, tolerance and breadth of vision; above all a deep sense of responsibility, of duty, and of service . . . Its function here differs only in degree, if at all, from that of any other type of secondary school, but, because it is concerned with a very large number of the ablest children, it has to that extent a particularly grave responsibility.

A mistress with twenty-one years' experience states a problem that is in the minds of many:

A difficult question to answer. I suppose the grammar school should, ideally, aim at developing the pupil (or providing rather an atmosphere in which the pupil may develop) intellectually and spiritually to his/her fullest extent. If that is so, the same should have been true of the grammar school twenty years ago.

If the function of the grammar school is also to provide an education which will enable the pupil to earn his/her living in a world increasingly competitive . . . there must be a widening of the curriculum and at the same time a resistance to the crowding out of so-called cultural subjects which seem to me more necessary than ever in a world of increasing leisure time.

Is the function of the grammar school also to provide the moral standards which twenty years ago were probably learned from a religious home-background?

A mistress with thirty years' experience, and a master with twelve, represent a fairly widespread opinion that it is the function of the grammar school to fortify the pupil against the debilitating effect of mass influence s

There are several functions, as I see it, for the grammar school and they are sometimes in uneasy relation.

First, we have to maintain standards of scholarship, to stimulate and begin to satisfy intellectual curiosity, to advertise the worth of learning among pupils most of whom live in a frankly 'Light Programme' atmosphere.

Second, for the 70 per cent who leave at sixteen without achieving any real scholarship, we have to provide a foundation on which they can build; to convince them that a normal human life includes an interest in books, music, etc.; to cultivate a habit of thinking about and discussing problems of politics, human relationships, etc.; to develop a realization that behind these lie principles involving questions of values and so ultimately of moral and religious beliefs.

Third, we have to train people willing and able to be leaders and to take responsibility – so grammar-school life ought to offer opportunities for initiative in word and action.

Apart from the social purpose of the school, and in spite of the demand for scientists and the resultant earlier specialization, I consider the purpose of a grammar school, perhaps its main purpose though least definable, goes back to the Renaissance: to give an introduction to the humanities and a training in intellectual processes, and thus provide a healthy counterbalance to the influence of the cinema, I.T.A. and Radio Luxembourg, not in a monastic or snobbish spirit, but to help pupils *not* to accept without question *all* the products and ideas of what J. B. Priestley calls 'Admass'.

The notion of character, strong if occasionally vague, repeatedly asserts itself. Sometimes this character is thought of as in a sense preliminary to the work of the school, and – separable from intellectual gifts – as partially a determinant of the success of school work. Thus, as we have already seen, there are said to be boys and girls of 'character' whose performance sometimes ultimately surpasses that of their fellow-pupils possessed of mere 'intelligence'. This inherent character is one of the elements the decline of which is associated with a lament for the fee-payers' children of past days. But in another sense it was and is the supposed function of the school to *produce* it: terms like 'character-building' are used fairly frequently. The exemplary pupil-figure who emerges as a major assumption proves to be one whose lineaments have already been outlined: admirable if a little devoid of sparkle. Brilliance is, of course, highly appreciated; good manners are very desirable; but industry, pride in work, public spirit, truthfulness and stability – these are essential. Barbarian and Philistine both contribute to the ancestry of the ideal grammar-school pupil, but the Philistine characteristics are dominant. Hard work, in particular, is often thought of as good in itself: indeed, it is at times uncertain whether study is of chief value as the product or as the inducer of strenuous application:

I feel most strongly that we are trying to educate too many to too high a level in the grammar schools, and that the numbers entering them should be reduced, but if the social climate is inimical to such an idea, then we can play a valuable role by insisting, even for the less academically gifted, on the traditional standards. Work is a habit, I feel, and if we can inculcate that habit, then the fruits may be seen much later, to the betterment of society.

As might be expected from the evidence of an earlier chapter, preparation for examinations is recognized by many teachers to be associated with the function of a grammar school, though none is so openly cynical as to assert that it is the only function. A fairly representative, if ultra-candid, view of examinations is:

(a) To push as many entrants as possible through G.C.E. 'O' level in as many subjects as they can manage, thereby ensuring that those in our community with above-average brains can use them to best advantage in the jobs they will get. Nothing was more appalling in the early years of the century than the wastage of working-class talent.

(b) To do its best to safeguard and hand on liberal traditions in an increasingly hostile world.

I do not mention concepts like 'good citizenship', 'serving the community', etc., because I believe it more important for our products to consider what it is they are serving.

Other alleged functions of the grammar school, some of them named by a fairly large proportion of the teachers, are: to concentrate on theory rather than technique, to inculcate respect for the right authority, to encourage the wise use of leisure, to maintain standards of scholarship, to give children a foretaste of types of human aspiration and aspects of human personality, to lead them towards worthy and interesting (as distinct from merely well-paid) occupations, to provide equality of educational opportunity for pupils within a certain range of ability, to encourage a humble awareness of one's own gifts and powers together with tolerance of those of others, to foster wide interests, and to give firm discipline. It is essentially, as a headmaster says, to give an education based on books. As for the cultural values already mentioned, their association with the function of the grammar school is expressed in the words of one mistress:

To protect as far as possible, even if only in a small way, the culture of European civilization, now assailed by barbarism from the East and from the West.

An important new problem is raised by a master of long grammar-school experience, whose comment gains significance from the fact that he has also taught in other types of secondary school:

In my opinion, the strength of a grammar school lies in the social activities that take place within its confines. Before the 1944 Act, the master who took a post in a grammar school was paid on a higher scale than in other types of school. Therefore the man who accepted a post in a grammar school understood that more was expected of him than mere classroom teaching, and so the grammar school was staffed with men who willingly gave their out-of-school time to running activities in which they were interested. That tradition still holds today.

However, the introduction of the 'basic scale' has imposed these duties on the masters who teach in secondary modern schools, and while many secondary modern schools are now introducing more out-of-school activities, not all these activities are being taken by a master because he likes to do it, but more because he is asked to do it. This has not the same value as in the grammar school, and the pupil is the first person to sense this.

The grammar school still gives to a pupil (even if unsuccessful academically) something that cannot be given by merely changing the names of the schools.

He might well have added that, in some districts, certain out-of-school activities carry 'overtime' payment in modern but not in grammar schools. Furthermore, to acknowledge that teachers may justifiably wish to earn a salary comparable with those of other professions need not prevent us from recognizing that the system of so-called special-responsibility allowances, besides producing ludicrous anomalies between school and school, or even within schools, has introduced more particularly a mercenary motive. This cannot but damp the spontaneity of grammar-school teachers in their concept of professional service, and thus undermine many of their former assumptions about the nature of their work.

Any theory of organized education must include an answer to the question how far the school is properly the mere instrument of the adult generation in any culture-pattern, testing its efficiency by the success with which it is able to transmit intact the traditions of the group; and how far, on the other hand, it is the function of the school to dissociate itself from, and at the same time to affect, the contemporary pattern – either by intelligently anticipating innovations which the inertia of the unthinking majority may cause to be postponed too long, or by emphasizing its conservative and traditional force amid disintegrating influences. A grammar-school mistress, looking back on a long teaching career, realizes that the question becomes particularly difficult and even more important when, through a shift of school population, what is traditionalism for one section of society becomes an innovating force for another. She says:

Twenty years ago the main function was clear – the school offered what was demanded (an academic education, character training, cultural standards and physical education) by parents and girls of a fairly fortunate and enlightened type. *Now* the grammar school must endeavour to provide the same, not to supply a conscious demand but to fill what is often an unconscious or unexpressed *need*. It should adjust its methods to keep in step with changed home conditions, changed ideas of leisure, etc., but it should *not* change its real values. It should still aim at providing an education in the true sense of the word, and should not be tempted into becoming a training establishment for 'job' takers. There is more need than ever to inculcate standards of taste and ideals of service, intellectual honesty, etc.

It should not stagnate, but neither should it be too eager to rush ahead (e.g. in employment of the latest mechanical aids to easy study). It should train its pupils to take the objective view when facts are distorted by emotional presentation. I think that the function has not changed, but the need for the school to perform that function has intensified, while difficulties have increased.

In the eyes of these teachers, then, the function of the grammar school is partly individual and partly social; it is concerned with intellect and character, often in a curious and not easily definable association; it has to serve the needs of the time, and yet both to conserve and to innovate in opposition to the time; it should be able to presume a close understanding with the home, and yet must preserve a certain aloofness from the home. Moreover, it is now faced with the task of transmitting to some of its pupils, and even to their parents, what were formerly unquestioned personal standards; it has to cultivate an understanding of the increasingly difficult contemporary world, but at the same time protect its pupils from mass media; it must train its pupils for careers, while not losing the ideal of learning for its own sake; it has still to educate for leadership, though the notion of leadership may be changing. These and other notions of function are bound up with many assumptions expressed and unexpressed, some of them perhaps mutually incompatible. A master of experience, yet with several years' service still ahead, may speak for many thoughtful contemporaries:

I used to regard grammar-school education – originating in the humanistic tradition of the Renaissance – as, basically, simply education *sans phrase*. I would have acknowledged that it was, or over and over again had been, cumbered with obsolete husks of pedantry. But that is what it meant for me and represented my personal aim in my teaching. I think I still hold this view, in the sense that much as one pressure or another calls upon us to produce scientists and technologists, I still think that the first and basic thing is to produce the beginnings of reasoning, upright, fair-minded men with some access to the heritage of 'culture' – some likelihood of readiness to acquire taste for at least facets of the riches of our tradition. (I hope I am sounding broadminded enough in range.) But however much an enduring 'soul' of this must be at one with the past, it has in *body* to be 'bang' up to date. Therefore, there is enormous need to modify and revise the curriculum, to ensure its making complete contact with the conditions of today. Perhaps revision has become a matter of running hard merely to keep in the same place. This of course is where science and technology come in, but as humane not merely utilitarian studies. We have got to satisfy the urgent demands of the rising generation and also remain true to our fundamental awareness of our cultural roots. I think perhaps there is a difference in this from, shall we say, a smug narrowness more evident twenty years ago.

PART THREE

Those who are Taught

7

The Learning of Subjects

CHILDREN entering the grammar school begin to think in terms of
'subjects' and to associate these new concepts with feelings of
success and failure. In a sense, of course, they have known 'subjects'
before. They have met 'history' and 'geography' in the primary school,
and are all too likely to think of themselves already as 'good at tables'
or 'weak at composition'. But in the grammar school they face the fully
developed system of subject-periods, specialist teachers and end-of-term
examinations. Most children soon learn to place these freshly identified
subjects in order according to two principles which may or may not
coincide – success and preference. Naturally, their notions of comparative
achievement or liking need not correspond with any absolute judgement.
The very intelligent child may not be weak at anything; the thoroughly
discontented may find nothing to like. But a 'best' and 'weakest' subject,
or a 'most enjoyed' and 'least liked' lesson, most children are likely to
have. They carry, accordingly, two mental lists, on which subjects and
lessons are arranged according to strict precedence; and once an item is
fixed on either, it is somewhat difficult to dislodge. Its position, indeed,
tends to become part of the learning-situation itself, by constituting one of
the major assumptions brought by both teachers and pupils to their task.

One might suppose that a subject frequently given as 'best' would
seldom appear as 'weakest' – but that is not how the results come out. In
the children's evidence, if a subject appears at all it is almost as likely to be
the one as the other. Some subjects are mentioned again and again, others
hardly ever; so that we possess a clear picture of the order of importance
in children's minds of grammar-school subjects. Religious knowledge,
little regarded, is at one extreme; languages and mathematics are at the
other.

Looking at boys and girls separately, we see similar broad tendencies.
There are fluctuations, but languages and mathematics remain highly
charged subjects for both sexes. English, however, has greater significance
for girls, science for boys. Many boys are conscious of lack of success in
languages, many girls feel a comparable weakness in mathematics. But

before making a generalization such as 'Girls are unmathematical' we
should note that mathematics shares with languages the strongest indications of success for girls, and that for boys languages come third on the
list, after mathematics and science.

Children in 'Y' forms less often give estimates of 'best' for science,
languages and mathematics than do those in 'X' forms. Yet even in 'Y'
forms these subjects have fairly strong associations of success. Both sets of
'weakest' estimates show little deviation from the average. The arts are
associated with stronger feelings of lack of success in the second than in the
fourth-year; nor can this be entirely because – for many fourth-year
pupils – these subjects drop out of the reckoning, since both second- and
fourth-year estimates of 'best' are near the average. In the fourth year,
many of the pupils who feel themselves to be studying these subjects
seriously may well be doing so (probably retaining them as public examination subjects) because they are judged to be good at them. It is, however,
worth recalling in this connexion that the estimate of 'best' in 'Y' forms
is only a little higher than that in 'X' forms. It can be seen that estimates
of both 'best' and 'weakest' for science are markedly higher in the older
than in the younger group. This suggests that the science subjects considerably increase in importance between the second and fourth years.[1] Very
significant is the steep rise in estimates of 'weakest' for languages in the
older group, suggesting that notions of linguistic difficulty have much
increased. It may be noticed that in each year estimates of 'weakest' exceed
those of 'best' in both languages and mathematics, but that in the fourth
year the gap is much larger in languages than in mathematics. There are
also indications in the papers that when English is entered as 'weakest'
some form of language-study, particularly grammar, is usually meant;
and there is some evidence that teachers in general cause a fairly clear
distinction to be drawn in their pupils' minds between language and
literature.

As might be expected, the average figures conceal wide differences
between schools. Let us begin by looking at some examples of 'best'
ratings in second-year 'X' forms. In one boys' school, for languages the
figure is 10 out of 35, in another 1 out of 31; in one girls' school, for
mathematics it is 11 out of 31, in another 2 out of 32; in one girls' school,
for history it is 11 out of 30; in two girls' schools history is not mentioned. Comparable examples could be found for 'Y' forms or for 'weakest'

---

[1] No firm statement can be made about *increase*, *decline*, etc., since the information is given
by different groups of children. If they may be taken to be representative, we may conjecture
some probable tendencies of development.

subjects. Why is it that in one school's second-year 'X' form 15 girls give French as their 'weakest' subject, while in another it is not given by one? The differences are just as striking in the fourth year. In the boys' school first mentioned above, 10 out of 20 boys give French as their 'best' subject in a medium-graded fourth form; in another school's 'X' form 15 out of 31 give it as their 'weakest'. In a 'Y' form of one girls' school 11 out of 20 give mathematics as their 'weakest' subject; in another 1 out of 21. It may be remarked, incidentally, that 'X' form figures show a greater tendency than 'Y' form figures to be bunched together for 'best' subjects, but it is difficult to know what conclusion, if any, should be drawn. For 'weakest' subjects, bunching seems to occur with equal frequency for both 'X' and 'Y' forms. Perhaps children in 'X' forms tend to know success with greater certainty than those in 'Y' forms, whose figures thus form a more random set; whereas few children are left in any doubt about their least successful work.

It must not be thought that these figures represent a capricious choice on the part of the children. On the contrary, there was every indication, both in their demeanour when answering the questions, and in the papers themselves, that the decision was taken with great care. Sometimes an appeal was made on the spot: 'I can't decide whether it's geography or Latin. I got a lower mark for geography, but I find Latin more difficult in class.' Often remarks are added to the answers. Typical comments are:

'I love it.' 'I can't understand the master's explanations.' 'Mathematics, but I think I am improving.' 'It used to be French, but we have a new teacher this year, and I am understanding it better.'

Moreover, the results on the whole tally with one's independent observations, where these exist, of the quality of the teaching. The boys' school already mentioned as giving the high ratings of 'best' for French is known to have an unusually good French department. In a girls' school where the geography mistress is known to give much attention to the problem of preserving the confidence and interest of weaker pupils, 7 out of 28 girls in the fourth-year 'Y' form give geography as their best subject (this is the highest proportion in any school) and none gives it as her weakest. In a school where the Latin is known to be in the hands of a very weak teacher, 15 out of 32 second-year pupils give it as their weakest subject, and none gives it as the best.

A survey of the results would tend to confirm several opinions already held about the grammar school. It suggests, as has been said, that English, science, languages and mathematics are in general the subjects in which success or the lack of it is significant for the children. The fact that practical subjects come low on the scale does not in itself support an assumption that more intelligent children are weak, even comparatively, at practical subjects. If this were so, one might expect a large count of 'weakest' against few of 'best'. The figures are interesting rather as indicating the degree of importance with which several people, but chiefly the staff, invest subjects for the children. It appears to be generally assumed by all parties concerned that the two curricular elements of primary-school days, on which so much emphasis was laid, still persist; that English and arithmetic have become elaborated into a curriculum whose main pressures are linguistic on the one hand, scientific on the other. Granted this, the figures give rise to some interesting questions and observations. Why is religious knowledge at the bottom of the scale? Is it because teachers feel strongly that, religion being the common need of all, it is inappropriate to load it with notions of success; or is it because, being often a non-examined subject, for most children it just does not count? The high peaks of 'weakest' in languages for boys and in mathematics for girls may be due, if not to inherent sex differences, to socially determined sex preferences: but they also suggest that language teaching may be weaker in boys', mathematics teaching in girls' schools. The fact that notions of 'weakest' predominate over 'best' for these two most loaded subjects suggests that teachers conscious of the importance of their subject and the need for success in it may tend to over-emphasize its disciplinary aspects and to generate negative feelings about it. If this be so, it is interesting to notice that science, also often given as 'best', is not so frequently given as 'weakest'. It is noticeable, too, that though very many girls consider mathematics their 'weakest' subject, their proportion of 'best' is surprisingly near that of boys.

No simple generalizations can account for the picture given in the children's evidence. Their assumptions of success appear to be derived from two powerful, complex and somewhat contrary sets of influences. The first represents the expectations of society and its general idea of grammar-school functions; the other, the child's own temperament and ability, individual parental attitudes, local environment, the tradition of the school, and the influence (not necessarily the teaching-skill) of particular teachers. This second set of influences is extremely important, and children's remarks make it quite clear that in particular the teacher's power to communicate feelings of success and failure cannot be over-estimated.

If we look at individual children, we find that they by no means automatically associate greatest enjoyment of a lesson with highest success in the subject, or least enjoyment with lowest success. Some such correlation is seen in the body of answers, but there are interesting variations. In English and mathematics, the idea of being unsuccessful does not appear to carry a correspondingly marked lack of enjoyment, whereas in languages the lack of enjoyment is if anything even more pronounced than the sense of failure. As might be expected, physical activities are more popular than 'important', while English, foreign languages and mathematics seem to be enjoyed considerably less than they are associated with either success or lack of it. The popularity of the sciences is most marked (though they carry also a fairly high rating of 'least liked'): two children in five name a science lesson as one of the two they most enjoy. In contrast, nearly thirty per cent find least pleasure in a foreign language, classical or modern.

Comparing second and fourth years we see, as might be expected, that physical activities are considerably more popular among the younger than the older forms. This probably indicates not that physical activities are less enjoyed as children grow older – the low figures for 'least liked' are almost identical for both years – but that what Wordsworth calls

> The coarser pleasures of my boyish days
> And their glad animal movements

are being refined in adolescence and are taking their place amid a host of competing pleasures, some of them of a more markedly intellectual kind. Perhaps another illustration of this is the very marked rise in the enjoyment of science lessons. In fact, the sciences show a sharp increase in ratings of both 'most' and 'least enjoyed'. One might have expected some decline in enthusiasm, as stricter disciplines begin to replace the fun of playing about with fizzy mixtures, magnets and balances: the interesting thing is that an increase in appreciation almost keeps pace with this.

The comparison of 'X' and 'Y' forms shows, not surprisingly, that physical activities figure as 'most enjoyed' nearly twice as often in 'Y' forms as in 'X' forms. This is almost certainly associated with the fact that they are more often the 'best' subject in 'Y' forms; but also, no doubt, with the slower assimilation of intellectual pleasures, which of course is the chief reason why a pupil goes into a 'Y' form in the first place. Science, languages and mathematics are much more positively enjoyed in 'X' forms, but we should note that about a quarter of even 'Y'-form children name a science lesson as 'most liked'. The surge of dislike of foreign-language study in the fourth year is clearly marked, and is highest in 'X' forms. It is indeed significant that nearly one-third of the ablest children name a language lesson as 'least liked', while the slightly lower percentage in 'Y' forms is doubtless attributable only to the fact that many children in these forms have dropped one or perhaps all foreign languages by the fourth year.

The greater popularity of the arts, geography, English and languages among girls and of science among boys may be noted. It should nevertheless be observed that the sciences have the highest total of lessons most liked by girls. Dislike of mathematics is expressed twice as often by girls as by boys, but the girls' figure of 'most enjoyed' is not very markedly lower than that of boys.[1] A closer analysis shows that for both sexes, while the appreciation of English and geography remains constant in the second and fourth years, that of languages and mathematics is markedly lower in the fourth year, that of the sciences markedly higher, and that of history is lower for boys and higher for girls in this year. Other details invite consideration. Are girls' apparently greater preferences for the arts (painting, music, etc.), English and foreign languages due to a sex difference in aptitudes, to the fact that these subjects are given more time and are taught better in girls' schools, or to social assumptions that the sciences are the sphere of the boy, the arts and languages that of the girl?

As before, a glance at individual lists reveals great differences between school and school. More than a third of all the answers from one boys' school (not the one previously referred to) give Latin lessons as the 'least liked'; in another, there are only two such answers. Biology is in general a popular subject, and even more popular among girls than among boys; yet 7 out of 25 girls in one form like biology lessons least. History is outstandingly popular in both years (and in 'X' and 'Y' forms) in one boys' school. The average figure of 'most enjoyed' for art in the fourth year is about six per cent, but in one co-educational fourth-year form 10 out of 28 give this rating for art.

It is clear that for the pupils the day of the 'grand old fortifying classical curriculum' is over. There is no evidence in these papers that the classics, even in translation, occupy a large part of their consciousness. Yet it would be a great mistake to jump to the conclusion that science is now all that matters to them. The fact that foreign languages appear to have a higher aggregate of importance than either the sciences (taken together) or mathematics, suggests on the contrary that the curriculum of the *grammar*

---

[1] This is particularly true if we look at single-sex schools. The complete figures are: In boys' schools, 22 per cent; in girls' schools, 20 per cent; in co-educational schools, 20 per cent of boys and 13 per cent of girls. (Note: *two* lessons were named.)

school is still felt to be strongly concerned with linguistic study. It should also be remembered that the subject-division used for purposes of classification had to be arbitrary, and that a different grouping might give a rather different picture. If, for example, we take history and English to represent for the middle school largely literary interests and therefore consider them as one subject, we find that together they outstrip the sciences and mathematics and rival foreign languages in significance, and that in popularity they exactly equal the sciences and are inferior to no subject.

Although, then, the popularity of one or more of the sciences is clear enough by any reckoning, there is no need to suppose that modern schoolboys or schoolgirls assume in advance the insignificance or unattractiveness of other subjects. The chances are about equal of engaging their interest in either scientific or literary studies. Boys appear to be more predisposed towards the first, girls to the second, but there is little evidence here to support the assumption that sex difference is an overwhelmingly conditioning factor. Perhaps the most disquieting elements of the survey are the apparent insignificance of religious knowledge and the frequent dislike – even though their importance is conceded – of foreign languages and mathematics. The estimate of religious knowledge reflects general contemporary opinion, and is illustrated by a boy's remark:

I dislike hardly anything. But I think assembly has no practical use, except for reading notices of general interest in school, which might quite easily be put on the notice board.

Neither French nor mathematics often draws the appreciative comments that are occasionally given for other subjects, particularly sciences, English and history. Both subjects, however, are associated with a number of remarks expressing bewilderment, dislike, or fear of punishment. In the eyes of the children, teachers of these subjects appear with some frequency to be insufficiently clear in their explanations, to go too quickly, to be 'boring' (a word that embraces many pedagogical errors) and to be impatient of learning-difficulties. That these associations are not inevitable and that all subjects are closely dependent on the influence of individual teachers is illustrated by the fact that in one school these qualities are attributed with considerable unanimity to the teacher of physics – a subject which is popular elsewhere. But it is also clear that assumptions of various kinds strongly influence the processes of both teaching and learning.

A headmaster takes morning prayers. He is, let us suppose, a convinced

Christian, who feels that he is doing something more spontaneous and more genuine than formally obeying the 1944 Act's injunction that the school day should begin with an act of worship. But what if the assumptions of the assembled school are largely those of the boy already quoted – and, moreover, are shared by some of the staff? It will be difficult for him to pierce that shuffling impatience or polite attention without appearing either clownish or priggish. The master who gives religious instruction may be on good terms with his boys; but he feels that the study of his 'subject' is strenuous. It includes hard moral judgements and abstruse theological concepts; the historical and textual study is difficult, the poetry grand but austere or deceptively simple. How is he to communicate all this to the cheerful pagan who assumes no need of salvation, whose ignorance of the Bible is almost complete, and whose opinions of our Christian heritage, if he holds any, may well be based on the Sunday-school notions of religion scornfully publicized by an eminent scientist? How much easier, in these respects, is the task of the colleague in the physics laboratory! Even the least intelligent of his pupils has heard of volts and barometric pressure, radar control, cathode tubes and magnetism, and is not only willing but eager to see in the laboratory toy of balls and wire a model of the solar system and an allegory of the force that keeps sputniks in their orbit.

8

Background Influences: Families, Friends & Out-of-School Interests

CHILDREN bring to school a network of assumptions woven of parental attitudes, family structure and habits, friendships and all the influences of life outside school. Before they even enter a classroom these assumptions have already largely determined their capacity to receive certain kinds of knowledge – and, moreover, to learn in the precise way in which the school wishes them to learn. At the outset, then, of two children with similar intelligence one may be predestined to learn with ease, the other with difficulty. Once inside the school, they meet another complicated tissue of assumptions that may or may not approximate to those they already possess. These new assumptions held by others begin in turn to exert their influence, generating powerful feelings of acceptance and rejection and subtly reacting upon a child's own view of family and neighbourhood.

We do not always realize the strength of these invisible forces. The mass media and the teen-age culture, which offer such exciting alternatives to the stuffy demands of the pedagogue, may for the moment be ignored; so may the cynical *Zeitgeist* that silently discredits generous impulses of enthusiasm and belief. Powerful as they are, they lie nearer the surface than do the assumptions, communicated by parents and family, that make life itself intelligible to the young child and remain as strong conditioning forces in adolescence. And it is these assumptions that, as often as not, the school challenges, not the less significantly because the challenge is sometimes at the point of apparently trivial symbols.

Sit up straight and hold your knife and fork properly. (Who said it was 'properly'?)

You don't end a letter with 'and oblige' or sign it 'Mrs. Smith'. (Why not? My mother does.)

After our harvest festival we will send the produce to hospitals.
(My father says it's the Ministry of Health's responsibility to see that hospitals get adequate supplies of fruit.)

Read *The Ode on a Grecian Urn* for homework.

('Thou foster-child of silence and slow time' – it's nearly time for *Wells Fargo* – yes, Mother, I can keep an eye on Tommy for half an hour: it's only reading homework.)

One of the schools visited was a small 'first choice' school in a beautiful city. Originally a private foundation, it perhaps inherits some prestige from the days when secondary education for the middle classes was expensive and dependent upon private enterprise. The parents of rather more than four pupils out of five have themselves had a grammar-school education. In contrast is a large school in an industrial area. Nearly 70 per cent of its pupils come from families in which neither parent has been educated in a grammar school. Almost all the brothers and sisters over eleven years of age of the children in the first school are receiving or have received a grammar-school education. This is true of only one-third of the brothers and sisters of pupils in the second school – and this in spite of the fact that the rate of grammar-school admission is slightly higher in the second district than in the first. In the first school, again, the sixth form is nearly a quarter of the whole school: in the second, less than one-twelfth. Perhaps most significant: in the first school, 80 per cent of the children express not merely acceptance but keen enjoyment of school; in the second, a mere 28 per cent. It is an almost inescapable conclusion that initial family assumptions, though not the only determinants, are powerful influences for or against success in grammar-school learning.

The figures for all nineteen schools surveyed suggest that co-educational are more likely than single-sex schools to have pupils who do not possess a grammar-school 'background'. The boys' and girls' schools with the highest figure for single-sex schools are in the same locality, a large industrial Midland city. Both are large and enjoy considerable prestige in relation to the other maintained grammar schools. But the city also has two large and highly reputed direct-grant schools, to which no doubt many parents with a grammar-school education tend to send their children as holders of either special or fee-paying places.

The lowest proportion of pupils with 'friends not at grammar schools' is found, perhaps significantly, in a school whose headmaster openly and frequently emphasizes the exclusive nature of grammar-school education and the desirability of avoiding distracting social contacts. Very low figures are, as might be expected, those for a boys' and a girls' school in a London 'dormitory' town with a largely middle-class population. The schools with the highest proportions are a boys' school in a small west country seaside resort, a co-educational school in a northern seaside town and two co-educational rural schools. As the two seaside towns also draw from a large rural hinterland it may be supposed that an agricultural environment, partly because of a comparative scarcity of companions and partly through similarity of interests and pursuits, tends to discourage separation out of school hours.

There is a discernible difference in all these respects between 'X' and 'Y' forms. 'Y'-form children are more likely than 'X'-form children to have parents who did not attend a grammar school and also to have non-grammar-school friends, and much less likely to have brothers and sisters with a grammar-school education. Not only, then, will 'X' and 'Y' forms in the same school differ in average intelligence. There are also social influences that tend to accentuate differences between them.

It is impossible to estimate exactly the children's impressions of their parents' attitudes, past and present, to their membership of a grammar school. But a survey of five hundred expressions of opinion suggests that the large majority of parents, probably over 80 per cent, very eagerly wished the children to enter a grammar school. The rest consisted chiefly of those who were indifferent or only mildly keen, with a small addition – probably about 5 per cent – of parents who were opposed to the idea or in conflict with each other about it. After two or four years (there is little difference here) a small number of parents, representing perhaps one family in sixteen, appear to have increased their approval and co-operation. A comparable proportion has lost its enthusiasm, and the remaining parents continue to be indifferent, or retain or develop attitudes of hostility or conflict.

It may be estimated that of the children whose parents actively wished them to have a grammar-school education about half not only felt this eagerness but associated it with some tension, as is illustrated by the following groups of comments (boys and girls being represented in each group):

Second year

(1) 'Very very much. (They encouraged me, and were very disappointed when I didn't pass at first. They encouraged me to do my best at my secondary modern school) . . . (2) They are very pleased that I have passed. Glad that I tried hard.'
'Very much, for they knew my life would practically depend upon it.'

('X' forms)

(1) 'Very much. At the school I was going to they didn't teach very well, so mummy coached me in Arithmetic and daddy in Scripture . . . (2) They are very pleased and always await eagerly the day when marks are known.'

(1) 'They wanted it with all their hearts . . . (2) They are still very, very pleased.'
('Y' forms)

Fourth year

(1) 'VERY MUCH . . . (2) They want me to work and get on in life.'
'They wanted me to come very much and indeed I was given a wrist-watch and £1 for passing.'

(1) 'They were very anxious and would ask me every day if the results had come through . . . (2) They are still very keen and insist on my doing my homework before I watch T.V. or go out with my friends.'   ('X' forms)

(1) 'They were openly very enthusiastic about me coming to a grammar school and wanted me to come very much . . . (2) They are still very worried if I do not try hard enough and are very keen for me to do well.'   ('Y' form)

Consciousness of tension is not always painful. Though a minority has been aware of disturbing pressure, many children seem to have shared their parents' enthusiasm with pleasure.

Second year

(1) 'Mummy and Daddy did want me to come to a grammar school very much . . . (2) They feel quite excited about it, and share my school life with me.'
('X' form)

(1) 'They wanted me to come to the grammar school with great interest . . . (2) They are very pleased and are always willing to give me help when I need it.'
('Y' form)

Other children felt little or no tension, though aware at the time or in retrospect of their parents' interest. Several, indeed, express some scorn for the parent who would resort to threats or bribery:

Second year

'My mother and father were very sensible about this question, and told me they would very much like me to go to a grammar school but if I failed they would not make a fuss about it.'
'They were very keen but they did not try to worry me by saying too much, or disappoint me by promising me things if I did pass.'   ('X' forms)

Fourth year

'They expected me to, for they felt I could cope with the work. If I had failed my 11+ they would not have been very disappointed, though, because Daddy is a technical school teacher and both are very broadminded.'
'I think they were really keen but they never let on. They did not do the silly

thing of bribing me with a new bicycle. They explained the advantages for me of a grammar school education and then left it to me.' ('X' forms)

'Naturally they wanted me to come, but they were not frantic . . . They are glad I passed and help me as much as they can in making decisions on what subjects I should take.' ('Y' form)

At first sight it may seem that, whatever may be thought of the children who did not enter a grammar school, those who have entered are for the most part supported by highly favourable parental attitudes – so much so, in fact, that in this respect we need worry little about them. But on reflection, we should modify this opinion. In the first place it must be remembered that much of the enthusiasm is vague and diffused, or (as will be seen later) by no means always leads to the right kind of parental support after the child is in the school. Secondly, the existence of a proportion which cannot be exactly estimated, but may be as much as 15 per cent, of parents who are initially indifferent or even opposed to this kind of education, constitutes a problem and a challenge. Even if it were as low as 10 per cent, this would mean that, for example, sixty children in a school of six hundred were likely to be beginning their grammar-school life without positive support, wise or unwise, from their parents. It should also be remembered that the proportion, though lower in some schools, will be higher in others. Moreover, this is not a matter of simple numbers. Everyone familiar with any kind of community or association knows that members with neutral or negative attitudes can be tolerated to a certain limit, beyond which the association tends to lose its coherence and its purpose. If parental attitudes are appreciably transmitted to their children – and there is much evidence from this inquiry that they are – then some schools must be taking a strain that can only be held through the exercise of unusual gifts on the part of the staff.

Considerably more of those children whose parents are hostile to a grammar-school education, or in disagreement with it, are in 'Y' forms. How far this attitude is a cause of a child's being in a 'Y' form, and how far it is a consequence of the fact that a child not in the top rank of ability is not so likely to awaken parental pride and hope, can only be a matter for speculation. It is certain, however, that less successful children are likely to have their task made harder by the thought that their parents are indifferent or opposed to it, and teachers who deal with such children need to be aware of the conscious and, still more important, the unconscious loyalties, with which they may come into conflict.

Boys and girls show that they can be keenly and sometimes bitterly aware of their parents' attitudes:

(1) 'They were indifferent to the situation. I came here because they could not afford to send me to Public School and wanted me to be at home . . . (2) They feel they're saving money and beyond that I do not know their thoughts.'

(1) 'My mother very much and my stepfather was not so bothered . . . (2) My mother is glad and wants me to get on and my stepfather is not bothered.'

(1) 'They would not have minded if I did not come to one . . . (2) My father is glad that I came but my mother wishes I hadn't.'

Acceptance of his parents' limited educational aspirations is suggested by the remark of a fourth-year 'X'-form boy:

(1) 'They weren't really bothered . . . (2) They think I should have gone to another school to learn to be a draughtsman or a joiner.'

While some parents give their children the right kind of cheerful assurance, sharing both their success and their problems, others express their interest only by driving their children or by holding them austerely to a high standard of achievement. Further examples of both kinds of 'encouragement' may now be given:

Second year

(1) 'My mother was very anxious for me to get a good place in the world because she knows what it is to have a life of misery in poverty . . . (2) She is pleased but is now anxious for me to keep in an A form.'
'They think I should work harder and not fool around at all.'
'They feel that I am getting on very well here, and encourage me to work although I am expected to work *without* being told to.'
'They are still proud and pleased and help me in any difficulties I have.'
'Their feelings have not changed about me being at a grammar school, but they worry me about the work.'   ('X' forms)

'They are very pleased and are encouraging me in every way.'
(1) 'They were intent I should pass . . . (2) they are pleased but feel I should work very much harder than at present.'   ('Y' forms)

Fourth year

'They are quite serious about my going to a grammar school and help me as much as possible.'
(1) 'They wanted me to come very much and did their level best to see that I did come . . . (2) They are very glad . . . and insist on my working hard to achieve the best possible job.'
(1) 'They were very eager that I should come to grammar school, it appears to

me now, but they were convinced that if I did not pass, I would be receiving the correct type of education, and would not have made me think I had let them down ... (2) Now they are very pleased and encourage me to work, though they most certainly do not force me to work if I am tired or have worked a great deal of late.'

'They still feel the same as when I came and they assure me of this by always looking through my schoolbooks and if there's a bad mark they criticise me on it.' ('X' forms)

'They are very interested still and always give me quiet when I do my home-work.' ('Y' form)

Some parents who saw without much enthusiasm their children entering a grammar school, later show considerably more interest and co-operation:

Second year

(1) 'They did not mind where I went ... (2) They think it is a very good thing as I have a lot of things to occupy my mind.'

(1) 'They didn't want me to come ... (2) They are a little less against it now.' ('X' forms)

(1) 'Not a lot but they did not mind a lot either ... (2) Better than they did at first.' ('Y' forms)

Fourth year

(1) 'They did not particularly want me to come ... (2) They are very pleased.'

(1) 'They were not particular whether I came or not ... (2) They feel that I should try to get my G.C.E. now I am here.'

(1) 'Not really ... (2) They feel glad I came.' ('Y' forms)

To balance these, there are parents whose enthusiasm wanes. Sometimes this seems to be because of disappointment in their children's lack of progress, though it is difficult to say what is cause and what is effect in such a deterioration of attitude:

(1) 'Very much ... (2) [They think] the sooner I leave the better.'

(1) 'Very much ... (2) [They feel] nothing really.'

(1) 'They liked [the idea] very much ... (2) Not so much. Given up hope.' ('Y' forms, 2nd and 4th years)

Other parents begin to lose their enthusiasm when they realize that being at a grammar school exacts a price in money, leisure or the organization of home life. A doubt is implied in the comment:

'They feel that the grammar school education is really worth the large amount of homework and the extra expense of uniform.'

A more definite decline of support is seen in the following remarks:

(1) 'Desperately . . . (2) my mother doesn't like it very much now because of the homework.'

'They are still pleased I came but wish that I was able to leave sooner because Mother has to work to keep me supplied with uniform.'

'They think it is good as I can now check on bills etc. But my parents do not think that homework is necessary they say that we should learn enough at school.'

(1) 'They wanted me to come very much . . . (2) They aren't very particular which school I would have gone to. It is a nuisance having homework when I could be doing something useful in the house.'

(1) 'Before my mother died and my father re-married they wanted me to come a great deal . . . (2) My grandmother and my father think I would be better at work.'

It should be pointed out that many parents, while not withdrawing their support, seem to be seriously troubled, and not primarily for their own sakes, about the pressure of work, as is seen in two remarks typical of many:

'They moan sometimes if I take too long over my homework, so that we cannot get out together, but they would not like me not to be here.'

'They are pleased that I have succeeded in entering but express some doubt about the excess of homework.'

Evidence that children under pressure at school communicate a sense of strain to their families is seen in a boy's and a girl's remark:

'They take an interest in my school life [but] they think that perhaps it is having an effect on my temper.'

(1) 'They wanted me to come, but did not worry me in case I should fail . . . (2) Too much homework. I get bad-tempered when I can't do it and take it out of the family.'

Illustration of the strain that can be felt by adolescents who on the whole accept the demands of school and by so doing place themselves athwart the family assumptions and tradition are given in the extended remarks of two girls, both of whom write of school, 'I like it very much':

'They wanted me to come although they said very little about it . . . They are beginning to think that it might have been more practical if I had gone to a Technical School . . .

At home my parents are quite poor and so we have a small house with only one living room which can be used and therefore when I do my homework in the winter I have to do it in the living room. My parents have the television on and I am doing my homework in the room. My homework takes up most of the evening and therefore I rarely go out. I have a thirteen mile bus journey to and from school. People in my village are inclined to think that one gets stuck up when one goes to a Grammar School.'

'I like the school very much because fun is put with the lessons and that does not make them dreary even the worst . . . They only wanted me to come to the grammar school provided I was good enough for it . . . They are absolutely disgusted with it and really wish they had never sent me . . . The main difficulty is passing my G.C.E. English . . . Another difficulty about homework is that my Parents disagree with it. When I am busy doing it my Mother calls out and says "Surely no more homework. It is not fair if you work hard all day at school and have to come home to more work." I hear this said every night. I also disagree with homework as I feel tired when I arrive home.'

It may be added that, since the second girl enjoys most in school 'an English lesson when a Shakespeare's play is being acted', she is almost certainly well in advance, educationally, of her family. (Neither of her parents attended a grammar school.) One is not surprised that neither of these girls is in an 'X' form.

Two in every three of a sample of the pupils have television in their homes. Boys almost always give this information without comment. The girls' occasional remarks are mostly disapproving: 'No, *thank goodness.*' 'Yes, unfortunately.' Both boys and girls sometimes make remarks such as 'I am not allowed to watch it until I have done my homework,' or, 'I only watch certain programmes,' which suggest a consciousness that television may be regarded by parents or teachers as something of a rival to serious education. On the other hand, as their general remarks will show later, it is sometimes mentioned as one of the fields in which they feel that they are exercising new discrimination as a result of the taste and judgement developed by school.

It is difficult to form an accurate picture of the conditions in which these grammar-school boys and girls do their homework. We may note that there is a small number at the best and worst extremes – the one suggesting a room allocated for this purpose, the other (represented only by boys) suggesting no provision whatever. What 'bedroom' signifies is not easy to estimate, since it may indicate either an extremely unco-operative attitude towards homework or elaborate care. We should note that slightly over a third of the pupils (in addition to those who have a special homework room) show by their answers that it is their habit to withdraw to a room where they may have solitude and quiet for concentration:

'dining-room', 'drawing-room', 'spare room', 'a room where there is peace and quiet', 'the room where the children are not playing', 'the front room', 'the room without television'.

Some add that the room is heated. It may also be observed that, while the proportion of girls in 'X' forms having quiet provision is slightly higher than that of girls in 'Y' forms, that of boys is twice as high in 'X' forms.

Many children appear to do their homework in rooms – named as 'sitting-room', 'living-room', 'lounge', 'kitchen' – where family activities are going on. There is one striking detail, though: comparatively few of these are boys in 'X' forms. Why is this? If 'bedroom' signifies, as it may, a more serious provision for girls than for boys, then the evidence of co-operative family attitudes may be little different for the sexes. If it does not, the figures may mean that families tend to take a boy's work either more or less seriously than a girl's – to show, that is, either more co-operation or more hostility – or that boys themselves tend towards the extremes of casualness and seriousness. Or again it may be that girls, either from preference or because of family assumptions about the girl's role, tend to remain within the family circle more constantly than boys, so that a homework environment which seems to be for boys associated with a tendency to poorer performance in school work is not so obviously associated in the same way for girls.

These answers give no very clear total picture. We may tentatively say, however, that boys in 'X' forms tend to have markedly, and girls in 'X' forms less markedly, more favourable and fewer unfavourable home-work environments, in proportion, than do the pupils in 'Y' forms. There also seem to be some grounds for supposing that girls are either less often willing, or less often permitted, to concentrate on their studies away from the social pressures of the family.

It is cheering to observe that comparatively few of these children are often bored – though girls tend somewhat to the extremes of 'often' or 'never'. Boredom, whether frequent or occasional, is usually referred to school situations. Many children mention specific lessons; others speak generally of 'lessons I dislike'. Prolonged talk, whether on public occasions (particularly speech days) or private, is boring. So are long lessons, too easy lessons, lessons in which there is much listening and little activity, and having to study an uninteresting book. Teachers cause boredom when they talk about a subject with no life in it, repeat themselves and speak monotonously, go off the point, ask questions to which they have already given the answers, or go out of the room leaving the class to work. The picture of restless young people reluctantly submitting to enforced

passivity is supplemented by a list of some out-of-school causes of boredom: listening to an uninteresting talk or conference on the radio, listening
to music, listening to an uninteresting lecture. Some say that they are
bored in the holidays, particularly towards the end of the long summer
holidays. A few give a picture of boredom at home: they are bored
when they have nothing to do, no future plans, nothing to read; they
are bored when alone, or ill in bed, or when it is raining and they cannot
go out; one boy says that he is bored when he has no cigarettes. Other
occasional causes of boredom are given; among them are visiting relatives,
waiting for a bus, waiting for boy-friends, films, television.

An inquiry into interests and leisure activities gives a general impression
of considerable vitality. Many forms of vigorous physical exercise are
mentioned. Boys considerably outnumber girls in this section, but this is
largely explained by the fact that the boys' interest in sport is not always
that of players: some of them are keen followers of local teams. The girls'
interest in watching sport is negligible.

A quarter of the interests and activities may be called constructively
recreational. If domestic interests and activities may be admitted in this
category, the proportions of boys and girls are almost equal. Boys are
interested in 'building things out of wood', 'making electrical contrap-
tions', 'building radio sets, carpentry, model railways', 'making rocket-
propelled boats', and making models. Some of them play musical instruments. They take an active interest in cars and in trains. Some enjoy
photography. Some play snooker, billiards and chess. Many girls are
keenly interested in the home. They work in the house and garden, sew,
knit and cook. They help their mothers in various activities, and look after
younger children. Others, like the boys, play musical instruments; they
sing and they seem to show more interest than boys in listening to music
as well. They look after pets – budgerigars, dogs or horses – and sometimes
help in stables or kennels. Some paint and sketch, and some are immensely
interested in amateur acting.

A small proportion of the answers shows predominantly studious or
creative interests that may be thought either to overflow from or to
supplement work done in school. Such are bird and animal watching,
'adding to my collection of animals', keeping reptiles and fish, identifying
flowers, trees and insects, studying art, chemistry, Greek, 'going to the
the seashore and finding things', 'going down to the dry dock and
watching what they are doing to the ships'. (The writer of this last is a
girl.) A few of the other answers express interests more and less definitely
connected with the open air. They mention fishing, shooting, taking dogs

for walks, hunting and just 'going into the country'. A few boys are so keenly interested in farming that it is their chief out-of-school activity.

Very few answers give as chief out-of-school *interests* those which may be classified as passively recreational – that is, popular music, television, cinema, theatre, concerts, listening to records, listening to Radio Luxembourg. Yet these things much oftener represent spare-time *occupations*. It would be unwise to read too much into this apparent discrepancy: it may, however, mean that these passive recreations are sometimes sought *faute de mieux*, or from a desire to be like one's companions, rather than because of a strong initial interest. We must also remember that there are degrees of passivity. Television, cinema, theatre and concerts can all demand active interest and participation.

Few boys and girls give reading as their chief out-of-school interest, but it accounts for many more of their spare-time activities, particularly for girls, who here outnumber boys by nearly two to one. Not all this reading is of what the teacher would recognize as literary material. Considerable evidence outside this inquiry exists to show that not only school stories and other writing of a childish and ephemeral type but also science fiction (at all levels), stories of sex and crime, and cheap women's magazines make up part of the reading of grammar-school pupils. There is little sign in these papers of a taste for sustained and fairly difficult reading, though it is indicated now and again. It may be noted that the excess attention given by girls to reading is roughly compensated by the boys' interest in collecting. In its passive form this consists of collecting matchboxes, train numbers and car registrations, or of 'sticking football pictures into scrapbooks'. Its more active form is almost exclusively stamp collecting. Only a few girls appear as collectors.

Almost one-sixth of the interests and activities may be classified as gregarious. About half are concerned with some kind of youth organization – scouts, guides, Boys' Brigade, Girls' Life Brigade, A.T.C., Red Cross, St. John Ambulance, church and other youth clubs, Crusaders. The rest may be called 'merely gregarious', and are named as 'going out', 'meeting friends', 'mixing with a crowd of boys and girls', 'going out with boys', 'boys', 'girls', 'people', 'dancing', 'rock 'n' roll', 'coffee bar', 'parties'. In both categories girls outnumber boys. With the boys, organized activities exceed the unorganized. With the girls the reverse is true, and in the second category they outnumber the boys by eight to one. Other miscellaneous interests stated by the boys and girls are church, furtherance of the gospel, studying for sermons (this last by a boy who is a member of a strict fundamentalist sect), going out with parents, looking round other towns, games with the family, making up games about sporting activities, writing to pen friends.

Asked what they feel about leaving school, some of the fourth-form pupils give neutrally-toned answers. 'I shall leave when I have my G.C.E.', '. . . when I have learnt enough for a good career', 'I shall go to college'. Few indicate that they want to leave in the sense that they are tired of school. Some regard leaving school as a natural and proper transition to a new stage of life, to be anticipated neither with reluctance nor with eagerness. A very few say that they have not considered the matter, and slightly more express mild regret at the prospect. In all these classes, it is interesting to note, the proportions of boys' and girls' answers are almost identical. The largest proportion for each sex is represented by those who are extremely reluctant to leave; but there is here a discrepancy between the sexes, reluctance or fear being indicated by forty per cent of the girls and twenty-five per cent of the boys. Complementary to this is the fact that twenty per cent of the boys, as against eight per cent of the girls, say that they look forward to leaving school when the time comes. These last two answers are almost certainly associated with the fact that a boy tends to envisage his future career more clearly than does a girl.

The question on leaving school calls forth many interesting remarks. Boys make comments such as the following:

> I feel that I shall lose good friends and masters.

> I am nervous about starting a job on my first day.

> I am frightened by the thought of looking after myself.

> I get tremendous fun out of school life, which I shall miss.

A girl in a 'Y' form illustrates an occurrence familiar to headmistresses – the marked swing towards school that takes place sometimes in the fourth, though more often in the fifth, year:

> About a year ago I was really waiting to leave school; now I think that if possible I will continue my education until I am $17\frac{1}{2}$.

An 'X' form girl describes a fairly common situation, in which can be seen the feeling – very strong in certain sections of the community – that education is an 'extra', expendable when other needs are great; and also the unquestioned assumption that if only one member of the family is to have an advanced education it must be the boy:

I want to stay on at school, but my brother is at the University and my parents have to work hard to keep him there. I must therefore leave as soon as possible as I want to earn quickly.

Other typical remarks from girls are as follows:

I shall be happier and freer when I have left school.

I dread leaving my friends and having to meet and make new ones.

I shall be sad to think I may not see some friends and teachers again.

A new life will start, and that will be exciting.

Asked what they would like to do after leaving school if they were given unlimited choice, both boys and girls give answers which as a whole correspond fairly closely with what they think they will in fact do, though girls show a greater tendency than boys to curb their aspirations Where the pupils permit themselves slightly extravagant ambitions, those of boys appear as travel and exploration, or expert air navigation, and those of girls as travel, acting, ballet and work with animals. A few girls, too, would like to pilot aircraft. With girls the kennel or stable maid seems to have now exceeded the ballerina and air hostess in popularity. It is also interesting and slightly surprising to find that, among both boys and girls, those who aspire to teach appear to be more numerous than those who actually expect to be able to do so.

The chief obstacles to the realization of their ambitions are thought by both boys and girls to be money, and weakness in certain parts of their school work. The first seems to be regarded as absolute; the second they usually hope to surmount by 'hard work'. The pattern of final expectations shows about one-third of the boys in the learned professions (many of them as 'pure' scientists), and the rest about equally divided between clerical and bureaucratic work on the one hand, and the services (almost exclusively Royal Air Force and Royal Navy) on the other. There is a sprinkling of engineers and farmers. The abler girls look chiefly to the teaching, medical and nursing professions and to the higher Civil Service. Their total number is probably roughly balanced by that of the future clerks, secretaries, comptometer operators and receptionists. Many girls not very successful in school work wish to be hairdressers. The protective and fostering propensities of girls are seen to be an important influence in their choice of teaching (often specified as 'of young children'), medicine, nursing and work with animals. The clerical and routine occupations are often, no doubt, regarded as a means of earning money until they marry or as a supplement to the family income afterwards.

This middle-school population is seen to be for the most part lively, gregarious, friendly and physically energetic. Its boys and girls feel their ties to home, school and adolescent society. They have many interests and are seldom bored when life goes normally, but a large number of them can be rather suddenly deflated, having few resources for enforced inactivity or solitude. Their out-of-school interests tend to be active and practical, often (particularly for girls) centred in the home. Some – perhaps many – frequent coffee bars and dance halls. Most of them are not great readers. Many seem to find more interests and resources in school than away from it.

Their parents for the most part strongly favour a grammar-school education. But a few do not, and parents in general vary very much in the kind and degree of support they give to the work of the grammar school. Some send their children to bed early. Others allow them to stay out late and to go to bed late. Some see the necessity of making proper provision for study at home, others do not. Many encourage their children, but some over-press them – often with little understanding – to do well at school. Many others sow in their children's minds doubts of the validity of school demands and standards. Those who can take an informed interest in their children's work are probably outnumbered by those who, however sympathetic, are unable to talk the language of school.

At every step we see more clearly how delicate and how complex is the work of the grammar-school teacher. It is no longer sufficient – if indeed it ever was – to know one's subject. It is not enough to snatch time to add a few diversions to the programme. Mere 'contact with parents' will not suffice. In any case, as teachers themselves recognize, it is likely to be with the wrong parents for their purpose. No wonder that at the present stage there is waste. No wonder some with sixth-form ability do not stay the course, and many, though they get by, do not work to full capacity. No wonder that some children in modern and comprehensive schools, possessing apparently lower initial ability, are doing better than a section of the children in grammar schools. Ardent reformers, seeing this, blame the system. The grammar school has failed with its 'C' stream – therefore, away with the school! Grammar-school teachers, seeing it, are apt to blame the selection procedure. The examination does not test qualities such as 'perseverance', and children who do not possess such qualities cannot successfully be taught.

They are both wrong. There is no guarantee whatever that there would be less wastage of these particular pupils in a common school, though some of them would undoubtedly find their apparent level more readily, while their semi-failure was masked by the compensatory success of more industrious fellow-pupils. Nor must grammar-school teachers assume that persistence, industry, concentration are inherent in some pupils but not in others. But they may have to learn a new language, and a new art of imaginative projection.

9

The Receiving End

NONE of the three types of grammar school considered – boys', girls' or co-educational – is outstandingly more or less likely than the others to be actively enjoyed. According to these answers, nearly half the middle-school children in grammar schools enthusiastically appreciate their school. The proportions, however, vary strikingly from school to school.

Children in 'Y' forms are as a whole less appreciative than those in 'X' forms, and older pupils are less ready than younger to express keen enjoyment. This was no doubt to be expected. Pupils in 'X' forms may be supposed generally to feel greater assurance of success, and therefore greater pleasure, and many children at the beginning of their second year still preserve the vitality and enthusiasm that are a matter of common observation among first-formers. Though some are better adjusted at the age of fourteen or fifteen than at twelve or thirteen, for most the novelty of school life has worn off by the fourth year, and such things as hard work, the approach of the official school-leaving age, apprehension about the future or strains in social relationships might be expected to have their effect. Two-fifths of the fourth-formers, however, and a like proportion of children in 'Y' forms, express not merely tolerance of school life but positive pleasure in it. True, these figures are averages, and there are wide variations; it is also likely that a 'Y' form in a highly selective school may be as intelligent on the average as an 'X' form in a less selective school, so that there may be a closer relationship between general ability and enjoyment of school than the figures at first suggest. But even with these reservations, they give grounds for believing that middle-school apathy is far from inevitable, and that being in a 'Y' form need not spoil a child's enjoyment of school.

The number of those who say that they actively dislike school is very small. But it, too, is unevenly distributed. The answer does not occur at all in two boys' schools, two girls' schools and one co-educational school. On the other hand, it reaches more than six per cent in one school, which also has a low percentage of those expressing strong appreciation. Some closer attention will be given to the malcontents – forty-six in all – at a later stage. They demand it, chiefly because their papers represent only in more extreme form the dissatisfactions which some of the remaining children, despite an injunction to be frank, probably conceal under the more colourless answer of 'I neither like it nor dislike it much'.

There is a very slight suggestion that, other things being equal, a child with a 'grammar-school background' is more likely to appreciate his school; but, as he is more likely in any case to be in an 'X' form, the observation means little. Clearly many more important considerations determine a child's appreciation of school than the education of his parents. Family expectations and sympathy are, of course, a very different matter from parents' education, though the two have some connexion, as we have seen already.

It is indeed difficult to say objectively what things make for happiness in a grammar school. Social class does not of itself seem to be decisive. There is some significant sex difference. The size of the school seems to be unimportant: percentages of preference for a large school and a very small school are 67 and 66; two schools of the same size return percentages of 80 and 22. Buildings seem to matter little. A school returning a percentage of 64 possesses beautiful buildings and a delightful situation, which are mentioned appreciatively by the children. But 61 per cent and 64 per cent are given by a boys' and a girls' school each of which (particularly the girls' school) is housed in old-fashioned and highly inconvenient buildings. It does not invariably correspond with the academic aspirations of the school. The highest percentages of all are returned by two schools in one of which the sixth form is nearly a quarter of the school, whereas the other is struggling to maintain sixth-form courses. Nevertheless, there is some evidence to suggest that a large sixth form tends to make for satisfaction in a school, even though, if it is small, other factors may compensate. Part of this satisfaction may be mediated by the staff, which is usually likely to be more contented if it has a fair amount of advanced work. Happiness does not seem to depend on the school's being the only or the pre-eminent school in its district. Two boys' schools of comparable size and function in one town both return high percentages. The same is true of two girls' schools. But a boys' school known to be strongly preferred and a girls' school which is the only one in its district both return very low percentages.

There seems to be some connexion between geographical environment and enjoyment of school, since south-western schools, rural and urban, tend to return a higher proportion of appreciative answers. This may be due partly to a comparative scarcity of local employment, particularly for the more able. It has long been a tradition in this part of the country for those with good ability to get the best education possible and then to seek employment 'up the country'. Such a tradition predisposes children in favour of a grammar-school education. This is paradoxically compatible with the existence of an unusually stable social structure and the remnants of an older outlook – the important people in one rural area are still said to be the squire, the parson and the schoolmaster – and of a respect for scholarship. Such an attitude lingers even in the towns. Though there is a disposition to stand out for rights, there still remains much truth in the statement of a master in a city school:

> This is a district where scholarship and respectability count. There is also little of the north's fierce feelings about 'Them' – there is more of a tendency to touch the forelock!

Many teachers comment on the kindly and cheerful temperaments of the children: one master who came from a school in the home counties to a rural school in the south-west described the change in atmosphere as overwhelming. (It should be added, however, that teachers in this part of the country also frequently mention with some exasperation that these children are lazy and far too easily satisfied.) If there really is stronger likelihood of appreciation in these districts, it may be partly due to the circumstances already mentioned. Perhaps the outstanding beauty of the environment is not without its effect upon the attitude to education. Certainly the children are conscious of it – one boy, for example, while acting as guide from one block of buildings to another, spontaneously spoke with simple enthusiasm of the magnificence and interest of the coast. Yet the geographical influence, like others, can be counterbalanced and must not be over-emphasized. Not all south-western schools give high percentages of appreciative answers, and one of the happiest schools according to this reckoning is in the industrial north.

A strong sixth form on the whole helps children to appreciate school, though the force of their academic amibitions (which is, of course, reflected by the size of the sixth form), is not invariably accompanied by clear evidence of appreciation. There are indeed indications that a comparatively low degree of appreciation is associated with an atmosphere of drive and anxiety about academic success, chiefly as measured by public examinations. This is partly shown by the fact that in several schools with low percentages of appreciative comments the figures are very markedly higher for 'X' than for 'Y' forms. Examples are:

A. A boys' school (36 per cent appreciative answers)

$$\text{IV X:}\ \frac{12}{34} \qquad \text{IV Y:}\ \frac{3}{31} \qquad \text{II X:}\ \frac{21}{31} \qquad \text{II Y:}\ \frac{9}{28}$$

B. A girls' school (22 per cent)

$$\text{IV X:}\ \frac{7}{30} \qquad \text{IV Y:}\ \frac{2}{28} \qquad \text{II X:}\ \frac{13}{32} \qquad \text{II X:}\ \frac{4}{30}$$

C. A boys' school (29 per cent)

$$\text{IV X:}\ \frac{10}{27} \qquad \text{IV Y:}\ \frac{2}{26} \qquad \text{II X:}\ \frac{13}{28} \qquad \text{II Y:}\ \frac{6}{25}$$

D. A co-educational school (28 per cent)

$$\text{IV X:}\ \frac{11}{34} \qquad \text{IV Y:}\ \frac{0}{33} \qquad \text{II X:}\ \frac{18}{32} \qquad \text{II Y:}\ \frac{6}{26}$$

These may be contrasted with:

E. A boys' school (67 per cent)

$$\text{IV X:}\ \frac{25}{33} \qquad \text{IV Y:}\ \frac{10}{19} \qquad \text{II X:}\ \frac{22}{32} \qquad \text{II Y:}\ \frac{19}{29}$$

F. A girls' school (80 per cent)

$$\text{IV X:}\ \frac{26}{34} \qquad \text{IV Y:}\ \frac{21}{27} \qquad \text{II X:}\ \frac{26}{31} \qquad \text{II Y:}\ \frac{25}{31}$$

G. A co-educational school (64 per cent)

$$\text{IV X:}\ \frac{20}{34} \qquad \text{IV Y:}\ \frac{11}{33} \qquad \text{II X:}\ \frac{24}{32} \qquad \text{II Y:}\ \frac{19}{26}$$

Children's own remarks give some indication that they are conscious of and resist 'drive', as we shall see later. Nor is the presence or absence of pressure invariably connected with the extent of academic success. The school which appeared to have the most relaxed atmosphere of all (it is also, incidentally, the school with almost the lowest selectivity) has a quite outstanding record of examination results both on the average and for individuals. But it is difficult to draw conclusions, because we do not know the order of antecedence. We cannot tell whether children tend to enjoy their school in consequence of an easy and confident attitude on the part of the staff, or whether the staff only finds it possible to develop such an attitude when the children are already happy and ready to be interested. Conversely, drive and anxiety from the staff may stimulate resistance in the children, or may be the consequence of a desperate attempt to break down already existing resistance and apathy. But the member of the staff is the senior partner in this venture. It is his responsibility to break into the circle, not to become the slave of the process. The fact that half the children in these nineteen schools express strong liking for their school, and very few indeed positively dislike it, should give considerable encouragement to grammar-school teachers, particularly as appreciation does not seem to be prevented by district, size or selectivity of school, age, ability, or social class. Yet the evidence does not justify complacency. As has been said, the neutral remark almost certainly conceals for some a more positive dissatisfaction, while for others 'I like it very much' may be perfunctory. At the very least, the existence of 50 per cent of pupils (a figure which may rise to nearly 80 per cent in individual schools) who have not been roused to active enthusiasm remains a challenge to the teacher's art.

At one extreme in the scale of enjoyment are those children who like school so much that they say they can find nothing to dislike. At the other are the very few who can find nothing to like. Most children, however, whatever their total opinion of their school, have very definite likes and dislikes within the school situation. The most appreciated elements of school life are physical activities (of many kinds), companionship, personal relationships, school clubs and societies, and certain lessons. Teachers are associated with both lessons and personal relationships. The part of school life that is most disliked is undoubtedly homework, which is mentioned by over half the children. School meals, punishments and the attitude of prefects are all disliked by many. Some teachers, in their attitude, awaken resentment. Personal adjustment to the life of the school and relationships with other boys and girls cause unhappiness or difficulty – not all of it serious – to perhaps twelve per cent. School work is mentioned, though not with undue frequency. School restrictions annoy some children, and uniform is disliked by a few. Among other miscellaneous dislikes the discomfort of travelling to and from school is mentioned surprisingly often.

'I enjoy'

Much appreciation of school is connected with attitudes to other people; that is, to contemporaries and teachers. Friendliness is much valued, whether in a general atmosphere of goodwill or in the possession of particular friends:

'Because I have made FRIENDS VERY QUICKLY.' 'School is the friendliest place it is possible to go to.'

Closely allied is the feeling of companionship, the pleasure and security given by membership of the school community or of a smaller group (house, form or circle of friends) within the larger society:

'Although I do not like all the lessons, I enjoy the company of the girls, and there are many lessons I do like.' 'I like school very much because it gives me a feeling of security, and helps me to enjoy life to the full.' 'The sense of community is felt as a strong support.' 'Because our whole school is a very lively community.' 'I enjoy working in *most* subjects and my friends are all very kind to me and between us we can always find something to grin about.' 'I could not really stand any other than a Grammar School and boys are not too rough here and most pranks are reasonably fair.' 'I like this school very much and shall be sorry when I have to leave. School gives you team spirit.' 'I like it because you never feel left out.'

Often the fact that companions are of the same age as oneself is appreciated:

'Company, because the place where I live consists mostly of "victorian seniles".' 'Getting together with boys of my own age even though they live in a different district.' 'I like it very much because I like school life much better than being at home and I like being with girls of my own age as I have nobody at home.'

Companionship is sometimes valued because it is with others of the same sex:

'Because it is a boys' only school.' 'No annoying boys around. Many social interests.'

It should be added, however, that members of co-educational schools are found to express comparable pleasure in the presence of the other sex!

Sometimes companionship is valued as an extension of one's own small circle of experience, and the means of learning to tolerate and appreciate other personalities and opinions:

'The social atmosphere where there are clubs and societies in which boys learn to respect each other.' 'The general good fun making a lot of friends and now that I am older I can go on anything up to month holidays with them.' 'The company of other girls in class and their opinions in arguments and the chance of learning something new every day.'

There is no doubt that some boys and girls believe the comradeship of the school to be more than accidental, attributing it to the association, for a common purpose, of like-minded people – like-minded either because of an approximate similarity of intelligence or because of certain identities of interest and aims:

'Because we can discuss points intelligently, being all of about the same intellect. We work quickly and there is an atmosphere of selectiveness, both as regards pupils and masters.' 'Everyone knows everyone else and thus there is a friendly atmosphere.' 'The meeting of friends of one's own habits and academic knowledge.' 'School is like a family with set times for play and work.'

School societies mentioned appreciatively are of many kinds, and there is no attempt to divide them into recreational and serious:

'The various films and lectures we have in the Science Society.' 'The clubs in which we can fully express our own opinions and do things we like.' 'I enjoy the fact that I can make friends more easily in school than out of it. There are also the various school societies in which you learn, somehow, more useful things than facts.'

Teachers are repeatedly mentioned with appreciation, sometimes general, sometimes particularized:

'The times when a master sets a problem which is interesting and we work together to solve it.' 'I enjoy most of the lessons especially when a lively master takes us.' 'The friendly feeling of most masters.' 'The feeling of belonging to a worthwhile community and having mistresses who are understanding.' 'I enjoy lessons where the mistress is friendly and acts on a level with us, like when we have debates or form councils.'

Teachers are valued for being friendly, fair, well-qualified and good at their work. It is also desirable for them to have a sense of humour. Appreciation of friendliness, fairness and humour mingles with a philosophic acceptance of the fact that not all teachers will be congenial all the time.

'The staff can be very nice and helpful in lessons.' 'The mistresses are usually fair about marks.' 'I like it because the teachers are considerate, although they sometimes get cross.' 'Most masters are fair.' 'Most masters are nice at sometime in the year.' 'I find the girls and the mistresses friendly and helpful.' 'Most of the masters like to share a joke as we do and help us very much.' 'I have many friends here which gives a friendly atmosphere and *some* of the masters join in the fun of a joke, and lessons are carried on in a friendly atmosphere.'

Although kindness is liked, slackness is not. Teachers are commended for being firm and competent:

'I like it because we have interesting lessons and good mistresses.' 'Because there is a good staff and the boys are nearly all friendly. We are taught well.' 'The teachers in school life are strict and therefore you get better teaching.'

Interest in individual children is also highly estimated:

'I like a grammar school because the teachers take more interest in you than they did at the last school.' 'The lessons are interesting and most of the mistresses are quite pleasant and most are interested in the form as individuals not as a crowd.' 'I like the quaint building and the personal attention given by the teachers.'

Almost every school subject is mentioned as pupils speak appreciatively of lessons they enjoy. A fourth-year 'Y'-form boy gives the key to the attraction which science exercises for many:

Experiments in Physics. It is such fun to stir up bubbling mixtures, test them with litmus paper and add things to them.

Spaciousness and variety in the curriculum are much enjoyed:

'The extensive choice of subjects.' 'The wide opportunities such as chemistry, physics. The new discoveries in different subjects.' 'The variety of subjects.'

Learning, both in and out of lessons, is frequently mentioned as a source of pleasure. Sometimes this is related directly and specifically to the method of teaching:

'I like the people and the method of teaching and ruling.' 'Because of the interesting topics discussed in nearly all subjects in Geography, History, Physics, English and Chemistry.'

At other times the emphasis is rather on the curriculum and the content of lessons (it may be noted that even here the enjoyment is often associated with companionship):

'Different lessons and you find more friends.' 'I find the work hard but pleasant. I am not very good at Craft and enjoy it here better than at a technical school.' 'Lots of new doors open to me, i.e. shooting, games, new interesting subjects.' 'Because there is a wider range of subjects (Biology, chemistry, physics).' 'New things and lessons have been brought into my life by a grammar school education.' 'It is a very great change from the junior school and there are a variety of lessons.' 'At school one can learn academic subjects which one is unable to do without having an education. One can also learn what other people are like.' 'It gives me a chance to try things I would never have thought of, e.g. playing games, speaking foreign languages.'

Some children reveal themselves as natural lovers of learning. They are found in both 'X' and 'Y' forms:

'I am always wanting to learn more as I find it very interesting.' 'I enjoy the interesting lessons which tell what happened 500 years ago or about other countries.' 'The feeling that all the time you are going to learn something new.' 'I like to be with people and to be able to learn things to satisfy my curiosity.'

Closely connected with this fundamental 'curiosity' is the sense that one is learning about life, expanding horizons, beginning to understand oneself and others and so to grow up:

'Because I have learnt a lot and grown up more since coming here.' 'I know it is doing me good and I have most friends at school.' 'This is the school I feel fits me best for adult life.'

Other sources of appreciation are found in what may broadly be called school atmosphere and association. These include a sense of tradition, of the mingling of discipline and relaxation, an awareness of standards in work and conduct, and a feeling that there is abundance of pleasurable activity and interest outside mere lessons.

This last seems on the whole to be thought of as an extension of the more organized work rather than as being sharply divided from it, though its value in providing contrast and relief is recognized:

'There are so many activities besides lessons that can be enjoyed.' 'I have made many new friends and developed many new hobbies.' 'Although I sometimes complain about the work there is always such a lot of activities that you should not really complain.' 'This school has more activities than the school I attended previously.' 'Life in a Grammar School is more varied than in a secondary school.' [The writer has recently been transferred from a secondary modern school.] 'Because there are so many new subjects and interesting clubs to belong to.'

Discipline and freedom, work and play, are all enjoyed at times:

'I like everything about it and in it. Working and playing.' 'It is not very, very strict but you are kept in good order.' 'I like it because there is not too much stress on work, as we have 3 lessons per week of Games or Gym.' 'Because of the routine, although sometimes this is boring, but it is often a comforting thought to know that your time is planned.' 'I like the atmosphere and although it is strict it is very enjoyable. There are also many privileges.' 'I like the fun of school life and the work and play that mixes together so well.' 'Because we have pleasure, and yet we also work.'

Tradition is sometimes thought of as the tradition of a particular school, sometimes as that of a more general fellowship of learning. It is valued by many:

'It is pleasant to think that one is learning and also passing on a grand tradition and also the friendliness of the girls.' 'Because I feel rather proud to belong to such an ancient and historic school.' 'I like the school very much because of its traditions and the school atmosphere.' 'Because I am proud to belong to a school with such a good reputation and I like most of the masters.' 'Our school has a good reputation and also much history to it.'

(These answers, it should be said, are all from different schools.)

Independence, too, is valued. There is room in the grammar school for the girl who likes 'the feeling that you are doing things for yourself'. And the following remark, though perhaps not strictly relevant, reminds us that school has still to provide for the gentle and reflective spirit: 'I like the travelling to school in the morning when you can see the beauty of things.'

It was to be expected that boys and girls would show appreciation of the significance of the grammar school in fitting them for a career, or, at any rate, in increasing their market value when seeking employment:

'I like it because I know I have a chance of having a good job when I grow up.' 'I like school because it gives you a good career.' 'My education gives me a chance to meet more people, and I like to think that I have a good start in life.' 'School gives me something to work hard for and helps me for my future job and living.'

Yet, although such remarks occur in every school, and although awareness of the 'career' value of the school figures largely in another connexion, it is comparatively seldom given as a reason for enjoying school. This, no doubt, is as it should be, since to realize the usefulness of a thing is by no means the same as taking pleasure in it. Consciousness of the part played by the grammar school in promoting social mobility, which has been implied in some of the remarks already quoted, is perhaps a more positive source of pleasure. This is less often associated simply with ambition or with the thought of rising in the social scale than with a sense, of course imperfectly defined by such young thinkers, that education is preparing them to transcend social barriers – that, as Matthew Arnold said, 'Men of culture are the true apostles of equality.'

'I like the comradeship of school, and the chance which the school gives to enter into all spheres of life.' 'In a grammar school one gets a cross cut of the whole community and one learns how other people live.'

Enthusiasm for school, often so warmly and so spontaneously expressed, has its negative side. Eager and attractive sociability can be seen as evidence of an increasingly 'other-directed' school population, and the recurrent reference to friendliness may suggest that a vague gregariousness is replacing more precise and discriminating relationships. The love of comradeship and of activity can be read as a fear of loneliness and restless avoidance of boredom:

'I would be bored if I did not go to school, and having been to school since I was 3 years old, I cannot imagine life without it, and I think I would miss it very much.' 'Because at school you are with your friends whereas when you are by yourself you are bored.' 'I enjoy the comradeship of other boys and do not like to be alone for too long.'

Even in the most sincerely commendatory comments on all that school has to offer there is sometimes a suggestion that this is appreciated chiefly as 'entertainment'. (The word itself is used occasionally.) There is, furthermore, unmistakable evidence that many homes are unable to provide either the companionship or the stimulation which these boys and girls need: school is, in fact, clearly seen by some as a compensation for what the home cannot give:

'I like it very much because I find it very interesting and there is no time to get bored, as I often do at home.' 'The reason I like it is, because, during school holidays I get very bored and I am glad to come back usually.' 'Because if I was home their would not be much to do, but school takes up most of the time for me.' 'I like it because I have many friends here, and when I have to stay at home I get very bored. If I have to stay inside, I have nobody to talk to all day because both my parents and my elder sister go to work. My other sister works in her spare time.' 'It fills in my spare time in the evenings. And I find the subjects most interesting.'

Yet, when we have made complete allowance for negative, passive or compensatory evaluations, the majority of appreciative remarks leave an impression of keen and positive enjoyment. And when we look particularly at those who say of school, 'I like it very much', we cannot doubt their enthusiasm. There is a sense of wonder, of delight in the unexpected, of constant alertness, of unmistakable vitality:

'It's fun.' 'The atmosphere is splendid.' 'I like it very much because I do not find many things difficult.' 'I like it because there is always something to do and always nice things for us to go to and we have fun.' 'I get all the help I want and feel that I am doing well at this school.' 'It is a great satisfaction to be at a grammar school.' 'I like my school life very much.' 'The school cultivates interests of all kinds.' 'I like the lessons and also the traditions of the school.'

Undoubtedly, for very many of these boys and girls – by no means all of them among the most socially 'privileged' or highly intelligent – there is contentment and a sense of fitness. Something, some blend of temperament and endowment with the school curriculum, atmosphere and other circumstances, has made them feel that school is 'right'. It is of the utmost importance to try to discover whether this happy combination is accidental – subject to random influences, or at least to circumstances beyond our reach – or whether it can be so controlled as to communicate this high morale to the other half of the school population.

'I dislike'

Few children express violent dislike of school. But even among the most appreciative some aspects of school are less pleasing than others, and in this whole middle-school population certain objects of dislike are mentioned with some regularity.

Homework is by far the least acceptable element of school life. Some children make it plain that they object, not to homework in itself, but to homework that demands an excessive amount of time, and there is frequent complaint of the injustice of teachers who set work which takes appreciably longer to do than the time allocated to it in homework timetables:

'A *large amount* of written work and learning work.' 'I dislike homework which takes more than the set time.' 'Being set too much work for homework. The maths master often sets us 2 hours' prep when we should only have half an hour.' 'I don't like so much homework. I wouldn't mind a little but certainly less than we get now.'

Many of the answers are vigorous protests against what is felt by both boys and girls as an almost intolerable burden and a restriction on animal spirits:

'The homework which seems to weigh one down, especially during the summer months.' 'Homework can be very troublesome at times, especially at week-ends when one wants to go out.' 'I dislike homework because when I come home at night I always feel a little exhausted.' 'The time taken by homework. Not the actual work. I feel I have that hour and a half almost cut out of my pleasure. I do not dislike the homework, but wish that I could have the time taken by it added on to the day.' 'I dislike the homework most, this is partly because I have to travel a long way in the bus. Carrying my satchel to and from school wears me out. In the summer I get ever so hot with my blazer, cap and tie on.' 'Homework should only be given in winter. In summer it is warm and light and is the most likely part of the year you go out.'

For some pupils the comparative freedom of their modern-school friends intensifies the sense of oppression:

The fact that all the amount of homework we are given prevents us from going out at all during the week, all I do is to go home have my tea, and do my homework, whereas my friends at the secondary schools go out several times a week.

And for a discontented girl, homework is foremost among the things that typify the irksome régime of school:

Small hours of work at school and huge amounts of prep, stricked discipline, uniform, especially winter uniform, plugging of classical music.

Punishments are understandably disliked, though the occasional need for punishment seems to be acknowledged. Such penalties as order marks or 'losing marks for the House' are almost invariably met with derision. Impositions and lines arouse great resentment, in boys particularly. Both boys and girls greatly disapprove of detentions, and repeatedly insist that this form of punishment is demonstrably ineffectual, since the same people occupy the detention-room week after week. The pupils, on the whole, feel that their contract with school ends with the close of the school day; after this, they may of course voluntarily give time to school activities, but any compulsion to stay is felt to be an infringement of the rights of the individual which is not even justified by misdemeanour in school hours. Criticism, then, on the grounds of ineffectuality or injustice, is made of all the forms of punishment in school. Corporal punishment is mentioned comparatively seldom, but the answer of the boy who says, 'Caning, although I have never been caned yet,' though superficially amusing, may nevertheless stimulate some quite serious reflection on what could have prompted such a remark.

But whatever criticisms are made of particular punishments, it is evident that the occasion and spirit matter more than the actual penalty. Punishment which seems to the pupil hasty, excessive or unfair is strongly condemned. This is one reason why punishments from prefects are so much less tolerable than those from teachers: another is, of course, the indignity. The teacher who forgets proper decorum is also criticized, as when a boy writes, 'I dislike being hit about the head and face by a teacher.' (It should be emphasized that this kind of statement is rare.)

Prefects are a focus of dislike for many pupils, the great majority of them boys. Some representative remarks are:

'I dislike any prefects who are prejudice in their actions and decisions.' 'The most unfortunate thing is the number and severity of impositions set by prefects.'

'Tyrannous prefects.' 'Bigheaded prefects.' 'Some (only some) over-officious prefects.' 'The power of prefects who can give punishment as they please.' 'Prefects, their powers are too great and it goes to their heads, they strut around like kings.' 'Being sometimes given two detentions for a small offence (by prefects mostly but sometimes by masters).' 'I dislike the haughty superiority of some sixth formers . . . and the domineering attitude of some mistresses.' 'Lines and detentions and school dinners and bossy prefects.'

Although teachers are so often mentioned with warm appreciation they are felt on occasion to mar the enjoyment of school life. Sometimes tension between teacher and child is attributed to a general incompatibility. ('Teachers you can't get on with.') Sometimes particular members of staff are mentioned, very occasionally by name or nickname, more often in association with the subjects they teach. It is quite apparent that many pupils extend, even consciously, the personal sentiment to the subject. ('History and the mistress we have.') It is perhaps worth noting that dislike of lessons seems to be more often consciously associated with personal relations than appreciation is. A less conscious but still definite type of association is seen in a remark such as, 'I dislike Maths, French and a few of the masters.'

A generally stern, unsympathetic or unfriendly attitude is disliked by many. It may be contrasted with the friendliness and humour that are so warmly appreciated:

'The periods with a master who is very strict, does not let you talk quietly and does not like a joke.' 'A master who is to strict.' 'Being ordered about and dispised by a lot of mistresses who do not try to understand their pupils, but just teach and criticise.' 'When the teachers are cross.' 'Lessons with strict teachers.' 'Stern teachers.' 'Sarcasm of the mistresses.'

Some pupils resent a lack of respect or of imagination which, as it seems to them, results in refusal to consider their motives or allow explanations, misinterpretation of their actions, and the over-hasty imposition of punishments:

'Some masters when they think you have done something wrong do not give you time to explain but clamp down on you and put you in detention straight away.' 'Mistresses who do not allow one to explain your wrong-doings.' 'The way some mistresses have no understanding for us and make no allowances for trivial things which seemed to us to be big.' 'One or two masters who will not listen to another point of view.'

Occasionally there is a feeling that members of staff abuse their power:

'I dislike bullying which goes on sometimes (by master and boys). I also dislike boring lessons.' 'The feeling that some mistresses accuse wrongly, realise this but still rather enjoy it. Watching a mistress repremand a girl who is too scared to stand up for herself.' 'When I believe the teachers are unfair and I am not allowed to say so.'

The disciplinary policy of the staff is under close scrutiny and there is great resentment of any favouritism or unfairness. Disapproval in one school of 'the masters who punish one boy only if two or more are doing wrong' is balanced by the protests in another against the punishment of a whole form for the misbehaviour of one member.

A distinction may be drawn between, on the one hand, the feeling of incompatibility of one pupil with one teacher, and, on the other, a degree of hostility between 'Us' and 'Them'. It can even indicate a certain differentiation among schools, according to whether teachers are mentioned singly or generally; there is a clear difference between the remarks 'A master who is sarcastic' and 'The feeling that the masters are to a certain extent your enemies'.

Dislike of professional incompetence is well expressed in the terse remark, 'Teachers who fail to convey to you what they are trying to teach.' A few children dislike having the progress of the lesson held up while explanations are given to a slower member, but more resent the teacher's refusal to allow a question or give adequate explanation, and strongly dislike the sensation that the lesson is leaving them behind. Both boys and girls show considerable sensitiveness to pace of speech and to pitch and timbre of voice: 'I dislike the masters who make a long speech, never varying their tone.' There is some dislike of repetitive or monotonous work, but teachers who have tried certain ways of varying the pattern of their lessons are warned that digressions and the interpolation of personal anecdotes are on the whole disliked. Improving lectures are as unpopular as ever: 'I dislike the unnecessarily long talks given by our head about little things.' Associations with both monotony and edification may be in the minds of pupils in two schools who write with emphatic dislike of speech days.

Uneasy personal relationships are not confined to those of pupils with teachers. They may be connected with some suggestion of class bitterness:

'In certain cases the snobbish and unfriendly attitude of the boys.' 'I have lost most of my friends and can't speak to my parents freely.' 'I have lost many friends since I started this school. And people call me a snob.' 'Because I do not think that most of the teachers are strict enough with us and the lessons are rather boring. There is also *snobbery*.' 'I dislike it because I don't get on at all well with the teachers and I feel out of place because I wasn't born here.'

Sometimes there are unsatisfactory relationships between sections of a school – for example, seniors and juniors.

'The bullying. There was a lot of bad feeling between junior boys and the boys in the middle forms, when I first came here. But this seems to have mostly disappeared now.' 'I dislike the way the lower school is treated by the higher school.' 'Unfriendlyness to new comers by the higher forms.'

Just as boys and girls evidently appreciate kindness and friendship, so they are seen to suffer when they meet hostility:

'I dislike being bullied and beaten up. Also I dislike rugby as we are made to put on ridiculously short shorts and dreadfully cold shirts. I also dislike lines as they are a waste of time and do not stop you doing the same thing again. I do not like having my, or my friend's ball being taken and thrown or kicked far away.' 'The way in which most of the girls tease me.' 'The quarrels that go on especially with girls.' 'If girls refuse to be friendly and if teachers do not see your point of view.'

School work in general is seldom stated as 'most disliked'. Particular lessons, however, are fairly often mentioned, and many pupils say that their greatest dislike in school life is of the least congenial lessons. As might have been expected, lessons are usually disliked either when they bore the pupil or when they are associated with a sense of failure:

'Boring subjects.' 'Lessons in which we are supposed to sit and look or listen to something or someone.' 'Lessons where you have to sit for the whole time, doing one thing, such as translating.' 'Lessons that I do not understand.' 'My worst lessons.' 'French because I am not very good at it.' 'Dreary lessons.'

Examinations are disliked by an appreciable number of pupils, though a few find them exhilarating; the competitiveness associated with examinations is mentioned with both approval and disapproval.

Some boys and girls seem to be unable to find any point of interest in their work or any relationship between it and what they feel to be 'life'. This feeling of irrelevance is sometimes though not always associated with a strong sense of failure:

'I find that I cannot get on at all well with some subjects, yet I still have to plug away at them, though I will never use them.' 'I dislike a lot of the subjects I am forced to take and therefore I find the majority of my time spent at school very boring.' 'My school life has nothing to do with my outside interests. I find most of the lessons boring and dull.'

Closely connected is a dislike of the strenuousness demanded in school work and a consequent resentment of the constraints imposed:

'School subjects are hard, we have too much prep.' 'School is awfull nattery teachers lots of Homework etc.' 'One is made to work too hard and is given too much homework.'

Dislike of constraint is not confined to, or even chiefly associated with, the demands of study. School is sometimes felt to impose intolerable restrictions on a full and active life, to be dull and out of touch with modern interests, and to be deliberately trying to prevent the young from growing up. The internal discipline of school is also resented:

'I hate the routine and the way the staff are always telling us what to do and what not to do.' 'We are all treated like babies and not even allowed to grow up at school parties. When other girls who have left school can act their age.' 'I like to be outside and doing things that I prefer than being shut indoors and writing. Particulairy when it is lovely weather.' 'I think our school is too old-fashioned and it restricts any kind of modern pleasures e.g. jiving. It won't let any new ideas be accepted.' 'I dislike the way everything is run exactly the same year in year out.' 'I hate sticking to the same routine every day.'

The discontented pupil frequently longs to be at work, chiefly because work is a mark of adult status, but often also, one feels, because of strong hints from home that money ought to be earned or that school is a waste of time:

'I want to leave school to be a hairdresser but I can't leave till I'm nearly 17 without paying.' 'My friends are mostly at work, and since my mother died I have lived with my Aunt. I would be more use to her at work.' 'I have left my old friends and I can't go out to dances with my friends for homework. And a lot of expence for my parents.' 'I feel as if I would like to be at work and I dislike being treated as a child.'

As already shown, a few children, while rebelling against school, condemn it for having not too strict but too lax a discipline:

'Not enough discipline. Drab uniform looks awful because of laziness and slopiness not corrected. Many lessons boring owing to not strict, brisk mistress.' 'It hasn't enough discipline therefore you cannot learn so easily.'

Though uniform is strongly disliked by a minority in most schools, only a very small number of children finds it the most disliked element in school life. It draws its share, however, of the annoyance felt by an appreciable number at what are felt to be excessive or petty restrictions or unnecessary compulsions:

'The compulsory games.' 'The many restrictions which to myself seem annoying and petit.' 'Having no choice about certain school functions such as having to go to sports although I would go anyway.' 'The strict rules and having always to wear a beret with uniform.' 'When people restrict you in your activities by saying that you still go to school – They forget that others of the same age are going to work.'

The Pattern of Adjustment

Boys and girls in these schools are thus seen to be affected by many of the things which may be supposed to interest young people of their age in any type of school: the physical conditions of school, the atmosphere of quiet bustle, games, meals, recreation, school regulations, and their relationships with their fellows and with authority. It is significant and encouraging to find that so many of them are characterized by an immense zest for learning – savouring with delight the range and variety of the school curriculum and excited by the sense of limitless reserves of knowledge waiting to be explored. Moreover, their very pleasure in companionship, though sometimes attributable to the fear of solitude and of silence that characterizes our time, itself often implies a principle of selectivity. Occasionally this can be seen as little more than a rather pathetic social insecurity – 'Girls who do not live in bad areas' – but more often it shows itself in the recognition of a fellowship of learning. There is considerable understanding of the fact that a social unit exists or comes into being less through mere proximity or accidental coincidence of interests than through the possession of a common object, and that the object of the grammar school is learning. This introduces an important principle of spontaneity into their work and their associations.

This sense, often not fully articulate, of the peculiar nature of school fellowship affects not so much the *extent* as the *kind* of appreciation that is given to the staff. Most highly valued is the master or mistress who can create a partnership for tackling a problem of learning or can enter into a discussion on apparently equal terms. It is also true that, by this very art of the teacher, children who are not originally initiates are invited into the fellowship. Whereas some children are apparently at the outset lovers of learning possessed of a passionate desire to know, others have that love awakened through the respect and interest accorded them by a trusted member of the staff. Hence the resentment against teachers who do not like a joke, or who will not listen to explanations. By such refusals they are implicitly excluding from the fellowship.

Some, then, of these enthusiasts, appear to love 'mere' learning; others, perhaps the majority, are brought to learning through its association with a personal guide. Further classes may perhaps be distinguished, among whom are the manipulators and experimenters, such as the boy who likes stirring up bubbling mixtures and adding things to them, and those with quick human interests, such as the girl who enjoys hearing about people in other countries or other periods.

One problem of the grammar school is suggested by the fairly frequent resentment against prefects, especially in some boys' schools. It is not enough to laugh this off as being 'the nature of the beast' for middle-school boys. One must remember, first, that the complaint is not inevitable – in some schools it is not found; secondly, that in other types of school, boys of this very age are themselves prefects (and perhaps, it must also be remembered, exercising similar 'tyranny' – so that there is no justification for a hasty assumption that the right answer is to decapitate our schools by removing the sixth forms). One cannot help suspecting that the purpose of prefects has in many ways changed from that of the days when Dr. Arnold set out to civilize his school through the sixth form. Certainly there is reason for believing that some boys of seventeen and eighteen are feeling a licence to behave arrogantly to their immediate juniors, and for wondering whether this is the best training for 'leadership'.

Although girls also occasionally fall foul of prefects, their chief resentment seems to be against irksome restrictions, over-anxious cultivation of public spirit and tone ('I hate "House spirit",' says one schoolgirl) and of 'being treated like babies'. How to cultivate the right attitude to a rapidly maturing girl is indeed a problem.

The general impression is of a school population many of whose members enjoy meeting their friends, are on fairly good terms with their teachers, appreciate the opportunities that school affords for sport and recreation, chafe somewhat at restrictions and the demands of homework, accept the necessity of a certain amount of application and can respond favourably to variety and liveliness in the school curriculum without being deeply engaged. Some – a very few – are antagonistic. A large minority is seen to be both studious and spirited. A smaller minority, while not in rebellion, has little grasp of the intentions of the school and looks outside for its main interests. It is this last group which presents the most important challenge to the grammar school.

10

A Sprinkling of Malcontents

THE boys and girls who express keen enjoyment of the grammar school represent on the whole those who are well adjusted to the school's methods and objectives. Their motives and the character of their enjoyment differ in subtlety; some are clearly more academically gifted than others; many show a common-sense recognition of the fact that school life will have its ups and downs. But it may be assumed that they have no unbearable feeling of failure in school work or of being persistently bored, oppressed or outclassed. It is true that some, as has been seen, are conscious of school assumptions that may be incompatible with those of home, and that his can result in quite serious strain. Still, for the moment they have thrown in their lot with school, so that in a strictly limited sense and on its own ground it may be said to be succeeding with them. They are, moreover, a minority, though a minority that must not be ignored: the majority of appreciative pupils is supported by adequately favourable family attitudes.

The unhappy, unsuccessful, bewildered or defiant boys and girls two per cent of the children questioned – exhibit directly the extreme of failure in adjustment; at the same time they may be taken to represent the discontents and inadequacies of the large number – over nine hundred in this survey – whose acceptance of a grammar-school education is at best incomplete. The forty-six disaffected pupils are distributed in fourteen out of the nineteen schools, the proportion in co-educational schools being slightly higher than that in single-sex schools. There are approximately equal numbers of boys and girls, in both the second and fourth years. There are twice as many fourth-year as second-year pupils, and three times as many in 'Y' forms as in 'X' forms. Neither parent of half the number of pupils (or two-thirds, if 'Don't know' answers are also counted, as they probably should be) has had a grammar-school education. Both parents of three pupils (and eight fathers and ten mothers in all) were educated at grammar schools. It may also be of interest to know that the proportions of homes having television – slightly under three-quarters – is not markedly in excess of that for the total number of pupils. This much-discussed modern medium, therefore, is not here shown to have any direct connexion with acceptance or rejection of school.

When asked what they enjoy most in school life, ten of these pupils return negative answers:

'Nothing.' 'Holidays.' 'Going home on Friday.' 'I enjoy the knowledge that I am receiving a good education, nothing else.'

Physical activities are mentioned by twelve, friends by six, and out-of-class activities by seven pupils. Only two mention lessons, and these, significantly, are in the active and practical subjects of woodwork and cookery. The rest of the answers are individual:

'Library.' 'Writing essays.' 'When the headmistress has a little talk to the form privately.' 'Wandering about the trees in the far corner at break or in the dinner-hour.'

Homework is most disliked by fourteen of the pupils, relationships with teachers by eight, and work in school by five. (One boy mentions 'writing pages and pages of notes'.) Many, especially girls, feel irritated by rules, restrictions and routine, and express themselves forcefully.

'The prison like rules and the mountains made out of mole hills.' 'Pointless rules. Too much team-and-House spirit.' 'The rules, being enclosed in one building all day.' 'The way everything is run to an exact schudel.'

Some of the dislikes are connected with difficulties of personal relationships:

'People, look at you, if you say anything to them and say, "Eh, she's only a school girl".' 'When the form laughs at me, so I make a mistake.'

The out-of-school interests of this group appear to be chiefly vigorous physical exercise, the opposite sex, youth clubs, the cinema, and collecting and listening to 'pop' records:

'Dancing and collecting records.' 'Pictures and dances.' 'The opposite sex and youth clubs.' 'Boys.' 'Rock and roll and Tommy Steele.' 'Girls, I have two ' 'Horse-Riding and Fox-hunting.'

More individual interests are named as follows:

'Farming.' 'Train spotting.' 'Learning about the engines of cars and any other motor driven vehicle.' [The writer of this remark is a girl.] 'Activities of our Chapel. But my hobby is Aeroplane spotting and the study of aeronautics' Reading.' 'Nature, and the countryside.'

Their spare-time occupations correspond:

'Going into the snack bar with a group of girls and boys and listening to the latest records on the Juke-Box.' 'I knit, read and collect records.' 'My spare time is filled by playing snooker and tinkering with cycles.' 'Go to dance, pictures, help in the house, watch television, and just playing out.' 'Make model Aircrafts and Kites.' 'Play soccer if a ball is available. At nights I play out.' 'I go to clubs and I like drawing on scraps of paper.' 'Watch T.V. or go to the pictures.' 'Keep records and make scrap-books of Tony Curtis and Tommy Steele.' 'Ride my horse. Read when time.'

Asked whether they often feel bored, nearly all these pupils reply emphatically that they do: only seven or eight say the contrary. The proportion is significant here: in the total number of pupils, comparatively few admit to boredom. Many of the answers point to physical restlessness, dislike of 'talk' (this is very frequent), and impatience or absence of interest in lessons. It may or may not be a coincidence that three girls, all in different schools, say that they are chiefly bored in French and biology lessons. Perhaps most important is the indication of a lack of resources in spare time, which is associated with a strong dislike of solitude. Representative answers are:

'I feel bored sitting by myself as I am very talkative and when I have to listen to something in which I am not interested in, such as the majority of my lessons.' 'I feel bored just listening to people talk, I like to do things, I like to be active (Rock and Roll).' 'When people talk a long time about Polatics and about the government.' 'Yes, when a master keeps on telling you the same thing over and over again.' 'I sometimes feel bored on a Saturday afternoon, when I cannot go to see a football match. IN SCHOOL AS WELL OF COURSE.' 'When there's nothing to do, I feel bored. Sometimes when there is nothing on T.V. or no-where to go, you get fed up.' 'Yes, when parents lecture me or others about talking to boys in the street.' 'I only feel bored when I have too much energy and I have to listen to pettish lectures about nothing.' 'YES! I feel bored when teachers are explaining work, because they do not make the work sound interesting and they think that we can do it straight off after just explaining a thing once.'

Many people will have a fellow-feeling with the boy who says:

'I feel bored most in the lovely summer evenings when I look out the window whilst doing my homework.'

and feel concern for the girl who is so obviously lost:

'Yes, I often feel bored for no real reason. I rarely go out, as I have no-where to go.'

Seventeen pupils report parental attitudes which may be broadly regarded as 'being on the side of school'. There is only one suggestion of an increase in parental approval: 'They are glad I came here because I am not quite so much of a tomboy as I used to be.' All the rest of the remarks – that is, nearly two-thirds – suggest parents whose enthusiasm has declined (the largest number) or whose attitudes express indifference, hostility, conflict or indecision:

'They were not bothered whether I came or not . . . They still feel the same way.' 'My mother did not want me to go to a grammar school but my father did . . . my mother is still against it but my father has since died.' 'Yes. But now all this expence they do not.' 'My mother was very keen indeed . . . She is now unsettled about it.' 'They were very keen but did not say much . . . They want me to stay on to take my G.C.E. but I'm against so they are letting me leave.' 'They wanted *ME* to come because *they* didn't pass for grammar schools. They were glad that I had passed . . . They feel now that considering the little progress that I have made that it was a waste of time.' 'My father did, but I'm not sure about my mother. Dad wants me to stay until I'm 16. Mum wants me to leave at 15.'

Some of these pupils have lost a parent, and find adjustment to school difficult in consequence. The father of one girl has recently died, and she feels – or is made to feel – that her mother cannot afford to let her stay at school until she is sixteen. A motherless boy is living with a relative who clearly thinks that he should be at work. A girl – an only child – lives with her mother and grandmother, who are both anxious and indulgent and do not understand the grammar-school tradition. A boy, fatherless and probably illegitimate, has been made very conscious that his education is a burden for his mother. Conflict between father and mother, as has been illustrated, can be focussed in the question of the child's school career, with unsettling results. Several pupils, girls particularly, have made their attitude to school the battle-ground of adolescent self-assertion against their parents. For example, a girl in an 'X' form wants to leave school. Her father wants her to qualify for 'a job that I will use this sort of Education in'. She considers that she will win, 'because I have a habit of protesting until I get my own way and though it disappoints them, my parents hate sulks, especially Daddy from whom I get my impatient temper . . . Upsets frequently caused between Daddy and me because of what I want to do and what he wants me to do.' Sometimes there is evidence that the demand made by school on one's time and attention is threatening deeply valued family relationships.

I hardly ever get out for homework. And with having a brother and sister [1]

---

[1] They are aged two and three.

I have to shut the family away from me when doing my homework, and by the time I have finished my brother and sister have gone to bed. So there is very little I see of them. For before I came to this school I used to take them to bed and before I took them I could take them out. BUT now through this school I cannot.

My younger brother [1] has his holidays rather different to me. He goes to a Junior School and he breaks up at a different time to us (usually before). My mother works and has either to stay at home to watch him or leave him by himself. When I am at home I look after him.

I have very little spare time after finishing my homework to talk to my parents. Consequently I feel as if I'm growing away from them. Life is all rushing about from the time I get up to the time I sleep.

Even among the seventeen parents who seem to favour education there are several – perhaps the majority – whose attitude cannot have encouraged an easy acceptance of school. For some of these adolescents the school has become the symbol of rejected parental authority; for others it seems to be breaking the family tie; others again have parents who would support school, but whose behaviour towards their children seems to be nervously propitiatory. Some parents have made their children painfully aware that, once at the grammar school, they must get their money's worth:

My mother says that she is not sending me to a grammar school for nothing cause people who go to ordinary schools can be hairdressers, so she won't let me be one.

Some try somewhat ineffectually to uphold the claims of school:

My mother keeps telling me to go to bed earlier and to get my homework done before I go out.

Some insist on the routine of homework and in other ways enforce the injunctions of school so firmly that the adolescent regards school and home together as conspiring to prolong the status of childhood.

Only one of these pupils at present wants to stay long at school. Another, though not enjoying school, feels some trepidation at the thought of leaving and four realize that their parents will insist on their staying until they are seventeen or eighteen. All the rest are determined to leave at the earliest possible moment, and at least six openly intend to leave at fifteen.

It may now be useful to look more comprehensively at a few of these discontented pupils.

Robert is in a fourth-year 'Y' form. He has a younger brother and sister.

Aged eight.

Neither of his parents attended a grammar school. There is no television in his home. He does his homework in his bedroom and goes to bed at 11 p.m. He has many friends who are not at grammar schools. His best subject in school is English and his weakest French. The lessons he likes best are in English and mathematics. He enjoys games periods, and dislikes 'French and Physics lessons and getting blamed by a teacher for something I have not done'. He dislikes school because there is homework. In his opinion grammar schools have no superiority 'because at other schools you get more or less the same lessons and once school is over for the day it is.' His parents were and are 'not bothered' about his attending a grammar school. His chief interest is boxing, and in his spare time he goes to a cinema or youth club. He looks forward to leaving school and would like a career in the Merchant Navy. School, he says, has brought him no advantages and one disadvantage: that he has to leave his friends early to go home to do his homework.

John, aged twelve, has an elder sister, two younger brothers and one younger sister. Neither of his parents had a grammar-school education. He has many friends not at grammar schools. His home has no television. He does his homework in the living-room or bedroom and goes to bed at 9.30 p.m. in summer, earlier in winter. His best subject is mathematics, and his weakest 'French which is rotten, I wish all french teachers would ~~go to Hell~~ drop into the sea'. The lessons he most likes are games and woodwork: he dislikes 'ROTTEN FRENCH (Bah)'. He enjoys holidays and school games and girls and dislikes 'Rotten teachers'. His keenest interest is in farming. He hates school because of homework and teachers. On the whole, however, he thinks a grammar school to be superior, because it has a good timetable and 'you learn a little bit more and you get on with respecable people'. His parents wanted him to come to a grammar school and are glad he is there, but he himself is longing to leave. He is often bored in French lessons. His present school differs from his primary school in having a proper timetable and teachers who 'pay more attention'. At his primary school the teachers 'did not care much' and had pets, of whom he was not one. He very much dislikes his long journey to and from school, although sometimes he has a good game of cards in the train.

Pauline, aged fifteen, has grown-up brothers. Neither of her parents attended a grammar school and they have given her no indication whether they think it a good thing for her to do so. She has many friends not at grammar schools and she is interested in boys and the youth club. She does her homework in the living-room and goes to bed about ten. She likes mathematics and is good at it and she dislikes French 'because of the teacher'. She has lost interest in school and sees no point in learning classical or modern languages, as they have very little use for most people when they leave school. (She wants to be a comptometer operator.) She has lost touch with many old friends, and, as few grammar-school people live near her, she makes her friends at the youth club. She is bored with homework, and does not like the way in which people expect her to know everything because she goes to a grammar school. Pauline adds a post-script:

I believe that the teacher has a very big influence on the subject. For instance I liked French very much in the 1st year then in the 2nd a teacher took me for French who for some reason unknown did not like me. I quickly lost interest in the subject and dread to go to it because of what the teacher will say to me. I think that girls should be allowed (at 15) to wear make-up and jewellry because by then they should know how to use them properly by then.

William is an only child. He is in an 'X' form, and is fourteen. His parents did not have a grammar-school education, and his mother is glad for him to be at a grammar school. His best subject is religious knowledge, and his favourite lessons history and English. He likes writing essays but dislikes writing notes. He hopes to become a minister of religion and will stay to complete a year in the sixth form, although he dislikes school. He is bored in many lessons and does not like being made to persist with useless subjects. He says:

Owing to homework I have not as much spare time as I would like, so I have had to give up a number of evenings when I would be out. Owing to the amount of filthy language it has been hard to keep a clean tongue.

Peter, aged thirteen, enjoys nothing in school and wants to leave as soon as possible. He adds a postscript:

I like girls. I think about girls. I cuddle girls. I like to play football. I like teddy boys, coppers and farming. My favourite team is — F.C. I like watching them play other teams. I don't like prefects. Some of the teachers aren't very nice. I like to study other countries. I like drawing maps. The teachers I don't like have nick-names. [Here follows a list of masters with their nicknames.]

George, aged fourteen, in a 'Y' form, dislikes school because of 'the masters'. He has an obsessive interest in football, likes nothing in school except games, and longs to leave. In his spare time he plays football and writes books about it. After leaving, he says, '*I would like to be a soccer player*, because where else can you get £50, for 90 minutes work.' The obstacle to his choice is that 'The Headmaster might not let me play for a professional team; *but I will by leaving.*' He writes of coming to a grammar school:

It as brought me nothing but disadvantages. The people I used to know, walk past me as if I was nothing, just because they think I am a snob. Well; that is why I am going to try to get into a professional football team, to show them that I'm not a posh snob, although I know a lot of our school are. I *DON'T* want to work in a solicitors office, or just an office, because most of the swots will end up there, like *HOTHOUSE PLANTS*; dead unhealthy. I want to have the lovely smell of the open air in my lungs, not the smell of a clammy, dingy closed-in hole, like an office.

Margaret, aged twelve, has two little brothers and a younger sister. Her mother was educated at a grammar school, her father probably was not. She does her homework in the study, and goes to bed at 8 p.m. She likes the headmistress to talk to the form, and is sensitive to the other girls' laughing at her in a lesson. She finds her school work difficult and the homework excessive. She reads in her spare time. Her assessment of the effect of school is:

My schoolmates are very well off and as there are four children in my family mummy cannot afford new things every week like they have. I do not make friends easily and at a primary school it was much easier as the people were more of my own class and they are not so uppish. Some people are inclined to be snobbish. There are sets and groups of people who agravate you and say awful things about you behind your back. Some people like you for what you've got and not what you are.

Jean, aged fifteen, is in an 'X' form. Neither her father nor her mother attended a grammar school. They wanted her to come to one and are still pleased because they think she has good opportunities. There is no television in her home. She does her homework in the dining-room and goes to bed between nine and ten. She has many friends who are not at grammar schools. Her best subject is biology, her weakest Latin, which she also dislikes. Her favourite lessons are in science and English. She likes some of her school work, and appreciates having friends of her own age, but she dislikes 'just being one in a large community'. She would like to be at work because she would then be treated more as an adult, but knows that she must stay until she is eighteen. Her greatest interest outside school is dancing, and she enjoys going to stay with her married sister. She often feels bored at school, but hardly ever at home. She would like to be a doctor and wants to get married. She finally writes:

As I have got higher up in the school I have found that life has become altogether happier. When I first came to the school I was at an 'in-between' age that was very difficult. Now my parents, neighbours, and my sister who is much older, treat me as one of them. I also like wearing nicer clothes, and going out with my friends, sometimes boys. Coming to this school has made me express my opinion much better, and I have formed my own views about different subjects.

But often I have the feeling that I shall never get through exams etc. and I get very depressed. Sometimes it seems so difficult to do well, even though I would like to. Girls, I have found, who do not go to a Grammar School, consider us all to be 'snobs', and I do not like being termed in this category.

I think that I appreciate things more now, but I do not think that this is to do with school, but just that I am older now.

Mary is in a second form. She is the middle one of five children, two boys and three girls. The home has no television, and she says, '*I disapprove of television greatly.*' She does her homework in the dining-room and goes to bed between 8.30 and 9. Her father went to a grammar school, her mother did not. Both parents think that school is doing her good. She is fond of nature and the countryside and enjoys rambles and cycle rides. The regularity of school life irritates her. She likes her best subject, French, and dislikes her weakest, mathematics. She writes:

I think I would prefer to go to a Secondary School as there is more art and craft and games. As I am not very bright I think this life would suit me better. But Grammar schools are very good and I am obtaining all the knowledge I can and am trying to appreciate it . . .

The only difficulty I can see is the five and a half mile bus journey to school every day and having to get up at six instead of half past seven and having less time at weekends to play instead of homework, and mummy, who exepts more of me now. I miss the drive round the farm with daddy on Saturdays and Sundays, and how he used to let me drive the lorry although I was only 11. This I miss most.

I can see no advantages at all.

These nine pupils are all very different from one another. Together they indicate something of the great range of ways in which adjustment to school may be unsatisfactory; and singly they represent types of family settings, temperaments, abilities and interests that are found with some frequency in the whole school population questioned in this survey. It is therefore useful to consider what their papers reveal.

Behind Robert, John, Pauline and probably others we see parents who (in the phrase used by many of the teachers questioned) 'haven't a clue'. It is true that whereas Robert's and Pauline's parents are indifferent to the school, John's are in favour of it. But their support is now probably no more than a residue of the bewildered pride they felt a year previously. It is quite unlikely to withstand the stresses of what will undoubtedly be their son's repeated failures and the disapproval of school, or to be translated into positive encouragement and understanding. Jean's parents, on the other hand, though themselves without a grammar-school education, have so unquestioningly accepted it with all its implications for their daughter that it is not even a point of disagreement or protest. Though she dislikes school, she knows that she will have to stay and do her best. It is fate.

Robert, John, Pauline, Peter and George say that they do their homework in bedroom, living-room or 'any room'. Experience has shown that in families with the social assumptions indicated in their papers, it is rare – indeed, almost unknown – for a bedroom to be furnished as a boy's or girl's private room, to be heated, or to possess any study furniture. It is likely to be used only for sleeping, and to be shared with brothers or sisters. If homework is indeed done there, cold and discomfort are at most seasons likely to ensure that it is scamped, so that the child can return as quickly as possible to the warmth of the living-room or the friendliness of the streets. But usually, though the bedroom may be officially allocated for homework, it is in fact done in the living-room, against a background of television, radio, playing children, or adults' talk, and often amid the protests of parents who either pity their son or daughter for having to suffer the imposed discipline or resent the intrusion of this alien breath into the family atmosphere.

Margaret and Mary (they are not in the same school) lead well-regulated lives at home. They do their homework in a specially assigned room, and, unlike many in this group, go to bed early. Both appear to be law-abiding children, doing their work conscientiously but finding difficulty in maintaining the standard expected of them. Margaret suffers an added strain because of her touchiness. She is solitary, excessively class-conscious and very vulnerable to real or fancied slights. Like many shy children, she evidently finds it easier to adjust herself to authority than to her peers; and this, rather than snobbery, may well account for their teasing. Mary is resisting some of the disciplines and burdens of growing up, and realizes dimly that school is but one of the factors in the process that is leading her away from the old childish trust and dependence upon her parents. The programme of her working day is also representative of many that, involving early rising and fatiguing travel, appear to impose a quite severe physical strain on children. (John, it will be noted, also complains of the tedium of daily journeys.)

William, an earnest and humourless boy, is the only son of a widowed mother who is probably both anxious and over-protective. His complaint of 'filthy language' need not perhaps be taken too literally: nevertheless, he is one of an appreciable minority of boys who complain of bad language or bad habits in their companions. At the very least, this minority illustrates the difficulties that inevitably arise when children from sheltered homes are thrown into contact with those whose social group knows few refinements or restraints. It is quite evident that William lives in a different world from that of Peter and John.

George's anger, his fanatical devotion to soccer, and the almost lyrical energy of his language, suggest immense frustration, and the violent capitals and changeable handwriting of his paper indicate his unhappiness. It is interesting to note how the grandiosely mercenary tone alternates with the expression of passionate longing for the open air. He, like Robert, John, Pauline and Peter, has fallen foul of his teachers, and resents the hostility that his behaviour has undoubtedly provoked.

Jean has considerable insight and a sense of purpose. Many of her interests seem to be natural and desirable, and the cause of her dislike of school is at first not very clear. We detect it, however, in her desire for individual significance, her longing for adult status, and her fear of inadequacy in work. One feels that a little apparently casual attention and encouragement at this stage would give Jean valuable assistance through a painful though probably transient phase of adolescent misgiving. But how is a teacher to discern, among hundreds of girls all looking much alike in their uniforms, the one who at this moment, in spite of her enjoyment of science and English, is unsure of her powers?

Reviewing the evidence gathered together in this chapter, we see that it is not lack of intelligence alone that can account for a dislike of school: some of these children are intelligent. It is not poverty or social inferiority: some are well-to-do and of good social standing. It is not lack of parental enthusiasm: some parents are co-operative. It may, however, be said that according to this survey, although no single cause or group of causes can be held generally accountable, one or more of the following tend to be associated with a rejection of school: lack of parental understanding or sympathy with the assumptions of school; a strong discrepancy in the social assumptions of school and home; the presence of companions with a markedly different social background; acute home anxieties arising from bereavement, divorce or poverty; disruption, through the claims of school, of a cherished family pattern; physical discomforts and fatigues, especially those associated with travelling and a long school day; the feeling of excessively prolonged junior status; failure to find significance in the school curriculum; the loss of old companionship; personal animosity between teachers and pupils; rebellion against parents; jealousy of elder brothers or sisters; feelings of inadequacy in school work; fear of examinations; sense of threatened individual significance; fear of responsibility or of growing up; dislike of routine; dislike of indoor pursuits; physical restlessness; self-distrust. Some of these are seen to be centred in family conditions, some in individual temperaments and endowments, some in social expectations, and some in the internal régime of school.

These pupils illustrate some of the problems that today beset the secondary grammar school. Should it, for example, provide more art and more comparatively unorganized outdoor activity for Mary, or is her own conjecture right, that she would have been better placed at a secondary modern school? Is William a more satisfactory pupil than the rebellious and – as unquoted parts of his paper show – sexually preoccupied Peter, and is it possible or necessary to capture Peter for academic study through his discernible enthusiasm for geography? Will John – though he may well have mathematical ability – stay the course, or is it in terms too alien for his comprehension? If he stays, will it be possible to give him anything more than an efficient training in techniques, and is it an essential (as distinct from desirable) function of the grammar school to do more than this? The opinions of the teachers, already analysed, suggest some uncertainty about the answers.

II

Conceptions of Grammar-School Function (2)

IN the opinion of the majority of the children,[1] the grammar school is without qualification the best type of secondary school. Of those who do not claim an absolute superiority for the grammar school, most say either that no one type of school is better than another, or that different schools are suitable for different purposes or different kinds of pupil. Few consider the grammar to be inferior to any other kind of school, but on the occasions when another type is preferred it is usually the public or the technical school; much more rarely, the modern school. Comprehensive and multilateral schools are advocated by comparatively few.

Of the large number of pupils who consider the grammar school to be intrinsically preferable, nearly all include in their answers some attempt to define the programme and pattern of grammar-school education. First, and most important: many of them regard it quite simply as a better kind of education, in itself worth striving to acquire. There is a feeling that the grammar school sets and maintains standards of learning:

'I think that a grammar school gives a much better education. I was talking to a friend the other day who went to a secondary school and he is in the 3rd form and when I showed him my Maths he did not know what I was talking about.' 'Higher standards makes one work harder.' 'It is a much better education, and all the educated people come from grammar school.' 'Yes, secondary modern schools attempt a sort of semi-education, not elaborating upon many subjects.' 'I consider any broader, fuller education much more useful than a slacker, less compact education.' 'Yes. Better education which is a great help when you grow older, especially in the world to-day. It gives you a sort of responsibility, to your school and other things, that you were proved good enough for it, and you should try to maintain that. Also I think that when you know more you want to be respectable and not waste your knowledge in being a ruffian.' 'It is a better education and they teach better things.' 'In a grammar school there is a certain standard that you have to live up to.' 'It gives one a good education in the fact that one gets to be knowledgeable without being stuffy.'

[1] The proportion is, approximately, for boys three to one and for girls two to one.

The education is often felt to be distinguished by being predominantly intellectual and theoretic:

'You get more theoretical work than in a secondary school.' 'I consider a grammar school education better for those who prefer brain-work.' 'I don't think a lot of practical work important as you can learn it later on in life but you can't learn and enjoy learning other things taken when you are older.' 'It's more academical than other types.'

In the course of this 'academical' education, the pupil is offered a wide range of subjects. This is stimulating, and gives a sense of spaciousness in the world of the mind. Within this range, the inclusion of certain subjects is particularly important. We may note with interest, in view of the often-expressed dislike of foreign languages, that it is, nevertheless, these very languages that are most frequently mentioned as proper to a distinctive grammar-school curriculum:

'They teach more subjects in a grammar school such as French, Latin and German in languages and Algebra, chemistry and physics in other subjects.' 'We are taught languages and from that we can discover the original meaning of many everyday words.' 'It gives more scope and a wider range of subjects.' 'A grammar school teaches far more general knowledge and sense. It teaches languages which not many other schools do.' 'In grammar schools we learn Latin.' 'I think so, yes, because other secondary schools do not take many languages.' 'We are allowed to specialise in our choice of subjects and we have the opportunity of learning languages.'

The intellectual education of the grammar school is known to imply hard work, in both quantity and quality. Homework, though a burden, is also felt, particularly by some younger pupils, to be an honourable distinction, signifying that one is receiving a real education:

'At other secondary schools only a limited amount of maths is taught, not much homework (if any).' 'Yes, because when I think of two of my friends who are in secondary schools it seems to me that they get pretty poor education. One day I asked one of my friends "How much homework do you have?" His reply was "We do not have homework." Homework, I think is a good thing, because it helps you.'

But homework is only one external sign of the spirit of hard work associated with a grammar-school education, a spirit which some think should extend to uncongenial subjects:

'A grammar school provides masters for Latin and French which I do not like but it is good for me.' 'Most girls whom I know who go to other schools seem to dislike school. They want to leave as soon as possible and don't enjoy school life: and they take no interest in the lessons. They do not try to understand things which do not interest them and very often have "one track" minds.'

Most of the writers feel that the studies of the grammar school, whether enjoyed or not, have to be pursued seriously, with concentration and speed. Relaxation, of course, is also necessary, but grammar-school pupils must realize that the central purpose of the school is work:

'All of them are there to work.' 'I think a grammar school is better because it can make a boy or girl concentrate far more in a period of time.' 'Boys work without being pushed.' 'You have some fun but when you work you work hard.' 'About everyone works quite steadily.' 'A grammar school is strickter and therefore more work is done. At my friends secondry school, all they seem to do is have open nights and plays etc. and as far as work is concerned, all they do is make pamphlets. They have all the week to do homework and it seems to make them slacker.' 'I do feel that a grammar school is the best because the people who go there are people who are trying to really work and enjoy life. At secondary schools people only seem to want to leave school and very few really work. I do not think the new idea of dropping High schools is a good one.' 'The teachers give the girls in a secondary school plenty of time to do their work. While, in a grammar school you have to have speed.'

Of course hard work is sometimes associated with the passing of public examinations. These are, however, mentioned comparatively seldom, and when they are noticed it is usually in a context such as the following:

'In a way I consider a grammar school to be the better because I do think that if you are determined to work hard and try for your advanced school Certificate, and then go on, maybe to a University to get a degree and finally obtain a very good career, then you have indeed profited by a Grammar School education. However if your feelings towards work are totally contrary to this then I think it doesn't matter to you where you go. And if you have set your heart on a career which does not need a good qualification, then one is apt not to worry. Personally I am extremely glad that I came to a Grammar school.'

The writers recognize that in order to provide this strenuous intellectual education the schools must be staffed by well-qualified people, with both sound scholarship and the ability to teach:

'They have clever teachers who go into more detail preparing us for the G.C.E.' 'It is more exciting and joyful and you get taught more carefully and properly.' 'You have better teaching than secondary modern schools. Because you go farther into a subject.' 'The secondary modern school cannot, no matter what the argument to the contrary, be a first-class school. Primarily, they have not teachers of the same calibre.' 'The teachers at a Grammar School are more knowledgeable and find it easier to teach.' 'The teachers seem to put a little bit extra in the lessons.' 'Any thing one wants to know, one only has to ask and someone will give an answer even if it was not the one we were expecting.'

The staff is praised repeatedly for its industry and its willingness to help, in both academic and personal matters:

'Each boy is thought of as an individual, and if he is not very good at one subject the masters will go to very great trouble to help you. The house masters and form masters are always ready to help you if you are in any trouble.' 'If masters are helpful in the progress of a boy, they sometimes find family affairs to be involved and they often try to settle matters by giving each boy as much help as they can and he therefore gains considerably.' 'The mistresses are usually willing to explain things in break if they are not understood by a person in the lesson.' 'On the whole the teachers have more patience with the girls who intend to work than those who don't and most girls at the grammar school intend to work.'

Individual attention given by the staff is highly valued:

You get more singularly attention. Do more work in a day than secondary schools do in a week – a very good thing.

For this combination of hard, concentrated study and personal under-standing (both between teachers and pupils and among the pupils them-selves) it is felt that the grammar school must be somewhat exclusive – a minority school. Sometimes the minority is of class, more often of intelli-gence. 'Class' is here a misleading term. The notion, it is true, is shot through with snobbery, with desire for prestige or fear of losing it, or with a rather narrow respectability. Yet, on further examination, it is seen to have little to do with inherited importance or authority, nor is it closely connected with financial position, though some occupations carry more memories of economic anxieties than others. It seems to be much more closely associated with a conscious and deliberate acceptance of certain aspirations and standards of behaviour – the 'bourgeois virtues' mentioned in Chapter 1. In any social *milieu* where these virtues are unfamiliar, or are threatened, or are maintained with difficulty, their maintenance tends to be accompanied by snobbery, priggishness or prejudice. It is in the light of such understanding that the following remarks must be read:

'The class of people is much higher and it is easier to mix and learn with them.' 'You meet a better class of people and get into a better society.' 'The tone of the school is usually good. The chaps who attend it are usually decent types in so far as behaviour and manners are concerned and they are not so unruly, rough, offensive and rude towards the masters.' 'Most of the pupils come from good families.' 'It has made me friendly with a lot of boys of the right type.' 'I think most of the boys and girls who are teddy boys and girls and such like come from secondary modern schools. These people I think are only these things because they want other people to know their there.' 'The pupils are more sensible and have been brought up in a different way.' 'You meet the better class of people.'

More often the minority is seen to consist of those within an upper range of intelligence. The association of such people not only makes it easier to learn, but also has social consequences.

'Yes, because there are no dull lads or lazy boys at the bottom of the class holding the good ones back. And there is a better community.' 'All the pupils in a form have the same intelligence quota [sic] and thus advancement at work is speeded up. At a grammar school one learns more, which in itself is an interesting thing.' 'When you take the scholarship I feel that it separates us . . . In the Midlands (where I used to live) they had grammar schools taking in A's and B scholarships and therefore not such hard work. Now in that area they have the new scheme to have all boys in a High School and transport them to a grammar school at 4th form age, if they are good enough. (Many people leave at 4th form age in secondary schools). I therefore think that a grammar school education is better than the others because having earned a grammar school place you learn faster.' 'The people whom I meet are very much the same as me.' 'In a Grammar school you meet children of about your own intelligence, and so their thoughts and activities coincide more with your own.' 'Yes, I do consider a Grammar school to be better than any other type of secondary education because nothing holds you back. All the pupils work at the same speed.'

Occasionally exclusiveness based on intelligence, far from seeming to accentuate class differences, is seen as a means of diminishing them:

It gives just as good an education as [independent] schools do and it mixes the classes so that one realises that she is very lucky either in money or happiness. It does not mix the very dull girls with the very bright girls and this is a good point as it would only cause jealousy with the dull girls and superiority on behalf of the others.

There are many suggestions that intelligent companions make congenial friends who 'speak the same language', but the special value of grammar-school friendship is not always naïvely associated with intelligence: it is often felt, rather, to be a consequence of the strong sense of community that arises partly from the association of like-minded people for the pursuit of learning, partly from the traditional and now assumed connexion of the grammar school with social value. Something of this mixture of views is illustrated in the following remarks:

'The boys who are sent to a grammar school are intelligent and therefore make a better friend.' 'You are with people at your own standard. Make many friends and are taught languages in school time.' 'You know the girls you mix with must have certain knowledge and you feel more comfortable if you can express things in a way other people understand.' 'I have found out that I have made more friends at a grammar school than my friend has at a secondary modern.' 'Friends are easier to make.' 'I came to this school after two years in a secondary modern. I find the lessons much more interesting. I also like my companions much better than those at my last school.'

A grammar school education, in the opinion of these boys and girls, is distinguished partly by certain external signs and characteristic customs and partly by qualities which are less definable but which are felt to constitute the grammar-school 'atmosphere'. The most obvious of the external signs is uniform. It is mentioned rather infrequently, but those who do mention it usually approve of it as a badge of grammar-school status:

'The boys have to where set uniforms, and this is much better than many of the "teddy boy" suits worn elsewhere.' 'The uniform is something to be proud of even though you are compelled to wear it.' 'We wear a uniform and everyone knows when you have passed to go to a Grammar School.' 'Uniform is more rigidly enforced and it makes me more proud of my school.'

The games of the grammar school are felt by some to be distinctive, either in the choice of game (usually rugby instead of soccer) or in the organization of games periods and matches. It need not be emphasized how closely this is associated with ideas of 'class':

'In grammar schools rugger is usually played which I personally consider far superior to soccer which is played in secondary schools.' 'Our games are of a higher standard.' 'The schools can have many more sporting fixtures with other schools.'

It is important, however, for those who would accuse the grammar school of snobbery to note that such statements are very few indeed.

Turning from the tangible to the intangible, we find that the school is thought by many to be a distinctive kind of community with its own recognizable tone and atmosphere:

'There is a better community.' 'The whole school is united.' 'I have a feeling that I belong here, that I won a place here and am therefore part of the school.'

An example of the way in which the school can imbue with this spirit one of its least able members is given by a fourth-year boy in a 'Y' form, the lowest of four 'streams', who writes:

I think that a grammar school is best, because if you are clever there is no limit to your opportunities of a career. And even if you aren't clever there is always something you can do for the school, so that you may benefit from its name without being a passenger.

The atmosphere is often felt to have that civilized relaxation which is possible when all, teachers and pupils, are able to take certain common assumptions for granted:

'I think the masters are more inclined to treat you as equals here than anywhere else.' 'A grammar school is less strict than a secondary modern, the masters seem more intimate to you.' 'Although I have had no experience of other schools, I have one friend who goes to a technical school. From her description of her life at school I have found that grammar school girls are better equipped for life after school. A grammar school education seems to give girls more confidence, it contains much more interesting work and treats its pupils with more freedom and respect although still maintaining discipline. I should like to make it clear that I have not based all my reasons on the discriptions of my friend's school.'

As the last writer notes, this kind of freedom by no means implies a denial of discipline, which would indeed be undesirable. In a large number of replies, the pupils make it quite clear that they consider a characteristic discipline to mark the superiority of the grammar school:

'The grammar school has more encouragement and strictness about the place.' 'I think it's more strict and more educational.' 'The grammar school masters can keep control over their pupils.' 'I think the teachers here are very strict and get you on a lot more than soft teachers who don't care if you do a thing or if you don't.' 'The masters are a lot stricter in a grammar school, and they make sure you know what they want you to know.' 'Your life may not be as free as it would in any other school but you benefit from it in the long run.' 'I think a grammar school is better because at secondary schools they can do what they like. I mean to say girls and boys who go to Secondary schools can fool around, the girls wear lipstick and powder and some people are getting to be like teddy-girls or boys.' 'A grammar school teaches discipline and manners that would, perhaps, at other schools, be quite slack. The high standard of education and the briskness at which a grammar school works is good for the mind and keeps one "on one's toes".'

Some teachers may be flattered to learn how their authority appears in the eyes of a fourteen-year-old schoolboy, like the one who says:

The staff has most probably had more experience and can deal with strong situations.

Many pupils value more highly the discipline that comes from within, is stimulated by trust, and manifests itself in controlled behaviour:

'Although strict discipline is obtained, boys are trusted – can do most things without the supervision of masters.' 'I think that grammar school children are better mannered and more self controlled. I am writing that because I have heard the people from the secondary boasting about how they can cheek and get their own way with their staff.' 'In a grammar school people are more controlled.' 'At some secondary schools I have heard that they are very cheeky to the mistresses and so they dont get much work done.'

The grammar school, then, is thought by many to be superior in setting a higher standard of learning, possessing better-qualified and more competent staff, demanding harder work, having more intelligent and purposeful pupils, inculcating a strong sense of community while at the same time mollifying rather than exacerbating the effect of class distinctions, and creating a characteristic atmosphere in which both relaxation and discipline play their part. These attributes are associated with the tradition and reputation which, whether they belong to a single school of many years' standing or are part of a general educational pattern which embraces the newest foundation, are a source of pride and confidence:

'Most grammar schools have a better reputation . . . something to be proud of and to live up to.' 'I do consider a grammar school to be the best type of school because of the tradition behind it and the reputation it has built up; now the name of our school is praised in universities.' 'A grammar school has a more interesting history than any secondary school and a reputation to keep up.'

Many pupils, perhaps about one-third of the total number, regard the grammar school as a means of preparation for certain types of career – though very few of these assert that such preparation is its sole or chief function. The function itself may be considered in several ways. In its lowest and least analysed form, it is seen as the provision of a useful 'name':

'There is a better education and reputation which help towards a well-paid job.' 'Even the name of the school helps when one is applying for a job.'

In a slightly more particularized way, the school is felt to offer courses leading to a qualification, usually alluded to rather vaguely as 'the G.C.E.', which – irrationally but very powerfully – will help its possessor to obtain a good post. This qualification is seen to be demanded by employers as a badge of a good education, though the actual studies it entails may not be directly related to the work the post will involve–'You can get better jobs with the G.C.E.' The school is valued by many as an avenue to the university, through a course related fairly directly to university studies. These studies may or may not be a direct preparation for the student's subsequent career:

'The education is better and I am certain that there are more chances of getting the G.C.E. at O and A levels and also scholarships from a grammar school.' 'From a grammar school it is possible to go to a university directly and G.C.E. may be taken in many subjects.' 'More opportunities are given in a Grammar school e.g. the G.C.E. The opportunity of going to College or University.'

The function as they see it, finally, is to provide a general education; this, while largely self-justifying, is also related to a career in that it enables its possessor to choose from a wide range of occupations. In other words, a liberal education:

'Because it develops your mind fully and helps you to understand things which you come against in your latter life. It gives you more variety when you chose a job. If you have had a grammar school education you can become an M.P., a school-teacher or a bank clerk.' 'A lot depends here on the interests and ambitions of the pupil. If he wishes to be a teacher, lecturer or scientist, there are few schools better than the grammar school and all those are private schools. If, however, the student has set his eyes on a career as engineer, draughtsman, or accountant, then the secondary technical school is obviously the better.' 'I think that the grammar school gives one the choice of being an ordinary worker or a scientist.' 'One can choose between more varied occupations, both on the arts and on the scientific side. The better education stops a person from getting frustrated in the things that person wishes to do later. I think it also helps women to have a better life, even if they marry, for they can help their husbands and children.'

This liberal theory merges into the notion, expressed by almost half the pupils, that it is the grammar school's function to promote the development of integrated people and to pass on a desirable tradition in the art of living. It is closely concerned with manners:

'It gets all the mannerly people together.' 'It teaches you good manners and helps you to live properly.' 'Everyday I am in contact with the local district secondary modern boys and girls on the bus and I dislike their attitude and behaviour.' 'I think the schools such as this devote more time to brainwork, cultivation of good speech and manners.' 'The grammar school is very particular about etiquette and posture and things which are most important.' 'You learn very nice manners in a grammar school and are kept under strict rules.' 'One can get just as good education at other types of schools, but a grammar school puts a finish on you that other schools cannot.'

The grammar school is also felt to be directly concerned with the development of the mind ('It gives you a whole mind because of the length of education') and very much concerned with character:

'Most of your companions are about the same degree of intelligence as you are and pieces of information passed on go to make up one's character.' 'A grammar school . . . helps us to grow into adults in a good way.' 'At a grammar school we are taught to be individualists . . . We are better citizens of the world when we leave Grammar school and the people who have been to grammar school are those which the country relies on whether in a crisis or not.' 'It helps you to understand things in a different way and develop your caracter.'

One form of this character-development is a growing maturity – a maturity that is fostered by the expectations of older people. The school régime gives confidence:

'I have learned to stand on my own feet and make my own decisions.' 'One gets better training to be a leader of men, and to go out into the world with confidence in oneself and in the future.' 'It has given me more courage to do things which I was unable to do before.' 'Your knowledge is extended, and when you go out into the world you can stand on your own two feet, and know what you are doing or saying is right.' 'It helps you to speak out amongst other people and not to be shy.' 'Independence of other people and forming opinions alone are more noticeable in grammar schools.'

All this is associated with an understanding of the world or of life. These terms are not defined, but appear to include the phenomenal environment, the management of human affairs and the empire of the mind; in other words, the beginnings of science, humanism and pure reason:

'It gives a better understanding of the outside world and what takes place there.' 'It makes you open your eyes to the things which you have not noticed before like looking into television and wireless sets to see how they work.' 'We have more knowledge of the world around us, and can put it to a more practical purpose.' 'It helps to widen one's outlook on life, to read intelligent books and take an interest in what is happening in our present times.' 'It gives you a better interest in life.'

The school is felt to be a preparation for adult life in a sense beyond that of training for an occupation, though this may be included:

I feel the training and the discipline which is given to us gives us a better lead in life, and therefore from leaving school we approach the 'outside' life better.

The individual is not so much at the mercy of mass influences:

'It teaches you to amuse yourself constructively without the help of the cinema
etc.' 'You find that most grammar school friends amuse themselves in a much
better way because some secondary modern pupils go jiving in the evenings and
go to common clubs and make a nuisance of themselves.'

Most important of all, perhaps, the education given is felt to promote
communication:

'You can talk to people and know what you are talking.' 'It is better for a
person if he can talk sensibly and knowing what he is talking about in a conversation.' 'I am sure that to have a knowledge of being able to speak to people is
better than anything else I can think of.' 'There is more freedom of speech and
you can say what you think.'

   Of those who do not think the grammar school actually superior, a few
give personal reasons which are of little significance in the argument,
though of great interest as indicating some of the attitudes with which a
grammar-school teacher may have to deal. Is there any hope, for example,
of setting the girl quoted below on the path of scholarship?

   No. At my other school I sat for the 11+ and failed while a really backward
girl pasted I consider this unfair. Then I was given another chance my parents
didn't want me to take it and neither did I. I told the maths teacher and she was
furious (as I would have been as I was getting 15 good marks a week for maths).
But I did not want I was all right where I was. I was excellent at Science, Geography, English, MATHS, History. But they had their way and I sat. I pasted 2nd
chance and here I am lucky if I get one good mark (that is usually for P.T.).

Others base their opinion on accidental details such as the local secondary
modern school's superior buildings or equipment. A few, again, disapprove of the games arrangements in their particular schools. More important and interesting opinions are those which concern the function,
atmosphere and effectiveness of other kinds of school. Thus, some prefer
the personal education given by the secondary modern school:

   No, I have been to a secondary school for a year and the atmosphere was much
better than at a grammar school. The pupils did not gain as much knowledge but
they gained an ability to mix well and do things with their hands. I do not think
knowledge superior to such talents.

In contrast to the boys and girls who value the grammar school for its
tension, pace and concentration there are those who like the more
relaxed tone of the secondary modern school. The work is thought by

some to be easier and more enjoyable, and the virtual absence of home-work invites admiration and envy:

Although a grammar school gives you a higher standard of work and enables you to have various certificates a secondary school does just as much in helping to give you much more pleasant life with your schoolwork.

The education in a grammar school is better and the type of people are better but it is much too 'HIGHBROW'. At other schools people are much more free to do as they like.

No I do not think grammar schools are better as many of my friends who go to secondary school are equally as clever as I am. They leave school earlier and help their parents out in money problems. Also secondary school girls are happier and enjoy themselves before they are to old to do so.

A grammar school is worse than a secondary modern, because secondary have more freedom and are happier and their outlook to life seems better because their parents dont get stuck up and expect too much of them they don't get much home-work. They have more time for outside hobbies. Most secondary schools are now bilateral take G.C.E. and R.S.A. comparing the two is like a prison to a holiday camp and school uniform is not compulsory.

The modern school is sometimes praised for its lack of competitiveness:

In a secondry school people get on with each other much better. There are no arguments and such like beginning about who came top of the form. There is less fight in exams.

Again, the grammar school is adversely criticized for teaching useless subjects and for having too narrow a curriculum:

'It prevents enough practical work as is really necessary especially in the Sciences, as time is wasted on useless subjects.' 'I feel that in a grammar school one is being put in a definite groove, without consideration of the boy's talents or likes, and with reference to this school I feel that there is not a sufficient choice in the curriculum.' 'Grammar schools are inclined to be a bit too much academic, with not enough art, craft, and needlework. This gives the girls a setback when they go out into the world for some don't know how to do almost anything around the house.' 'It is no better than a secondary school in so much as in a secondary school you are free to choose your own future and fullest help is given, while in this school your future seems to be made up by the teachers, who rather push you towards being a teacher.'

The grammar school may, in fact, be relying on an empty reputation:

'From the educational point of view, yes. It does give you a bigger chance of getting a really good job when you grow up. [But] I know a boy who goes to a secondary modern school and he seems to know just as much as some of my friends here. He knows a great deal of general knowledge and history.'

Secondary modern schools are thought to provide better facilities for practical and domestic work:

'In the secondary school, where my brother used to go they have pottery, boxing and when they have woodwork they go to a different school, which is what I want to do.' 'At other schools cookery, needlework and other useful things are emphasised, and games take up much of the time. Here, we barely touch any of these, but are always working at our books.' 'In the new secondary modern school they have different subjects which would be very helpful in future careers. For instants they teach Engineering and Metal Work. They also have the General Certificate of Education.'

These other schools may be just as good a preliminary to suitable employment:

'I think that if you are willing to work and work hard you will get just as much benefit out of a secondary type of education. My brother for instance did not pass for a grammar school, but worked hard and has now got a very good job in an electrical office.' 'In a secondary school you learn a trade and you are certain of getting a job but in a Grammar School if you fail the G.C.E. you will have a hard time finding a job.' 'Both teach similar subjects and in both schools you have a chance to get good jobs if you work hard enough.'

They are often more directly pointed towards particular work:

The grammar school gives you a wider outlook on life than any other school but if you are aiming for a certain profession in future life, then it might be wise to go to a school which trains you for this subject.

Moreover, they lead to money-earning at an early age: 'My friends are working and earning good money but I am not.'

Some pupils feel that one should not ascribe superiority or inferiority to any type of school. Schools should be judged individually, and any school may be good or bad:

I do not think a Grammar School is better than any other school. You still have the same activities and nearly the same lessons. The school life is just the same and you still have your friends. Any other school teaches you discipline and will power and how to live a good life just as well as a grammar school.

Schools may not, in any case, have the significance that the inquiry suggests:

It helps in many ways but it is not better. It does not really make any difference to a person growing up. For its their home life that really counts.

It is also unjustifiable to make distinctions which suggest a differential valuation of people:

No because the people that attend a grammar school are no better than those that attend a secondary school.

So far the comparison has been between grammar and modern schools. Some, however, compare the grammar school unfavourably with the public school:

'I think a bording school would be much better than a Grammar School. It helps one to stand on there own feet and work out difficulties for themselves.' 'A school like Eton or Winchester has more attention taken towards it. The boys get an individual upbringing.'

A few have heard about comprehensive schools and think them based on a sound principle:

I think the schools where there are a grammar stream, a technical stream and a secondary stream. They make a better atmosphere amongst the teenagers of a district as there is not so much resentment from those who do not have a grammar school education.

But by far the greater number of those who deny superiority to the grammar school do so not because they disapprove of it but on the grounds that it is suitable for one kind of person, the intellectual. Different schools, in fact, are suited to pupils who differ in either endowment or expectations:

'It depends on the pupil concerned. Certainly I think a grammar school education is best for me, because I like the "sit down and think" side. But for boys who are all athletics and sport, and who enjoy working with their hands, this is the wrong sort of education.' 'I think that a grammar school is good for a boy of good intelligence who is prepared to work and bad for a boy who just can't pass examinations.' 'I do not consider this is true because each school serves its purpose for the kind of pupil attending it. Secondary modern scholars are more suited for practical work, and would flounder hopelessly if they attempted to do Latin, just as Grammar School children would have no flair for metalwork, unless they had unusual talent.' 'For myself I'd say yes because I do better at Maths, English, history, Latin etc. than at woodwork, art, biology. For others it depends what subjects they like, do best in and what they want to be when they grow up.' 'No. Each school is designed for its own particular type of pupil. e.g. most secondary modern boys do not wish to do homework.' 'Personally a technical school would be disliked by me because of the fact that I am not good with my hands and a secondary modern because of the same reason and the fact that I do not generally do in my spare time the sort of things that boys in those schools do when they leave school.' 'For a girl who wishes to leave school at 15, and wants to get married as soon as she can, a secondary school is what she wants, because she learns more home life.' 'I think that grammar schools are better for girls who are prepared to work hard and concentrate. I do not think a grammar school is really any better than any other secondary school because it is just another type of school. There are schools to fit different kinds of girls such as girls who are good at making things and for girls who are not really interested in school work.' 'It really depends on the child. If he or she prefers the type of education which consists of mainly theory work the grammar school is quite definitely the right kind of education for that person. But if the child prefers a lot more time to be spent on things such as cookery, needlework, art, woodwork etc. than on Maths, English, Geography etc. the secondary school is the better type for him or her.'

Clearly, then, these middle-school boys and girls, whether or not they consider the grammar school to give the best kind of secondary education, show a large measure of agreement over its nature and function. To them, it is exclusive, though not narrowly so, admitting pupils of high and fairly high intelligence. The curriculum is organized to maintain academic standards, and is distinguished by the importance attached to linguistic study. It concentrates on theory and is not greatly concerned to demonstrate the immediate relevance or applicability of its programme. The school trains pupils for public examinations, success in which is a qualification for many kinds of work; and it prepares a substantial minority for entrance to the universities and the professions. Its prestige is usually high, because it has its place in a long tradition. Though games are valued, the grammar school is an institution of serious purpose, exacting strenuous and not always enjoyable effort from its pupils in both lessons and homework. Conduct, appearance and manners are all important, and discipline is strict, though strictness may be compatible with friendly relations between staff and pupils. There is no time to be lost, and the necessary seriousness, speed and concentration of the work make inevitable some exclusion of popular interests, as well as the postponement of money-earning and adult status.

The Horatian joys of this type of education are not to everybody's taste, and the tension for individuals can sometimes be severe, especially when a mediocre intellect is not fortified by family attitudes sympathetic to the austerity, hard work and discipline of the grammar-school tradition, or when the community and academic pressure of the school are felt to cause an almost unbearable separation from earlier associations and companionship. On the other hand, besides those who by both endowment and upbringing are easily and painlessly assimilated to the grammar-school pattern, there are also many for whom its intellectual experiences are felt – though not without some strain – to transcend the attendant social conflicts and penalties; many others who, though not highly intelligent, share their family's enthusiastic admiration for the grammar school and what it is felt to stand for; and many, finally, who, attracted by a hitherto unknown experience of community, captivated by unusually lively and skilful teaching, or won by the personal encouragement or challenge of a percipient teacher, are making their first important ventures, not without trepidation, into a world the strangeness and potential hostility of which are seldom even dimly appreciated by their elders. It is appropriate, therefore, to conclude this survey of the middle school by looking more closely at the picture they spontaneously give of themselves, their tastes and pursuits, and their adjustment to home and school.

12

'School and my Life'

BOYS and girls do not see themselves in terms of statistics or norms. They speak as individuals and see their school experience – how could it be otherwise? – in directly personal terms. Let us, then, observe a selection of their own final comments, made in answer to the question: 'Thinking of your home, your school, and the district where you live, what special difficulties or advantages has coming to this school brought into your life?'

BOYS' SCHOOLS

Second year, 'X' forms:

Before I came to this school I didn't have any homework, so I could go out to play every night, it is a long way to go to school everyday and I get fed up of seeing the same places. I don't like the masters of this school they are more striked than the ones of my old school.

More friends. As I have less of my own time I do things more vigorously and enjoy them more. I appreciate good music, i.e. skiffle, Jazz, Calipso etc. more as well as symphonys which practically drive me mad when playing the violin. School often makes me make various large decisions which are good for a person.

Second year, 'Y' form:

There is a minor difficulty in homework. I have a sister of eight who is very energetic and possesses a nice singing voice. It is hard to tell her to shut up because although in the living-room, her voice penetrates through into the sitting-room.

An advantage is the fact that I am always learning and doing something new. I enjoy this, because 'learning the unknown' as you might put it fills me with ecstasy.

Fourth year, 'X' forms:

I think this education gave me a wider view on life and that it made me understand people more. One fault I think it is inclined to make one a bit big for his boots and possibly talk big to less fortunate children.

Another difficulty is that with a better education one is expected to get a good job and as this is only a small town one will probably have to travel up country to get a job.

There is also a certain gap between me and my parents owing to the differences of education. On the other hand I am able to understand them more and get at the inner meaning in their arguments and talks to me.

Coming to this school has greatly stopped my free time, but I do not mind as I feel I will leave school prepared to be a good citizen.

I don't think much to some of the programmes on T/V but the instructive ones are usually very good. I have learnt to appreciate some types of music and hate others (e.g. rock and roll). I have learnt to distinguish between newspapers that have party leanings and think that party is always right to a paper that states the facts with the least amount of bias of opinion.

My home life has changed a great deal since I came to this school. At home I have less spare time, and the spare time that I have I often put to good use. I do not talk to my parents as much as I used to do, and coming to this school seems to have given me the advantage of listening, understanding, and talking to my brothers' more sophisticated friends. Coming to this school has made me more talkative to the neighbours and more understanding about small children. I think that coming to this school has made me rather more proud, and my main difficulty is being too proud. In the district where I live, some of my friends who did not have the good fortune to go to a grammar school have left me.

From my old school I made a lot of freinds but I found as I went to a grammar school and they didn't, they seemed to treat me as though I were a snob, and they had a stupid idea that boys who went to a grammar school were a load of cissy's, I taught them otherwise and so many of these old freinds are freinds no longer.

My new freinds I find have interests of the same intellectual standards as myself and due to this we stick together and next year we are clearing of on a tour of our own for three weeks. I find now that due to my learnings at school I know what my father is talking about when he discusses his car.

Before I came to this school I did not understand many quotations that were given in books; now I do. Now I can appreciate some books which before I thought were utter tripe.

Sometimes when I cannot do a piece of homework I have to leave it until the following morning and my parents say that it makes me bad tempered and tired because I lose sleep through worrying. In the area where I live I am the only boy (so far) who has passed his exams and sometimes when my friends come to play with me I am called a swot and a fool because I have to stop in and do my homework.

Fourth year, 'Y' forms:

One is able to speak much more freely with other people and this is helping to a person. In the home you are treated as a grown up person more so than if you were in a secondary school. If a person goes to a grammar school a person around you expects you to know things beyond ones capabilities.

GIRLS' SCHOOLS

Second year, 'X' forms:

One of the advantages is that I am aloud to get up early in the morning without being told to go back into bed. I have to get up early to catch the bus. But as I am at a grammar school I am expected to be good, keep my hair tidy, my fingers free from ink and also to enjoy doing homework.

I cannot go out much at night because of homework. I am taking a deeper and more serious attitude towards lessons although I dont like some of them. I have to get up earlier in the morning so that I shant miss the bus. The school has pulled me up from the indifferent ways of the other school. I find there is a deeper affection between me and my sister who is at this school also. I find my father is able to help me in the subjects at which I am worse.

Second year, 'Y' forms:

I have lost all my communication with boys. My mother and father always natter at me to do my homework wright and to try my best in everything which they did not before, I feel I can talk to the teachers and not be scared. I have learnt more about currant affairs and different countries. If I do anything wrong my father always says that I should not do that now I go to a grammar school. With it being a higher standard I always feel that I am poor in my subjects. At the grammar school you always seem to be paying money or making something which costs money. I can't wear any of my jewellry.

The homework is very hard for me to do, as my mother has bad arms and I have to do a lot of housework when I come home from school. My father is a bus driver and I often have to do his tea of a night. I also have to do my sister's tea when she comes home from work, but my eldest sister is married and she is in America.

Fourth year, 'X' forms:

At the primary school I lived almost opposite the school but now I have a larger distance to go. The homework is more and harder as would be expected but I don't mind this very much. Most of my friends go to grammar schools and we are always discussing school life.

A grammar school trains girls for their future life whatever it may be. We are taught to behave ourselves and even to walk properly. We are brought up to have better manners and to behave as young ladies. In spite of this we still enjoy ourselves at school.

At the primary school the classes were mixed but this school is for girls only.

This makes a difference as now we are a little shy of boys whereas we behaved naturally with them before.

The advantage is that I am learning more here than I would elsewhere, but girls often at Guides call me a snob and say I go to a snob's school because we have more prep and more school rules than they.

Also I often let all the prep pile on to one evening because I have not time for it on Brownie, Elocution or Guide evenings then I get all worked up about it and generally upset the whole household.

I think that coming to a large school like this and mixing with girls of all classes has made my speech poorer than it should be. With extra work and home work I don't have as much time as I would like for outside activities. I live a long way from the school and have to be away from home for eight or nine hours a day. The school has given me a bigger outlook on the outside world. The school has developed my talents of being able to do languages quite easily.

There have been many difficulties since I have been coming to a Grammar School.

(1) Always the question before I go anywhere is 'Have you finished your prep'.

(2) If by any chance I cannot do my homework mummy says that I should not have brought it home to do. I have a hard job to convince her that prep is compulsory.

(3) Another difficulty is that some of my friends who went with me to my first school will not now speak to me as I go to a Grammar School.

Now that I go to a Grammar School if I do something which is not really right and yet not really wrong, immediately the comment is 'You go to a Grammar School now and people there don't do those sort of things'.

Things done in the home such as cooking, mending a fuse, I begin to realise how they are made. They seem to link up now and become part of something.

Fourth year, 'Y' forms:

My neighbours never speak to me while I am in School uniform because they say I look 'snobby' in it. I try to undo this thought but I can't. Nearly all my friends go out and earn money and have lots of clothes but as I need school uniform I cannot have them and go places as much as they can. Homework is one of my difficulties. I think that we do enough work at school without doing sums and remembering dates when we arrive home. Because I am a *Rock 'n' Roll fan*, my father who is a *square* blames that because I never do well in school examinations. He thinks I should be 1st every time but I come 3rd and perhaps 8th.

I think coming to this school as well as my age has made me feel more grown up. I now feel free to talk to my mother on any subject. On the other hand when I use a slang word it is usually said 'And that's a grammar school girl for you'. I hate this. Coming to this school I have made many friends but I still have my one friend, she has been my friend since I was two. Also coming to this school has made me very self conscious, I mix with girls of all classes but some seem to look down at me, because my skirt or something isn't regulation, my mother doesn't attend the Parent teachers meetings and she can only afford to buy me the necessities.

I am afraid that coming to this school makes me sometimes dissatisfied with home and home life. I am glad I came though because I like it and can use the good education.

Difficulties at home. My mother has many friends and nearly every night when I go home someone is in the house talking and laughing. This sometimes causes arguements between my parents as my father tells mother that she cannot expect me to work when laughing is so plain to hear. Another is that my sister often wants records blaring on and although I am upstairs I can still hear them and I complain to mummy who tells my sister to take them off. This annoys my sister and we begin to argue.

Difficulties at school. I don't think I have any.

Difficulties at district. At first my friends ignored me because they presumed I would become a snob but after 6–7 months they knew that I wasn't and began speaking to me again.

The neighbours nowadays seem to talk to me more frequently and about more adult things than they did before I came. Frankly I feel more grown up since I came here. I seem to regard things as more beautiful or dirty (as the case may be) than I used to do. I seem to appreciate things more. With regard to school I think that with coming here I have learned more than I thought I would. Not just English and Maths etc. but how to regard and rely on things better than I used to do.

This School has brought me many advantages. I have learned to appreciate, music, books, and many other aspects of life. I have learned how and what makes a decent person.

But allso many difficulties. My friends rather think I am a 'snob' and say 'Oh she goes to a Grammar School' and I find my self thinking deeper than them and feeling on a different level. My parents are rather inclined to think that I need 'pulling down a peg or two' even. They also are expecting a lot to much of me as they really don't understand what going to a Grammar School means. At school there is not enough closeness between the staff and girls and I think the Staff think we are a bit of a nuisance and don't consider our point of view. We do not get the advantages of mixing with boys as in a co-ed school and can not mix freely as many girls of secondary schools can. The district where I live, there are not many people who have had the chance of going to a Grammar School and I get the feeling that they think I do not deserve it. Also, I often think that maybe I am becoming narrow minded.

When first I came, I thought 'teddy-boys' and such were ridiculous; now I even envy them their freedom, because school almost entirely rules my life, both at home and anywhere else. My parents think that I should only have a thought for superior things (i.e. classical music etc.) and I spend much of my time trying to be what I am not.

CO-EDUCATIONAL SCHOOLS: BOYS

Second year, 'X' forms:

People expect more of you than the other children, you are respected more. At home the television stays off until you have done your homework. With homework some nights you get out but mostly you are kept in swotting or writing as the case may be. It sometimes takes you along time to get into the confidence of other children as you are a 'grammar bug' (this is slang for a person who goes to a grammar school). Although there are all these disadvantages I would not go to another school other than a grammar if I could help it.

Advantages. One advantage is that you are separated from the people who are not at your standard of work and do not have to put up with louts and hooligans. Another advantage is that many more chances to a good life are given to you. You are encouraged to get on in life and be a scholar.

You are encouraged to go to university and be a scholistic man.

Disadvantages. one disadvantage is that many people who are not worthy come to a grammar school and there only interest is to start working.

Second year, 'Y' form:

Difficulties. (none) besides just getting home $\frac{1}{2}$ hour later and eating school dinners more.

Advantages. Excuses for not going messages. Such as 'I must finish my homework'. Homework makes me stay in and not going kicking my shoe toes out playing football, we play football in the street usually and have often been caught by police. But my homework keeps me out of this kind of trouble. On Friday nights I am allowed out till as long as I like, because I have stayed in all week and there is no school the next morning.

Fourth year, 'X' forms:

You can answer some questions that people who go to other schools cannot. Its difficult to do a lot of homework at night when the family want to watch T.V., and also when my sister brings in her friends its hard for me to tell them to be quiet. School has also knocked out most of my pleasures owing to getting a lot of homework and not being able to give the right amount of concentration to it. I now criticize most plays on T.V. and tell my mother about them. My father keeps telling me that he will back me up in my school work and help me to get as far up in the world as I can we generally have a talk on Saturday nights.

My home is not suited enough for me to do my homework, there are two rooms one of which I have to do my homework in. Each has a television or radio. The district does not really appreciate the amount of work a grammar school pupil has to do. I realise it to have become more dirty. My old friends of my first school have lapsed beyond me, I no more communicate with them and they perhaps have forgotten me.

Neighbours seem to respect you more and when you walk down the street and pass them I smartly touch my cap and say hullo and they reply back and that I think gives a good name to the school. The school has learnt me more manners and respect for other people. If you go to a grammar school and work hard you will be repayed in your later life.

CO-EDUCATIONAL SCHOOLS: GIRLS

Fourth year, 'X' forms:

People of my old school are jealous. They regard me as an outcast. These however are only childish people. My real friends are not so silly. My homework ties me down too much – I am not used, yet, to the staying in, never being able to go out when I want to.

However, my life has changed greatly; before I used to be unable to control my temper. Now, I am able to put into practice the self control I have been taught. I have not a lot of time to do homework in, as I have to help my mother.

My parents expect me to be top in everything. They say that I am not doing my best. I am, however, trying my hardest.

Most of the people in my village regard grammar school children as being childish, mostly because we wear uniform.

People take a different attitude toward me now. They think they have to talk on guard all the time, but I like people who are free, and frank with one.

Coming to this school has made me ask many more questions about things at home, has made me understand more things and made me more eager to learn more. It has made me take more pride in my appearance, my bedroom and everything about me. I cannot think of any disadvantages about coming to this school, living in the town where I do live and having a home like mine. I am proud of being a pupil in this school and should hate to leave.

Fourth year, 'Y' forms:

Nothing has changed much at home except that my parents make sure I do my homework every night. I get in for 9.30 p.m. on week days. 10.30 p.m. on the weekends. My parents still let me have as much freedom as they did before. I still go to 'Ritz' on Saturday afternoon bopping. I go to the Victory Club on Saturday night doing modern dancing, on Sunday night I go to the Ritz bopping but here my mother is strict, if I ever fail to be before 10 p.m. I won't be able to go dancing again. I love school, not just the lessons but the friendship I have and the sports and the wonderful place we have our school situated. I also like the general friendly atmosphere we have.

Most of my friends go to — Secondary School and that friendship still holds today. We are still as friendly with the neighbours, you see we are the only family up our Rise who have had a family where both of us went to a grammar school, but they still think the same as they did of us.

Difficulties are that I have to walk a long way to catch the bus. Has caused a lot of rows and arguements at home. It also means that a lot of expense has been wasted as I am not staying on after the age of 15.

Fourth year, 'one-stream' school:

When I first started at the grammar school, my friends of the primary school days called me a snob and though I tried to keep up the friendship it didn't work. Naturally, I have made some very close friends here and I must say these friendships are much firmer than any I had at the primary school. I have one friend at home, but at times I get a bit fed up with her because she is so silly about boys and talks practically of nothing else. I find now that I'm always criticising my mother's slightly Welsh accent and this annoys her and tempers fly. My elder brother and I seem to get on with each other much better than we did before I came to the grammar school, of which I am very glad because our constant squabbling must have got on our parents' nerves. I have also started writing stories in exercise books since I came and I find this helps me to express my feeling for horses and the world of horses and also what I think of certain subjects at school.

PART FOUR

Face to Face

13

Some Conversations

MUCH of the material of this chapter is drawn from personal interviews with heads and staffs from more than twenty grammar schools (not exactly identical with the schools that furnished the questionnaire material), sixth-formers of seven schools (three boys', two girls' and two co-educational) and a sprinkling of chief and assistant education officers and officials of professional organizations. All those interviewed might be regarded as being closely involved in the school situation and yet, unlike the middle-school pupils who answered the questionnaires, able for various reasons to see it with some detachment. Although there were some glancing references to other types of secondary school, those interviewed were encouraged for the most part to take the grammar school as 'given', and to base their comments on the existing situation. The comments could not be exhaustive, but their spontaneity compensates for their lack of comprehensiveness.

It will be convenient to consider the responses under the headings of system (i.e. both the place of the grammar school within the secondary system and also the internal organization of the school); work, curriculum and examinations; pupils; parents; staff; the purpose and character of the grammar school.

System

Officers of local education authorities are concerned, naturally, with selection, organization, and the percentage of pupils to receive a grammar-school education. This is not the place to consider details of organization. It may, however, be observed that, in the opinion of one education officer, the technical school offers nothing that the grammar and modern school cannot between them achieve. The grammar school, he says, really must take technology seriously, for within the framework of grammar-school assumptions it has the best chance of being humanized and civilized; technical colleges have cashed in on the lassitude and complacency of the grammar school, and he is alarmed at the growth of 'technical-college *training*' as opposed to 'grammar-school *education*'.

The complicated and difficult question of church schools must be passed over here; so must the many interesting developments in the modern-school field, such as the preparation for G.C.E. and other public examinations, experiments with 'biassed' courses, and the tendency to develop fifth and even sixth forms in certain schools. Conversations with representatives of local authorities were significant, rather, for some of the personal and detailed information that emerged. A chief education officer, for example, convinced from observation that the most potent influence bearing on a school is that of the head, is quietly watching one school in which, under a new headmaster, the sixth form has quintupled itself in five years, and another in which the head has, over a period, completely revised his ideas of discipline and punishment. Under another authority there are many small rural grammar schools, 'ruinously expensive to run' and demanding a somewhat high percentage of grammar-school places, but forming a pattern difficult to alter because some of the schools are so old. Glimpses like these reveal the strongly personal strain that runs through English administration, and emphasize how difficult it will continue to be in this country to devise any system that is not tempered by human and local considerations.

Most of the heads questioned had thought seriously about the size of the grammar school, and from their answers a fairly clear conclusion can be drawn. The headmaster of a small co-educational school (under two hundred) finds it very attractive, but recognizes the inevitability of change and expansion. The headmistress of a large girls' school (eight hundred) finds size an advantage in matters of staffing and equipment. But another, representative of many, considers her school of nearly four hundred 'the ideal size'; two headmasters with schools of between six and seven hundred describe them as being near the limit of toleration in size; one headmaster regards a colleague with a school of eight hundred as having an unenviable task; and the headmaster of a school of this size thinks, after several years of effort, that the cultivation of the individual cannot be satisfactorily achieved with such numbers. It seems clear that, judged by the criterion – an important one in the eyes of grammar-school heads – of ability to know and educate the pupils as individuals within a coherent community, a school of about four hundred is excellent, up to about six hundred and fifty is manageable, and over that number calls for a disproportionate strain on the part of head and staff if what is felt to be its proper character is to be preserved.

In the schools under consideration, the pupils represented a rate of selection that varied from forty to twelve per cent. Understandably, some of the schools with a less selective entry were troubled by problems such as premature leaving, manifest unsuitability of curriculum, etc., that were unknown to schools at the other end of the scale. It is fairly obvious that forty per cent is too large, yet too much attention can, it seems, be paid to mere percentage. The headmaster of an extremely selective school found, on his arrival, that both staff and pupils had to be convinced by demonstration of the possibility of high academic achievement; and, on the other hand, a school with a fairly wide selection (about twenty-four per cent) and a population whose intelligence quotients on entry usually ranged from about 96 to 125, seemed to be comfortably achieving very good academic results, and this without elaborate equipment, special coaching or 'streaming'.

At the time of the 1944 Act many people vaguely envisaged, as one of the workings of 'secondary education for all', a fairly ready interchange in both directions between different types of secondary school of pupils found to be unsuitably placed. This expectation was over-simplified and over-optimistic, though no doubt it was also in the event unnecessarily frustrated by conservatism and prejudice. However that may be, the testimony of these heads on the whole confirms that transfer from grammar to modern school 'just hasn't worked'. Some headmistresses have attempted to make two-way transfer effective; one of those questioned speaks, for example, of a girl who, transferred to a secondary modern school, clearly benefited, and became a prefect and eventually head girl in her new school. Some of those who tried to follow this policy, however, found themselves considerably hampered by education officers. These officers probably suspected, not without reason, that, if transfer were made too easy, certain schools would use it as a convenient means of getting rid of problem pupils. The headmasters in this inquiry were generally agreed that 'transfer from the grammar school never was a reality', though they occasionally, and their staffs frequently, lamented the near-impossibility of 'getting rid of an unwanted boy'. But there was much testimony, from both boys' and girls' schools, to the successful transfer of pupils from the modern to the grammar school. Interest in selection policy was considerable, though much more tinged with anxiety in some districts than in others. That the most careful of selection techniques may not work with automatic smoothness was illustrated by a chief education officer's story of a girl whom not only the 'eleven-plus', but 'twelve-plus' and 'thirteen-plus' selection machinery had failed to spot, and who came via secondary modern school and technical college, eventually possessing three 'A' level passes, to be interviewed for a county award.

Assuming what one headmaster called 'the given-ness of the grammar-school entry', most heads and staffs showed themselves to be thinking actively about matters of internal school organization, particularly classification, pace and 'streaming'. Headmistresses seemed somewhat more reluctant than headmasters to classify and label. One said 'We divide them into "A" and "B" forms, but I'm not sure that we're wise to do so.' Another places the children in 'streams' at entry, on the results of the selection examination, but has deliberately discontinued the policy of a more efficient reclassification at the end of the first year. With headmasters there was much more evidence of drive, ambition, and anxiety. A good deal of talk was heard of efficient classification, the creation of 'express' forms, and frequent adjuration to 'work hard and get on'. 'I tell them [in the sixth] that forty per cent just isn't enough, and put constant pressure on them to send the marks up.' 'You can't overwork a boy – it may be different with girls.' Yet among the men too there were signs of a contrary attitude. One headmaster of long experience, believing that a slower pace is the answer to many learning-problems, has instituted a halting-place in the third year which is so successful, and so little associated with any feeling of humiliation, that boys will sometimes ask to be halted, and subsequently do very well. In one of the most ambitious and efficient schools, possessing an 'express' course, the headmaster is experimenting with a reclassification based more on subject-preferences than on achievement, 'in an attempt to abolish "C" and "D" form mentality.'

Policy varies very much with regard to entry into the sixth form. One headmaster is so sure of the benefit of a stay in the sixth, however brief, that he will admit a boy even for one term. Others, undoubtedly more representative, will admit none unless they are seriously aiming at three 'A' level passes. It is well known that many headmistresses but very few headmasters have attempted to create a general sixth offering a genuine alternative course side by side with those aimed directly at university entrance; in this survey only headmistresses – and not all of those questioned – were found to be running such a course. The attitude towards the general sixth, where one existed, in other schools, is typified by such remarks as, 'a form chiefly for taking the November G.C.E.', 'a form for "returned empties".'

Most schools have a house system, and this assumes great importance in large schools, where it is used, sometimes according to an elaborate plan, as the chief means of ensuring surveillance of the individual pupil and of maintaining contact with parents. Often this second function is shared, according to rather complicated rules, with the form master or mistress, who also holds an office of considerable importance in the organization of most schools. In this connexion it may be noted that one headmaster much regrets the decline of the tradition of general-subjects teaching in the grammar school, believing that many 'C' forms would benefit very markedly from being more continuously with one teacher in their junior years.

Work, curriculum and examinations

There is much speculation on both the nature and the intensity of studies, which is focussed in two questions: the influence of public examination policy on the school's programme and the pupils' attitudes, and the reconcilement of general education with specialist study. The General Certificate of Education is felt to be the source of many problems. The headmistress of a fairly unselective school says that, although the intention behind the examination was excellent, it has never been suitable for a school of that type. A master in a boys' school feels that it penalizes the honest boy who formerly would have achieved a certificate with two credits and seven passes. There is a general feeling that the G.C.E. offers less inducement than did the old School Certificate to hard all-round effort. A headmistress says: 'Has the G.C.E. made it too easy to drop subjects? One could argue in favour of being made to stick at something' – words closely echoed by a headmaster:

The new examination is not like the old. I am in favour of the new, but the old did make them work in at least six subjects; now they can not only drop a subject but anticipate dropping it. But in any case they don't work as hard as they did before the war – there are too many other attractions.

This feeling that children work less hard is met in many staff rooms. Sometimes the new attitude is accepted with tolerance or even a qualified approval. More often it is regretted, and in some schools the inculcation of 'a spirit of hard work' is repeatedly said to be one of the distinguishing features of a grammar-school education.

Views of general education include consideration of 'mixed' sixth-form courses (regarded by some heads with interest and by others – particularly a few headmasters – with violent disapproval), and of the introduction of a general paper at 'A' level, condemned sometimes for its content and sometimes for its very existence. An experienced headmistress comments that if we go on at this rate we shall soon reach the absurdity of appointing 'specialists in general studies'. But another says:

My southern colleagues talk of 'vistas of unexamined knowledge' – but north-country children like to see something tangible for their pains.

Other attitudes vary from strong advocacy of early specialization to as strong an insistence that all pupils shall carry up to ten subjects as far as 'O' level. Supporters of the latter policy speak contemptuously of 'patching-up courses', or wonder why, with a sufficiently broad curriculum, pupils cannot be assumed to have received a satisfactory general education before reaching the sixth form. Those who advocate the former speak of 'enormous amounts of compensatory studies', or argue that specialisms should be taught in so liberal a manner that they constitute in themselves a general education. They also usually point out that a large number of 'O' level passes by no means necessarily indicates a general education – may, indeed, indicate the opposite. An interesting counterbalance to the argument that the School Certificate 'made them work' is given in the comment of a science mistress:

> The School Certificate placed a premium on factual knowledge, much of which could be learnt without comprehension. It is considerably harder now in science to reach an 'O' level pass than it was to achieve the old 'Credit', because the newer examination questions demand thought rather than repetition; and this is as it should be.

Any general notice of work and activities in these schools, depending as it does on brief visits and conversations, must necessarily be impressionistic and incomplete – nevertheless it should be given. One recalls the beautiful art work in one girls' and two co-educational schools, the very embodiment of individuality and zest; the half-dozen boys in one school who, not content with their already strenuous examination programme, decided to try 'O' level geology and religious knowledge 'off their own bat' – and were successful; the girls in another who, in their fifth year, spontaneously devoted much time to the rehearsal and production (sensitive and accomplished) of some sections of *Hamlet* and followed this achievement in their Lower VI year by a very good, and again entirely spontaneous, production of Anouilh's *Antigone*; the boy who, inspired by his geographical studies, spent a whole summer holiday making a competent survey by canoe of the local river and its estuary; the pupils in a boys' school who, under an able master, were learning exquisite style through acting Molière. Impressions such as these are but the surface evidences of a vitality that pervades the best grammar schools and is reflected in many of the questionnaires. They must be set against other equally evident characteristics – the frequent anxiety and pressure, the tendency to be bounded by examination requirements, and the feeling of teachers that adolescents nowadays are not only less ready in general for hard work but are also in some respects alien and unpredictable in their tastes. An English mistress with twelve years' experience illustrates this last characteristic in her comment:

Certain literature is now very difficult to teach. Milton is a foreign language. They can, with an effort, be induced to overcome their suspicion of Wordsworth and Keats, but not of Shelley. I am disconcerted by the lack of adolescent rapture.

We have seen the teachers' views of grammar-school work: now let us turn to the sixth-formers. Many of them commented, usually adversely, on the extent to which their school work had been dominated by public examinations. In one boys' school they spoke of the jerky rhythm of a school life punctuated by examinations, and the uniformity of syllabus and pace. There was the boy who, rather surprisingly, said that after studying *Northanger Abbey* for 'O' level he would have liked to pause and make a further study of Jane Austen. Another would similarly have liked to linger over analytical chemistry. In spite of this, most of them insisted that there must not be too much specialization and somewhat deplored the amount there was. They were sceptical of the ability of teachers to plan syllabuses without the guidance of examination requirements. 'Theoretically, it should be possible,' they said laconically.

In a second school, the sixth-formers were evidently affected by the pressure to 'get results' early, and asked many questions about the policy of taking 'O' level examinations in the fourth year, the stiffness of university entrance requirements and the unfortunate competitiveness which in consequence entered education at this stage. In a third, members of a sophisticated 'scholarship sixth' looked back with more objectivity on their school career. They felt that we should search for a satisfactory basic curriculum and, although they seemed to regard the examination system as a datum, said repeatedly that the syllabus up to 'O' level had 'very little relevance' (presumably to their personal education). There was considerable agreement that the 'O' level was useless to people like themselves. They had been conscious of a dramatic change in their outlook after entering the sixth form, but said that it was more vivid for the arts than the science people. There was a general feeling that not until they reached the sixth form had they become properly conscious of philosophic or religious problems or related their learning to themselves. They felt a growing appreciation of sixth form general periods. They spoke of the intense concentration necessary to advanced mathematical studies – a concentration which, they thought, might exclude other important speculations. An extremely intelligent young mathematician, unprompted, said that he was acutely conscious of his lack of training in human judgements. It was significant, in his opinion, that the arts people had up to that point made the most articulate contributions to discussion. A student of classics was sure that his work had forced him, even before the sixth form, to think of human values, religion and politics. Several science students spoke of the tendency of scientists to be naïve in their judgements of matters, particularly politics, outside the field of science.

In a girls' school, three prefects thought that school work was too heavily examination-bound. 'We are all our time passing exams.,' they said. 'It means that we are unable to do interesting things as they arise for fear of not getting through the syllabus.' The sixth form of a co-educational school said much the same. 'When we first come to the school we are told that there will be an important examination in five years' time. We work for it, pass it – and now are working for the next!' They recognized that the 'A' level programme was inevitable, but said that they felt it to be a heavy burden. They would have liked, if time permitted, to learn in the sixth much more about the organization of society, and about social conditions. (These particular boys and girls belong for the most part to a politically conscious working-class community.)

Pupils

All heads questioned, except those whose schools were highly selective, were conscious of the change in the social make-up of their pupils that had resulted from the disappearance of fee-payers' children and the entry of a new class of pupil through the selection procedure. On the whole they were inclined slightly to underestimate the social status of their children and to talk too readily (especially the headmasters) of 'first-generation' children.[1] A headmaster and a headmistress had noted a tendency for the 1957 entry to be a little more 'middle-class' in origin. An assistant master in one school, and the headmaster of another, commented on the fact that first-generation pupils of an earlier day, now themselves parents, are apt to send their children to public schools, so that even without the 1944 Act the secondary grammar school would have shown some tendency, socially, to fill up from below.

Some highly selective schools do not feel that incompatibility of social assumptions is a problem for them. A headmaster of one such school told how, fresh from experience of a school in which this problem was acute and real, he spent considerable time trying to persuade the parent of a

[1] Though, as the analysis given in Chapter 8 shows, the 'first generation' problem is very real for many schools.

promising boy to let him stay for sixth-form studies – only to be met with the puzzled rejoinder: 'I'm a Balliol man. Why should you try so hard to make me do what I already want?' But in most schools both heads and staffs frequently feel that they are trying to communicate with pupils who can hardly speak their language. One hears of a lack of the kind of general knowledge that is associated with the presence of books in a home; of the necessity to 'teach everything – from table manners to morality'; of the children of unmarried mothers, 'many of whom don't look after them as they should or take an active enough interest in their progress'; of boys and girls who come to school fresh from family 'rows', and of others abandoned by their parents at critical stages in their life; of pupils who, living in a social group that at best thinks of education in straightforward and very material terms, have little perception of the larger aims of the school and find it difficult to accept, particularly in the sixth form, the aims of general education; of premature leaving in a district where well-paid employment in light industries abounds, and the elder brother or sister who had no grammar-school education is 'doing well'.

There is general agreement that the poverty and distress of the 'thirties are now almost unknown, but that many pupils come from homes which possess neither a good cultural tradition of their own nor a humble admiration for 'educated' standards. Teachers speak of pupils who will never make scholars, not entirely through lack of brains but also, perhaps more essentially, through lack of 'clues'. Some pupils, too – girls especially – are expected to carry domestic responsibilities that are almost irreconcilable with serious study. On the other hand, we must not automatically assume that the absence of academic tradition in itself renders a home an unsuitable background for grammar-school pupils. Many 'scholarship' boys and girls of the past (and, indeed, many fee-payers) came from unacademic homes, and did well. They have their present-day counterparts. One headmistress spoke of girls who quite early in their school career surpassed their homes in learning, and this without agitation or conflict. The most valuable contribution from home, she considered, was humility – a quality certainly not always most conspicuous in the well-educated.

Other factors, not so directly associated with the home, affect the pupils. Problems arise when boys from the outskirts of a fashionable resort – boys with expertly dressed hair, who are accustomed to smoking, and sophisticated about their girl friends – mingle with shy country lads, or when the 'chips-and-pictures' girl meets the sheltered only daughter of strict parents. Teachers spoke, of course, of the influence of television (and here it may be observed that two headmasters protested vehemently against the 'dreadful types' given publicity at the opening of the schools' television service) and of the many other attractions that compete for children's attention. There is the attraction of the street corner – even the headmistress of a rather privileged school said: 'Though I shouldn't like to feel that my girls hung about in — Street, I'm not blind to the probability that some of them do.' Youth clubs and other organizations lay apparently justifiable claims to a boy's or girl's time. Professional sport and part-time employment have invaded the innocence of school games and internal loyalties: an approving reference to girls who 'would *even* give up Saturday morning employment in order to attend school matches', and a headmaster's angry comment on a boy who 'would not wear the school blazer and would rather play for — United than for the school' illustrate the uneasy equilibrium of the adolescent's attachment to school.

The staff of one girls' school mentioned the great problem of choice we imposed on children. Too much, they considered, was offered, both in and out of school, and the task of selection involved considerable strain. This brings us back again to the home, for such a strain affects the family routine. One heard in another school of a boy, a prefect – charming, well-adjusted and successful – who, on being given some advice on how to allot his time for home studies, unexpectedly burst into tears and said that there was no possibility of settling down to work in his home any evening before 7 p.m. 'An illustration', said the headmaster, 'of how one can be unaware of the stresses that affect even a relatively uncomplicated boy.'

Opinions varied as to the extent to which a boy or girl might be expected to succeed in spite of a background unconducive to ready adjustment in school, though all agreed that the higher the intelligence the greater the chance. In the opinion of one headmaster, home conditions can raise or lower the 'effective' I.Q. by as much as ten points, and he declared without reservation that if the home were too bad (i.e. 'broken' or unhappy) a boy or girl was certain not to succeed. In other schools one heard of boys and girls who, at first intransigent or bewildered, in their third or fourth year opted for school, and in spite of – one headmistress even said because of – unfavourable home attitudes, exemplified with great success what school was felt to stand for. Many members of staffs felt strongly that pupils who might statistically represent a wastage had nevertheless often discernibly absorbed 'grammar-school values', and had not only become more cultivated people but would also be likely to send their own children to a grammar school and prove understanding and co-operative parents.

Some teachers thought that many children ruled their parents, and that many parents failed to communicate a tacit understanding that both the length of school life and also the demands, sometimes unpalatable, of curriculum and rules have to be accepted. There was much evidence that children were affected by both their geographical setting and the contemporary climate of opinion. The headmaster of a school twelve miles from the nearest cinema, in an area where there is a residuum of respect for 'the scholar', knew that, though many of his pupils were 'first-generation', most were apt for learning. Much harder was the task of the headmaster and headmistress in two industrial towns, both of whom reported a recent wave of feeling in the school against working with the mind.

Considerable concern was shown over the problem of the lowest 'stream' and attitudes varied greatly, from that of the headmaster of a 'two-stream' school who thought that one must speak roughly to 'B' forms ('nothing penetrates – they are armed against it'), to that of another in a similar school who remarked: 'We develop brains in "A" forms and character in "B" forms' – going on to say more seriously that 'A' and 'B' indicated rather the need for different kinds of approach than for a rigid grading in terms of ability; a State scholarship had, in fact, recently been awarded to a boy who had come up through the school in a 'B' form. His view had much in common with that of the education officer who suggested that the question of the 'student type' needed investigation. The brilliant were not necessarily students, and real students, he thought, were often found in 'B' forms. As this inquiry showed, however, a greater problem arose when the lowest 'stream' was not 'B', but 'D' or 'E'. A 'D' form might be in terms of ability no lower, perhaps even higher, than a 'B' form in a two-form-entry school that was less selective, but the feeling of three forms on top of it was apt to be discouraging – a fact that has to be very carefully reckoned with in large comprehensive schools.

One of the strongest elements in the grammar-school tradition is the professional assumption of care and responsibility for the individual pupil. Its nature is not quite easy to identify, for it is compatible with a certain impatience of psychology, and a reluctance to admit any necessity for formal study of children, that still characterize the grammar-school world. An official of a professional organization said: 'The grammar school is unwilling to admit that the nature of children is a subject for study – yet it is often intuitively more successful than the secondary modern school.' A second master put it somewhat differently. Both the grammar and the modern school, he said, cared for their pupils, but in different ways: in the modern school there was a willingness to find out about such things as adolescent development; in the grammar school, a casual but deep sense of being answerable for the children.

Such a 'sense of being answerable' was seen at every turn in this investigation. Accounts of individual boys and girls were readily given – no mere anecdotes, but careful appraisals of capacities and adjustments, or records of early observation, patient guidance and quiet help over many years until successful achievement in personal or academic terms, sometimes gradual, sometimes sudden and spectacular, had been made. Practice varies, and some schools deliberately cultivate detachment; but the inquiry revealed in many schools a truly astonishing amount of contact with pupils as individuals, both in and out of school, and a quasi-parental concern for their welfare. Most schools quite clearly feel that their social and academic entity is a synthesis of individual relationships held in tension by the headmaster or headmistress, and regard with dismay the prospect of schools so large that such a structure is no longer possible. 'To talk of delegation of authority is to miss the point,' said one of those questioned; 'the head's function would change completely.'

Sixth-formers gave some pictures of themselves as pupils. Opinions were divided on whether experience in the sixth form changed a person, but the majority thought that it did so strikingly. They said that they talked much about religion and science, though in one school they admitted that they set bounds to their discussions of religion 'for fear of growing too heated' – a sign, perhaps, of the reluctance to become 'committed' that is said to characterize our age. They revealed the personal and accidental reasons which, for all their elders' careful planning, sometimes determine adolescents' choice of courses. ('I went into the science sixth', said a girl, 'solely because a girl I could never beat in the lower school went on the arts side.') They looked back on their school careers and recalled how an inspiring lesson, a moment of self-discovery, a timely change of pace and direction had influenced the pattern of their upper-school work. The story and experience of Christine are found, with variations, fairly often:

> I was transferred from an 'A' to a 'B' form [the second of four 'streams'] and came up through the school in a 'B' form. I was happier there – I did not feel inferior in comparison with others cleverer than myself. But I got my three 'A' levels. I am to be interviewed to-morrow for — Training College. The way to the

university is not quite shut, but I myself think I'm not a university type and would only do it with a struggle.

I was unsettled in the middle school and wanted to leave. But a change came in my outlook after the fourth form, though it was hard to see my friends independent while I was still a schoolgirl.

I feel that many children in modern schools waste their time, and all through their last year are longing to leave. (My cousin is in one, and I hear a lot about it). I should like to be a teacher but I dread meeting this attitude if I teach in a secondary modern school. I'm interested in the idea of comprehensive schools, but don't approve of them if they have to be of huge size. I think too that 'B' form standards might suffer.

The importance of the right companions was felt by several boys and girls who told of a decisive change in their attitude and performance when, deliberately or accidentally, they joined another 'set'. This was illustrated also by a headmaster who, talking of the slow emergence over many years of a difficult boy, said that a turning-point came when, in his fourth year, he was chosen for a major part in the school's Shakespearian production. This meant, among other things, rehearsals with a small group of influential sixth-formers. 'So he began to move in another circle.' This question of 'circle' is, as we shall see later, central to the very function of the grammar school.

Parents

The significance of parents in the educational partnership has already been touched on. As we have seen, the range of their social status is wide; so is that of their attitudes to education. A great distance separates the Oxford man mentioned earlier from the parents reported by a headmaster and headmistress as saying that since their children had grammar-school places they 'thought they'd let them come'. An equal distance, again, separates the parents – familiar to one headmaster – who, though pleasant and up to a point co-operative, regard education solely as the means to well-paid work, from those mentioned by a headmistress who, themselves not highly educated, respect learning and desire it for their daughters. There are also considerable differences in the amount and kind of contact it is possible for a school to maintain with parents: in a sparsely populated district or small town the parents are almost necessarily known as fellow-members of an identifiable society, whether or not there is a parent-teacher association. In a large city school, more artificial and deliberate methods of establishing contact are necessary.

Most schools have a parent-teacher association, but some, particularly girls' schools, prefer to keep in touch by means of periodic meetings and individual communication, fearing that a formal association might come to be run by a clique or would effectually exclude those elusive parents they particularly want to meet. Where associations exist, opinions differ as to their functions. 'I don't want to lay emphasis on making money,' says a headmistress. In the next school, the headmaster boasts of the funds his association has raised to buy additional equipment for the school.

It was found in the investigation that schools which could afford to take a somewhat lofty attitude to parents were those with a high proportion of 'grammar-school parents' – parents, that is, who could be assumed to be in fairly general tacit agreement with the school, and whose own tradition predisposed them to leave the school to get on with its work. (They were, nevertheless, often anxious parents, reported by one headmaster as overdriving their children and apt to ring up, quite unnecessarily, about the 'tragedy' of being in a 'D' form.) In most schools, however, parents were regarded as of great significance in the educational process, and the need – and difficulty – of establishing some identity of assumptions received much attention.

'My P.T.A. are charming – but they know nothing.' 'It's necessary to educate the parents far more than the boys – 80 per cent of my parents haven't a clue.' 'A girl thinks she wants to leave and earn money; it never occurs to her father to say, "No, my dear, your job's in school".' 'They have no idea of the scope of the grammar school, but are attached to the name.'

Commenting on the phrase used by the president of the I.A.H.M. at the British Association meeting in 1957 – 'Jimmy Porters taught by Lucky Jims' – a master in a boys' school said: '... but it is giving in to accept this; it is the parents who should be educated. There is, indeed, a need for more adult education, perhaps on the lines of part-time day release for apprentices.'

One headmaster reported a common difficulty with co-operative but bewildered parents:

There are many parents of sixth-formers – excellent university types – who come to me very worried because their boys have not made up their minds what they want to be. I often have to persuade them that it is normal and even desirable to go to the university without having decided on one's career.

Again, parents outside the tradition may show little regard for learning and yet be disconcerted and hurt when they come up against the effects of an austere discipline. A headmistress, faced with the difficulty of inadequate staffing in mathematics, decided that girls who had made little progress in the subject should in the fourth year be kept 'ticking over' on two periods a week until easier times came. The mother of one such girl protested vigorously against her being deprived of the chance to take it in the G.C.E. examination, though the girl had never made an effort in this subject nor had she been encouraged to do so.

Finally, many heads are troubled about the stubborn minority of parents who resist all attempts to bring them into contact with school. A thoughtful estimate is given by a headmistress:

> Parents have, absolutely, probably not changed much. I remember the people who were parents of children at a London elementary school before the war. But a new class of parent is getting its children into the grammar school – a class that does not refuse a grammar-school place, but has no idea what the school is driving at, and removes the child at the age of fifteen.

All these parents, the ignorant, the bewildered, the blindly indulgent, the resentful, the narrowly acquisitive, the apathetic – as well as the arrogant and the over-urgent – are an important and unavoidable part of the complicated task facing the grammar school today.

Staff

The present staffs of grammar schools tend to differ from those of twenty or more years ago chiefly in three distinct though interconnected ways: in availability, in distribution of age, and in social and academic assumptions.

Everyone knows of the shortage of mathematics and science teachers: in domestic science and physical education, also, teachers are too few. Though here and there a school in an attractive locality, or able for other reasons to keep its members of staff longer than is usual, was able to report full and satisfactory staffing, shortages in the subjects mentioned were found to be fairly general. What is not so widely realized is that in some places it is difficult to recruit teachers in any subject – and this, of course, makes it almost impossible for a head to achieve a satisfactory balance of staff. A headmaster said that it was rare nowadays to get any choice of applicants for vacancies in most subjects, and therefore impossible to discriminate for personal qualities. It is clear from many sources that heads fairly frequently find themselves compelled to make an undistinguished appointment to replace an influential senior member of staff who is retiring. A headmistress of long experience speaks of an unprecedented

number of staff changes in recent years, and the resultant sense of instability is clearly reflected in the comments from the questionnaires
returned by girls in her school. Moreover, as a headmaster observed, the
system of special-responsibility allowances provides a strong motive for
younger members of staff to move on in search of promotion after two
or three years.

The age-balance of the staff has been upset. A representative of a professional organization pointed out the absence of the middle generation of
women teachers – the stabilizing element in a girls' school. A headmistress
said that there was an excellent spirit in her staff common-room – better,
indeed, than that of many years ago – but many members of staff were
young, and it took all the resources of the second mistress and herself to
keep them stabilized. (The word is deliberately repeated, since it was used
by the speakers.) A master in his forties said:

> The men of my day signed on the dotted line not because they wanted to teach,
> but because they wanted to go to the university. Some got out through war
> service. It's all right if you like teaching – I myself do. But many stayed, and are
> miserable.

This is echoed in a remark heard in another school:

> . . . men whose hearts are not in their work, and who have gone bitter on the job.

There are different opinions about the social and educational background of the staffs of today. Some present-day grammar-school masters
and mistresses are evidently less socially secure than their predecessors,
being themselves the products of a 'first generation' schooling. They not
only make no attempt to inculcate standards of speech and manners that
were once the readily assumed concomitants of a grammar-school education – they sometimes do not practise them. (Though the fairly frequent
reference to 'manners' in the children's questionnaires suggests that an
appreciable amount of this tradition survives.) Their learning, too, in
spite of good achievement at the university, may be less firmly founded. A
headmistress spoke of the need for really scholarly staff, keen on their
subject. The scholarship of some was too shallow. She spoke of young mistresses who asserted that they did not miss their university studies – they
were quite happy in their school work. 'It is delightful in a way,' she commented, 'but they are incapable of sufficiently stretching the abler girls.'

Another headmistress felt this shallowness and ascribed it to fatigue.
'Compare an ordinary staff timetable', she said, 'with that of a teacher in
France. The public school also has the advantage here, as in so many

things. Think of the small classes, the greater leisure time – in particular the sabbatical terms. It is so very difficult for the staff of an ordinary school to keep up scholarly interests.' Headmasters, too, commented on the fatigue of their staffs, some accounting for it as the reaction after a loyal response to an appeal to raise examination standards appreciably within a short time.

Other aspects of the decline of tradition are seen in an occasional unreadiness to give extra and voluntary service. One thinks of the mistresses who, after 'standing in' for an absent member of staff, asked to be excused a hitherto regular out-of-school activity. A senior master commented regretfully on a change in attitude which he connected with special-responsibility allowances:

Before the war one was paid a higher salary in a grammar school but, once in it, one expected to do many things out of loyalty to the community, without receiving or expecting extra payment. The honour of being, say, a housemaster was quite sufficient reward. Now, however, it is the practice to link a housemastership with something payable – a 'post of special responsibility' – so that a housemastership is virtually a paid office. This leads to a feeling on the part of the assistant housemaster of 'Why shouldn't I be paid?' and even (though not in this school) of 'Why should I do that? It's a housemaster's job – he's paid for it!'

Despite such undeniable changes in outlook, the tradition of amateur service still remains, and is frequently felt to distinguish the grammar-school attitude. There was great indignation on one school staff because what it considered voluntary work (for example, out-of-school instruction in boxing) was paid by one local authority in its modern schools, and on another at the proposal of a local authority to pay teachers 13s. 6d. an hour for supervising homework.

Honest and generous service – evidence of this abounded, far outweighing occasional signs of a 'nine-to-four' attitude. In every school, too, one could hear of members of staff who made a distinguished contribution through personality or academic leadership: 'he created a wonderful atmosphere in the staff room'; 'she has scholarship, humility, and remarkably quick contact with her classes'; 'I have a brilliant staff.' One met the mistress to whom geography was, both for herself and for her pupils, an interpretation of life; the French master who inspired his advanced classes with zest and confidence; the physics master whose classes studied with delight a great variety of topics, including astronomy, until drawn into a narrower and deeper channel by the imminence of the G.C.E. examination. But there was also a strong suggestion that many teachers were more ready to follow, mechanically if conscientiously, well-established ways than to find a path for themselves, inspired by enthusiasm and conviction. The staff of one school said:

> We grumble about public examinations, but we should not like to be without them – we should be lost if they were not there.

More than one headmaster and headmistress spoke of the failure of the staff to run genuine non-examination courses at any level.

Nor is this conservatism confined to lessons and examinations. Several heads said that they had tried to revise the system or cut down the amount of homework, feeling the assignments to be unsuitable to many pupils today, but had been unable to secure the co-operation of the staff. The same sort of conservatism prevailed over syllabuses:

> A master will teach 1066 to 1485 year after year. If a boy won't take his history that way, so much the worse for him.

Many teachers, it was felt, had in mind also a stereotype of the kind of a boy or girl who was a suitable pupil, and little deviation was tolerated. There is an associated kind of intolerance, found in the teacher who is interested in teaching only intelligent pupils – the teacher of Latin 'who could never teach "B" forms, and has little interest in the lower half of "A" forms'; the mathematics teacher 'who must be given the ablest forms because no explanations are ever made and no patience is shown with the weaker pupils – yet the abler, with this teacher, often lose their genuine mathematical enthusiasm and take other courses'.

Teachers such as the last are, happily, not very numerous, though numerous enough to cause disquiet. They tend to be found chiefly among those who take the 'scarce' subjects. Their comparative rarity needs to be emphasized, especially in connexion with the opinions of some educational planners. According to these theorists, there is one type of teacher interested only in the older and abler, and another type – an 'all-rounder' – particularly suitable for younger pupils and a wider range of ability. As this inquiry shows, teachers whose range is really narrow are usually thought by competent judges to be quite simply bad teachers, only less unsatisfactory in their approach to the able than to the weak. There remains, perhaps, some distinction of type, which heads and staffs strove to define when questioned. One headmistress thought that she could discern the 'scholar' on the one hand and the 'general practitioner' on the other – and mentioned one of her scholarly teachers who, by the end of term, was finding it difficult to carry through her work with younger children and 'Y' forms, yet was a most valuable member of staff. Even this headmistress, however, added that 'pure' types were rare. Most of those questioned, both heads and assistant members of staff, were well represented by the headmaster who said:

At heart most of us want to be scholars, and value our advanced work. There are two reasons for teaching over the whole age range. One is the need of early recognition and help for the really gifted children: the scholarly mode of study must not be left to be acquired later – they need help from the ablest teachers from the very beginning. The other is the relief of alternation. Teaching is exhausting, but it is a refreshment to turn to the juniors after the strain of sixth-form work, and equally refreshing to return to scholarly work after the livelier pattern of junior teaching.

All heads were emphatic that good teachers were nearly always good with both seniors and juniors and that wherever possible they were asked, as a matter of policy, to teach both. School staffs agreed. It should be added that, though they were very willing to speculate on ventures such as the 'Leicestershire experiment" they were unanimous that if a choice – which they would regret – were forced upon them, they would choose the 'grammar' (i.e. the senior), not the 'high' school.

And then who would train the promising young ones?

The purpose and character of the grammar school

As indicated in Chapter 1, it is difficult to say what 'the' grammar school is. The schools visited for this survey differed in antecedents as well as in size and locality, and such difference had its bearing on their individual purpose and character. This school, for example, was formed from an amalgamation of a higher grade with a higher elementary school: in the higher elementary days a governor, incensed by a monitor's failure to touch his cap to him, threatened to restore the plate that had once been set in the school wall, inscribed 'For the sons of the poor'. That school, on the other hand, has always been coveted and has felt itself to be very much 'upper-middle-class'.

The following range of comments comes from the headmasters of boys' schools and co-educational schools:

'Has the grammar school ever been narrowly academic? Surely it must always cater for a wide range of ability, and has always done so.' 'I would send my own son here, for here, more than in most other types of school, he learns to be a person. There are many ways in which a boy can "find himself", not only through academic attainment.' 'Many marginal boys need to feel the "pull" of scholarship and manners found in a grammar school. The ideal of the grammar school is not exam.-passing but finding a niche in the community (though the demands of universities, employers and society make it difficult to realize this ideal).' 'The grammar-school, whatever its variations, is essentially for those who can learn from books. Those who learn by doing are not really for the grammar school, though they are in fact here and we ought to do our best for them.' 'There is too great a tendency now to concentrate on making learning easy, and to aim at quick impressions. "Flash it on a screen" occurs to us too readily. True grammar-school education is still verbal and bookish, and visual and other aids should be supplements only.' 'We are trying, above all, to give general culture. I see grammar-school education very strongly as a matter of communicating middle-class values to a "new" population.' 'The grammar school's main task is to protect children against Vanity Fair. There is a need to create a fortified "society within society". A grammar-school boy must be prepared in some respects to postpone growing up.' 'The purpose of the grammar school is to prepare its pupils for the professions, and to help them to get a good job.' 'When we succeed best in grammar-school education according to our own standards, are we succeeding according to the demands of the mechanical world? In recent years we have all become servants of the machine. In future more and more jobs will be machine-serving, either literally or serving the machine of State. There is a frightening division between work and leisure which threatens to become absolute.' 'The aim of the school is to cultivate the individual.' 'Personal qualities can be communicated, and personal contacts in the school are valuable. But there are limits to the elasticity of the school for the communication of the grammar-school tradition.'

The headmistresses say:

'The aim of grammar-school education is service to the community. I am horrified when I hear that the girls are thinking of it as the means to a good job.' 'The aim of a grammar-school education is to make a rounded person, not to concentrate on exam.-passing and jobs. It is concerned with manners (the girls should, for example, avoid dropping litter) and the creation of style: the public-school virtues, in fact – though without snobbery.' 'I want my girls to be educated so as not to be part of the sheep-like mass, in such things as their choice of entertainments. The grammar school adopts the public school's attitude, that it is the whole person that matters. Though the grammar school like the public school cares very much for brains, in the last resort character counts more.' 'Grammar-school education is an essentially abstract form of learning – learning organised in subjects. It consists in the acquisition of a wide moral attitude, first in the abstract subjects, then in life itself. It is a training to use one's powers of thought in any capacity, however humble, and is a preparation of that part of society which should have opinions.'

The staff's view of the grammar school has already been seen (in Chapter 6). Perhaps some opinions of sixth-formers may usefully be added at this point. A boy in one school said coolly that the school's purpose was to turn out managers and leaders, whose work it was to make decisions and organize life on behalf of those not intelligent enough to take the initiative. Another proper purpose was to provide the highly-paid employees of rich industrialists who, themselves having little education, could afford to pay experts. In another school, the boys' questions showed them to be anxiously comparing themselves with a neighbouring public school, envying its confidence and ease. In a third, the 'scholarship sixth' mentioned earlier said flatly that the use of a grammar-school education was to help one to rise out of one's class. (Most of them were of working-class and lower-middle-class origin.) Pressed to say what they meant by this, they said that in general the taste of the working classes was deplorable, because their members for the most part fell easy prey to vulgarizing mass influences. They were very conscious that their own education tended to unclass them, and many saw themselves in the role of 'outsiders'. They felt that a grammar-school education was useful as a means to a career, but considered its more important function to be that of producing 'cultured people'. They defined an educated person as one who had found a number of different ends to which he could direct his personality; who was familiar with and interested in a great variety of subjects; who was politically conscious; who could stand on his own feet, meet with ease people of higher and lower intelligence than his own, and choose his pastimes well. They had no doubt whatever that the grammar school was the best agent to produce such a person.

In a girls' school, the head girl said that the important function of education, which she considered a grammar school fulfilled, was to produce able people who could do things. No, said a young prefect, it was to develop human qualities; people had to learn to understand others, and to concede some of their own will. In another school, the girls thought that the grammar school predisposed one to learning. They were very conscious of the influence of the right or wrong group on the ability to learn, particularly in the unsettled years of mid-adolescence. In their opinion, grammar-school education was without question that education which was suitable for those who loved learning for its own sake.

This evidence may fitly conclude with a brief summary of the chief ideas raised during two conversations. The first was with the sixth form of a co-educational grammar school:

F.M.S. What is the distinguishing characteristic of a grammar-school education?

Sixth form. The pursuit of study to a stage beyond the preliminaries of learning – and for this surely a long school life is essential. The great difference of the secondary modern school is that most pupils there leave at the age of fifteen.

F.M.S. In some American states all pupils stay at school to the age of seventeen or eighteen. If ours did the same, wouldn't the distinction vanish?

Sixth form. Education would be rather like a convoy, keeping to the speed of the slowest ship, which would be a bad thing.

F.M.S. Germans and Frenchmen would probably agree – Americans wouldn't. But suppose we put the quicker and the slower into separate forms?

Sixth form. That would be better. But the school would still not be distinguished by the love of learning for its own sake.

F.M.S. Is this, then, what distinguishes a grammar-school education – love of learning?

Sixth form. Yes. In a modern school children learn to *do* things – things such as cookery and woodwork. Grammar-school children are interested in ideas, even of practical subjects.

F.M.S. But one learns a great deal of science in a grammar school. Might not scientific study be motivated by the desire to 'do things'? Your own sixth-form programme, for example, includes an immense amount of practical work.

Sixth form. No. There *is* practical work, but in a grammar-school practice is in the interest of theory, not vice versa.

The second summary is of a conversation with a grammar-school headmistress (not one of those already quoted):

Headmistress. The function of a grammar school is to evolve values that can only be achieved by slow maturing – hence it is for those who are prepared for and can benefit from a long school life.

F.M.S. If length of school life is in itself important, why shouldn't this benefit be accessible to the secondary modern school, merely through raising the school-leaving age?

Headmistress. Yes – that's possible to a certain extent, and some secondary modern schools are already keeping their pupils to the age of sixteen or even seventeen. But this slow maturing is more important for the intelligent.

F.M.S. Then the grammar school owes more to Plato than to Christ?

Headmistress. The personal qualities developed, particularly in the sixth, are more important than the subjects studied.

F.M.S. You get them into the sixth, in fact, on the pretext of making a specialist study of subjects, and then work on their characters!

PART FIVE

Survey

14

Academic and Social Assumptions:
Commentary

'**Y**ou cannot educate *mind* in vacuo,' said A. N. Whitehead. It is also true that you cannot *educate* in vacuo. Teaching and learning are almost inconceivable apart from a network of assumptions. The teacher assumes, first, that he has something to teach; secondly, that he has some*one* to teach. But this apparently simple statement conceals much complexity.

To have something to teach certainly implies the mere possession of skill or knowledge; but it further implies one of four things, or a mixture of them: that the teacher is willing, under pressure, to share this skill or knowledge; or has a spontaneous passion to transmit it – to found a sect, perhaps, or ensure the survival of a particular craft; or deliberately makes selection of certain subjects to fit a determined notion (sometimes highly simplified) of the pupil-product desired; or takes his orders from an authority – the State, perhaps, or a wealthy patron – which may itself have corresponding motives.

In the next place, the teacher must make certain assumptions about his pupil, foremost among which is that the pupil exists. He feels that the verb 'to teach' needs an object: in fact, as Sir John Adams pointed out, it has two – the subject-matter and the pupil. Teaching, in short, implies some intentional communication, the pupil being assumed to exist as the personal object of communication. But it is also necessary to envisage him as a certain kind of pupil, and even the most aloof and impersonal of teachers is not exempt from this necessity. The Reader in Arabian Entomology may deliver an hour's lecture without betraying the least consciousness of an audience; but he has actually made very definite assumptions about his students. He assumes them to be within a certain fairly narrow range of intelligence; to have particular antecedent knowledge; to be able to understand English (or whatever language he uses); and to be ready to try to understand him without any efforts on his part to flatter or entertain them. If these assumptions are wrong – if, for instance, he can be imagined delivering his lecture by mistake in a school for educationally subnormal children – no teaching can be said to take place, and he has no pupils though the room may be full. The teacher, then, assumes the existence of a certain kind of pupil. He also assumes either that the pupil (or those controlling him) wishes to learn what he has to teach, or that he himself, through personal conviction or as the instrument of authority, has an unquestioned mandate to make him learn it.

The pupil has certain assumptions that are complementary to those of the teacher. He assumes that there is something to learn and someone who can teach it. He may have a longing to acquire technique or knowledge felt by him to be of great significance, and seek out the appropriate teacher, as Eliza Doolittle came to Professor Higgins. In that case, having satisfied himself of the teacher's competence, he will assume his instructions to be valid and faithfully follow them in the chosen field. He may have a latent desire to learn, capable of being kindled by the teacher who sees in him a potential disciple; the authority of the teacher who kindles is then *ipso facto* assumed. He may wish ardently to be a certain kind of person, and place himself in the hands of the teacher who will show him the way; his desire may be as noble as that of the young man who asked, 'What shall I do to inherit eternal life?' or rise no higher than 'how to win friends and influence people' – it may indeed be ruthlessly self-seeking or even dishonourable. Whatever his personal motive, he will tend to follow his teacher's programme even in its uncongenial details, since, under an accepted leader, he assumes that the curriculum will be wisely selected and shaped to serve the desired end. Fourthly, he may accept the . ruling, as to the content or the ends of his education, of those stronger than himself. This is the position in which most children find themselves, at any rate to begin with; and in it the pupil's educational assumptions must be an extension first of parental and family assumptions and later of those of his social group.

So far the imagined situation has been very simple. It becomes indescribably complicated when, as is usual, the teacher is not a single prophet, mentor or tutor, but a member of a school staff, having colleagues and a large number of pupils and working within a highly organized system, and the pupil is not a single person pursuing a specific piece of learning, chosen or prescribed, or being trained according to a clearly perceived model, but is one of a great many people all receiving some vaguely defined 'education'. The situation is rather more intelligible if this education is deliberately chosen by the pupil's parents. A boy, for instance, who goes to a public school and Sandhurst is likely to come of a family with a military tradition; to have father, uncles and cousins educated in the same way, so that he is strongly disposed to accept a curricular pattern which, if it seems at times irrational, is not much more so than other patterns which the elders of a family impose on their young; to have schoolfellows with similar assumptions; and to envisage himself as an army officer. Much less intelligible, to both themselves and their parents, is the position of most children receiving a State-provided education today.

When the teacher possesses knowledge or skill which, either independently or as the agent of a superior authority, he is anxious to transmit, his effort to communicate is potentially at its maximum, while the desire of the pupil to learn is potentially at its minimum. (If it ceases altogether he is no longer a pupil.) The effort may be crude, as in the stock picture of the sergeant-major yelling at the 'awkward squad', or subtle; but if he, or the authority he represents, thinks the content of the lesson sufficiently important, the teacher will do his utmost, by force if necessary, to transmit it. It is easy enough to see this principle at work in the Victorian elementary school, where those who eagerly wished for education – and they were, it must be remembered, a significant minority, forerunners of the 'scholarship pupils' of a later day – were outnumbered by those who found no significance whatever in the difficult and remote matter they were expected to learn. (Quiller-Couch saw them as 'piteous bands of urchins chanting *The Wreck of the Hesperus* in unison'.) But how does it come about that the history of the university tradition also admits to records of schoolboy sufferings? The answer is, of course, that when a situation becomes traditional, primary ardour is apt to turn into dreary formalism; that when the original scholar is replaced by the pedant, the knowledge we communicate is no longer irradiated by consciousness of fresh discovery; and, perhaps most important, that most children are at times very unwilling representatives of their parents' aspirations and many are ill-equipped to fulfil them.

The substance of the present argument, however, is that – whether the teacher uses the cane, threats, bribes, moral suasion or visual aids – where lesson-content is assumed to be the constant, the pupil becomes the variable, and any one of these methods is used, whatever its incidental effects, primarily to ensure acquisition of knowledge. When, therefore, Caldwell Cook said 'the method of study is as important as the matter studied' he was enunciating a revolutionary principle which – except in the limited sense, not intended by him, that efficient methods make for efficient learning – is certainly not one of the traditional assumptions of the grammar school. Aspiring, diligent pupil and Olympian teacher; compelling teacher and reluctant pupil; the occasional happy coincidence of ardent pupil and generous teacher; all these, in the grammar-school tradition, rest on the assumption of the existence of a corpus of desirable knowledge which the teacher commands and access to which is regarded as a privilege.

What constitutes desirable knowledge? The first assumption is that knowledge – any knowledge – the act or state of knowing in itself – is in some sense a good. Into the university and older grammar school has flowed this notion, derived partly from the Greek ideal of enlightenment, partly from the Hebraic injunction to 'get wisdom, get understanding', partly from the medieval notion of human rationality, partly from the Renaissance concept of the mind of man

> Still climbing after knowledge infinite
> And ever moving as the restless spheres.

Here, incidentally, is an answer to the tedious question whether the older grammar school tradition was 'liberal' or 'vocational'. In discussions on education one hears *ad nauseam* the remark, made usually with a triumphant air of discovery, that grammar-school education was originally vocational *just as* technical education is today, that it is therefore nonsensical to associate it with disinterested learning, etc. To which it may be answered that such education was certainly closely associated with the Church and the professions and must have been regarded as the concomitant of a career and often as the means to it: to this extent, therefore, it was 'vocational'. But, leaving aside as irrelevant the possibility that some studies, whatever their occasion, may have a wider humanistic significance than others, there must have been many who, like Chaucer's Clerk, would see themselves rather as obeying the Hebrew principle than as acquiring a professional training. This feeling that knowledge is in itself good can still be traced in grammar-school assumptions, and is responsible for some of the noblest pedagogical aspirations, as it is also for the dreariest cramming.

A second assumption – rather different, though connected – is that there may be certain kinds of knowledge that are self-evidently valuable. Such knowledge is somewhat difficult to apprehend and admits of no proof. Commending itself as it does through direct perception, not discursive reasoning, it belongs, whether its subject-matter be science or arts, to the world of the artist's experience:

> When you do dance, I wish you
> A wave o' the sea, that you might ever do
> Nothing but that.

Now the sense of greatness is an immediate intuition and not the conclusion of an argument.

With the young of both sexes, Poetry is like love, a passion,

The kingdom of heaven is like unto a merchant man seeking goodly pearls . . .

This knowledge cannot be formulated in any syllabus, for it is distinguished by kind rather than content. It can be taught only by the communication of 'immediate intuition', and such teaching is seldom enough accomplished, or even attempted, in any type of school. Incidentally, it is perhaps more likely nowadays to occur – if at all – in the sciences rather than in the arts. But intrinsically desirable knowledge, together with 'knowing' considered as in itself good, is the logical correlative of the kind of person who loves learning for its own sake; and though such love is not exactly proportionate to intelligence, there are many reasons for believing that lovers of learning are more likely to be found concentrated in the grammar school than in any other kind of school. For this reason (and also because the saint and the philosopher as well as the pedant are among the predecessors of the modern grammar-school teacher) the grammar school today is still likely, despite the utilitarian pressures to which all schools have more or less succumbed, to preserve among its assumptions the belief that some knowledge exists which is valuable and desirable for its own sake.

As distinct from knowledge supported by the belief that all knowing is good, or from self-justifying knowledge, desirable knowledge may also be defined as that associated with an occupation or profession. The medieval workman had his 'mystery'; the doctor, the farmer, the tailor, all have their body of facts and techniques. It can also be the distinguishing mark of a class; as knowledge of courtly manners may characterize the aristocrat, academic knowledge the 'clerk', agricultural knowledge the peasant. It may be desirable in the eyes of Church or State. Any of these notions may enter into the grammar-school assumption of the existence of a body of knowledge proper to itself.

Up to this point emphasis has been placed on the view of the teacher as having something to transmit, and of the pupil as acquiring knowledge regarded either as an end in itself or as the means to another end. We should now consider the situation in which the teacher regards his pupil not primarily as the medium through whom certain knowledge is perpetuated, or in whom it is represented, but as a distinctive kind of person, whom knowledge can produce. The two are not easily separated. There is talk currently in America of the selection and training of men – and perhaps women – destined to be 'astronauts'. We learn that they are in the top two per cent of the population for intelligence as measured by intelligence tests, that they must be very good scientists, and that they have to respond satisfactorily to a series of 'stress situations' so trying that many apparently good subjects have in these situations shown psychosomatic symptoms and been eliminated. Clearly, then, they are already remarkable people; but the teaching that will be given them, involving the acquisition of much very difficult knowledge and skill, will tend to develop still further those very human qualities for which they have been selected: gifted, healthy and stable as they are, they will undoubtedly become more informed and expert scientists, better able to use their intelligence, and better fitted to withstand stresses. Moreover, this training and the work to which it will eventually lead will quite certainly make them into unusual and distinguishable kinds of people. One can have no doubt, in fact, that, after this teaching, they will be very different personalities, in degree and perhaps also in kind, from those they were before it began. Yet, when all this is conceded, a difference in teaching-emphasis can be discerned. The teaching is not undertaken in order to make them into certain kinds of persons, and however desirable particular moral or temperamental qualities – courage, for example, or an equable temper – may be, they are valued solely because they fit the pupil better for accomplishing his assigned task successfully, not because they are the elements of an artistically satisfying personality-pattern.

At the other extreme, one may think of a teacher (and a parent could, in this connexion, be regarded as a teacher) wishing his pupil to be, for example, a clear sceptical thinker, accustomed to detached observation and unlikely to be swayed by suggestion. The teacher in this case will adopt certain educational procedures – he may, for example, refrain from introducing the pupil to fairy stories. If he wishes him also to be, say, honest or athletic, he will take appropriate measures. Doubtless a modern sociologist could be found to say that the teacher or parent is directed by socio-economic influences that make this kind of teaching as much a process of fitting the pupil for an end as is the former. But the teacher's conscious aim at least is different: he thinks he is choosing a curriculum that will develop the personality-pattern – that pattern which exists in its own right whether the pupil is to be an engineer, a shopkeeper or 'just a housewife'.

An equally detailed inquiry into the position of the pupil is not necessary here. Broadly, we can say that it corresponds with that of the teacher, in that the pupil is capable of desiring (with greater or less distinctness) to be a particular kind of person, as well as to acquire particular kinds of knowledge. But two modifications should be noted. One is that the teacher may have 'personal' aims which, expressed largely in terms of a selected curriculum, may look to the pupil more like simple instruction. The other is that, conversely, children may feel strongly personal motives, particularly the imitation of an admired figure in fiction or real life, to accept instruction that from the teacher's view is designed with emphasis on the transmission of knowledge. Emulation, and affectionate or fearful obedience to the exhortations of parents or teachers, show variants of the same kind of motive.

Before considering what significance this notion of the 'pupil-product' has in the tradition of grammar-school education, it would be well to make a brief examination of terms; the present fashion has so extended the definition of 'education' as to make the word almost meaningless. We can paraphrase Matthew Arnold and say that schools educate, parents educate, playmates educate, the environment educates, 'life' educates. Education may be conscious, unconscious, positive, negative, good or bad. The widening of meaning probably began with the Romantics, but it did not immediately affect common use. We are apt today to speak of the education of the streets, or of an apprenticeship, or of a primitive tribe, and it is legitimate to talk in these or other ways as long as we and our hearers know how we are using the word. But the ordinary man of the past did not use it so generally: to him there was an evident and fairly simple distinction between the educated and the uneducated. He knew well enough that the uneducated peasant might have rich and genuine experiences and be master of elaborate crafts of which he himself knew nothing; he might even say that he preferred the uneducated; but he did not confuse himself by saying that the peasant was 'educated, but in a different way'.

The elements of education are reading, writing and reckoning, and when for various reasons a simplified and truncated education, that stopped short at these elements, was introduced, it was correctly called elementary. But education proper was academic learning. It was possible to point to an industrialist, and say that he was successful but uneducated; to a factory worker and say that through his own efforts he had become a well-read and educated man; to the ne'er-do-weel son, and say that he had wasted a good education. It should be observed that older generations of artisan workers, however high their skill and however elaborate their 'education' in the society of the workshop and in the trade union, tend still to use the word in this way and to regard themselves as being comparatively 'uneducated' unless they have acquired book-learning for themselves. They would concur perfectly with the master who, answering the inquiry reported in this book, referred to grammar-school education as 'education – *sans phrase*'. The product of this education blended book-learning and recognizable personal qualities, conspicuous among which was the power and habit of reasoning.

It is undeniable that the grammar-school tradition incorporates the notion of an *educated person*, as distinguishable from that of a person possessing a certain body of knowledge – and that teachers have tried to produce, and pupils aspired to be, that person. To trace adequately the evolution of the idea of the 'pupil-product' is impossible here: but it has strangely mixed and sometimes incongruous elements. Moreover, since by the twentieth century education through private tutors, even of the aristocratic and the wealthy, was almost negligible, the public and day grammar schools were virtually alone in transmitting the concept of an educated man or woman, as well as including some traditions which in earlier centuries had been outside the scope of the grammar school proper.

In different generations and classes the 'pupil-product' has been idealized in different ways. The man of erudition, the versatile thinker, the 'citizen of the world', the accomplished gentleman – and also, let us not forget, the independent and well-informed woman – these and other patterns have at times been before the minds of teachers and pupils. Though the concept changed, it is probably also true to say that at any given moment the teacher and the pupil had a fairly clear idea of what the pupil was expected to know, and what he should be; even if the teacher were an innovator or the pupil a rebel, each knew of a norm from which he was deviating. The early maintained secondary schools had to create a new norm; but they were in the hands of administrators, and to some extent of teachers, brought up in the old tradition. For practical purposes this meant the tradition of the great nineteenth-century headmasters and headmistresses: a tradition of sound learning, based firmly on the classics, with some infusion of useful and 'modern' subjects, and all associated with honourable life and Christian principles. And this, *mutatis mutandis*,[1]

[1] One of the modifications was to lay less emphasis on classical and more on modern subjects.

was to become, as we saw in an earlier chapter, the norm of not only a new generation but a new class.

With the fourth set of assumptions suggested – that the teacher might teach solely as the agent of authority, or the pupil learn only under compulsion – we need not long concern ourselves. An extreme form of such teaching was seen in the work of teachers who were passively acquiescent under the Nazi régime; learning of this kind was exemplified in the 're-education' techniques used in Japanese prison camps. Such extremities fortunately do not enter into the traditional assumptions of grammar-school education. They are familiar in a modified form, though, inasmuch as few teachers are independent private enthusiasts, and all English children are educated, however willing they may be, under the compulsion of their parents and the State. But even in a restricted situation where neither the teacher nor the pupil is a free agent, a considerable amount of teaching and learning may go on without undue strain, provided that the aims of the teacher are few and simple, and that the pupil sees them fairly clearly himself and also feels that the intentions of one embodiment of authority (the teacher) coincide with those of the other (his parents), or else that the same ultimate authority actuates them both.

The process we have considered so far is that of moulding or constructing, and rests on the assumption of an external pattern. This is as true of the pupil-product as of the body of knowledge and skill, and it almost completely characterizes the tradition of academic education. Keate is alleged to have said to the boys of Eton: ' "Blessed are the pure in heart." Mind that; it's your duty to be pure in heart. If you're not pure in heart, I'll flog you.' Dr. Arnold had a more precise understanding, and used subtler methods. But neither doubted that both knowledge and personal qualities had to be inculcated – significant word! There is, in fact, no room for Rousseau.

The essentials, then, of a stable situation of teaching and learning are as follows. The teacher knows something confidently; wishes or can be persuaded to communicate it; and knows to whom he is to teach it. He may or may not be much concerned with a 'pupil-product' but, if he is, he knows what he is trying to produce. (This can be equally true of a 'child-centred' education, though here the verb 'produce' is not quite appropriate.) The pupil is ignorant; wishes or can be persuaded to learn; and recognizes the teacher's authority to teach. He may see his education either in terms of acquiring knowledge or skill, or as enabling him to become a certain kind of person; if he does not see these ends clearly, he either embraces or accepts the authority of those who do, and if there are two or more authorities he assumes their concurrence. These essentials appear in different forms in different types of education. But when, in any type, one of them is very weak or even entirely absent, a condition of instability exists which may be the prelude to a superior reorganization but which while it lasts involves some waste of energy, diversion or resistance, and if it is much prolonged will result in the disappearance of the type. Such transitional instability characterizes the contemporary grammar school, as the results of the investigation used to support the argument of this book show. Let us now take a general look at these results in the light of the foregoing analysis.

The teacher knows something confidently. The investigation shows that there persist large numbers of teachers whose work is academically sound. No figures of degrees and classes were compiled, but conversation frequently revealed a good university record, and in more than one school the head spoke of a high proportion of first class and higher degrees possessed by members of staff. But on closer scrutiny, the situation does not look so encouraging. Although, in this limited number, the good degrees appear to be as likely to occur in mathematics and science as in other subjects, the converse is not true: these subjects show, in fact, a marked tendency to be represented by teachers with poor qualifications, particularly in mathematics. Moreover, in these subjects it is sometimes impossible to make any new appointment, good or bad. It is also quite evident that the good degrees are not equally distributed among schools, but tend to be concentrated in a few. Here the larger school has an advantage, since a larger absolute number of scholarly teachers, even if no more in proportion, probably tends to keep the academic level fairly high. A greater proportion (as distinct from absolute number) of teachers with good degrees tends to be found in schools either possessing a long-established reputation or situated in a very attractive locality. A grammar school with none of these characteristics may be performing an important function for its district, but has usually a hard struggle to maintain the academic level of the staff.

The consequences for education of a teacher unsure of his or her basic equipment of knowledge are not hard to foresee, and were in fact manifest. Here and there it was possible to see a head's efforts to cover up the tracks of a poor teacher, and his uncertainty whether to give this teacher the ablest pupils – who might be able to make something of even unreliable instruction, but might nevertheless lose their chances of themselves becoming scholars – or the weakest, who would in this position undoubtedly sink into an abyss of confusion from which they would probably never extricate themselves. Bewilderment or anger, corresponding roughly to what one already knew independently, is reflected in the children's questionnaires against such teachers. It cannot be assumed, however, that all is well even when the teacher has a good degree. As we have already seen, more than one head commented on the shallowness of learning, the absence of scholarly enthusiasm, in some well-qualified members of staff. At the same time the conscious and unconscious testimonies from sixth-formers and the questionnaire replies make it clear how important is the experience of contact with true scholarship.

There is a rather different sense in which the teacher should be assumed to know what he has to teach – that is, as the body of knowledge or skills proper to his work. Since most teachers are in the profession as the agents of some superior authority, however much room that authority may leave for the exercise of spontaneous enthusiasm, they may properly want to know the nature of their assignment in terms of what they are to teach. The old classical-mathematical curriculum, justified now as vocational preparation, now as the liberal culture of a gentleman (also in a sense vocational), now as mental discipline, now as a mark of social prestige, was fairly well defined. When variations and extensions were introduced – when Arnold advocated modern history, or Thring made music a serious element of education – they were introduced positively as exciting or interesting innovations, under the leadership of a powerful and persuasive personality, and were referred firmly to the classical base. But where is the agreed contemporary curriculum? Subject after subject has been flung into the 'bursting portmanteau'. The subdivision of learning has increased, partly as the result, partly as the cause, of this process. Let the pupil stagger as far as possible with the load, and either there will be voices raised in disparagement of 'mere facts', or the knowledge gained will be said to be so trivial as not to be worth acquiring. Let him select, and the cry is against unbalance and early specialization. And not only is the mere aggregation of subjects a problem: new and different species of subjects – entities like current affairs, citizenship and social studies – have reared their heads and disturbed the teacher's calm assurance that he knew what belonged to a curriculum. Amid all these uncertainties, almost every subject is suspect. Mathematics perhaps requires too specialized an ability to be suitable for all pupils, Latin is likely to be of 'use' only to a few, English is too vague (and a soft option anyway), chemistry narrow and illiberal. Specialist teachers become disheartened or arrogant about their subject, and it is not unknown for them to compete in their ambition or defensiveness to grab the brightest pupils for their own specialism.

Behind the whole present curricular situation lies the ultimate question: By what authority do I decide what to teach? That authority is not the Church; it is not the monolithic State apparently sure of its required techniques and indoctrination; it is not the tacit agreement of a homogeneous sub-society on what belongs to 'our sort'; it is the British public, expressing itself on the one hand tortuously and remotely through Acts of Parliament, and on the other through the occasional pressure of individual parents about individual children. Because that public is, like some Miltonic monster, amorphous as well as many-headed, it is difficult to simplify its demands – and teachers have in any case some inherited arrogance towards it, especially as it is apt to turn truculent when in some strictly limited situation the school fails in its opinion to deliver the goods. But the truth is that the teacher is being asked not only to satisfy his patron but also to some extent to decide what the patron wants or needs; in other words, a challenge has been thrown to grammar-school teachers – to lead in the creation of a new social order by evolving out of their own inner consciousness a contemporary pattern of 'educated man'. The Norwood Report offered an opportunity to take up that challenge. But practically the whole body of grammar-school teachers recoiled from the responsibility and turned instead to find its source of curricular authority in the syllabuses and question-papers of public examining bodies. How almost completely confined to this closed circuit grammar-school education is, the inquiry as reported has made abundantly clear.

He knows to whom he is to teach it. Who are the proper clientèle of the grammar school? High or comparatively high intelligence they must have, and the inquiry elicited many protests against 'too many grammar school places'. But how high? It is a curious fact that whatever the rate of selection, the estimate of the proportion of pupils in the school capable of starting Latin was roughly constant. Again, there was a strong feeling that qualities such as 'persistence', 'industry', 'concentration' must reinforce intelligence, and would to some extent compensate for a somewhat lower endowment. A sound middle-class background was also considered a strong, and indeed almost indispensable, reinforcement of the school's task with its pupils. A nice irony of history, that in a century the Philistines have become the repositories of 'culture'.

There is, it is plain, some understandable confusion about the sort of pupil the grammar school should educate. Gone is the old, relatively uncomplicated dualism which accepted that education, in the straightforward sense outlined above, was for the very intelligent and striving and also for those who desired it, could pay for it, and were sufficiently intelligent to make something of a rather unyielding curriculum. Those who attempt to envisage a suitable pupil are still referred, not surprisingly, to the stereotypes of this situation. But what of the pupils who are in fact in the school? There is evidence of considerable appreciation, in rather external terms, of their origins, capacities and interests – and also of a great variety of attitudes towards them:

'A number should not be in the school.' ' "Y" form boys benefit from even a rather unsuitable curriculum because they learn valuable things such as the habit of hard work.' 'Stretch them as far as possible and keep them busy.' 'Give them time – pace is important'.

In general, as the preceding chapter indicated, the teachers' impression of existing pupils is that a considerable section corresponds, in intelligence, expectation and achievements, fairly closely with the population of former days. About those pupils who are not making a success of their education some impatience is expressed, and several teachers take the uncompromising view that it is not for them to study the child or to make any concessions in the matter or manner of their teaching. The inquiry reveals the existence of a number of teachers who in actions and sometimes in words proclaim their intention of 'writing off' certain children. For the most part, however, the teachers' attitude is found to be neither aloof nor unsympathetic to these pupils. Many have some understanding of their position, and many more have clearly gone to considerable trouble to investigate their circumstances, to show patience, and to give them help and advice. What is missing is a sense that any part of the curriculum should be constructed with such children as a premise. They are regarded as regrettable accidents, 'wrongly selected'. Of course there are crude concessions to their presence: slower sets, the dropping of subjects, an occasional attempt to provide 'vocational' incentives. Nor is an interest in 'method' entirely absent. But such concessions are almost invariably made with a view of the learning-order and the examination which remains substantially unaltered. Any notion of the need for careful investigation into methods, periods and sequences of learning that differ according to different temperaments and backgrounds, without necessarily indicating absolute superiority or inferiority, does not appear to enter into the assumptions of the grammar school.

As to what makes the desirable 'pupil-product', the old view largely persists. Character and learning are still closely if sometimes uneasily associated; the most academic of teachers in an English school would hardly say, as he might well say in a French, that his business was to teach his subject and train the mind, and that the pupil's whole personality was no concern of his. On the contrary, aspirations to achieve 'a rounded character', 'a whole person', abound in the teachers' testimony. What is under-emphasized, if anything, is a passion for pure learning. Yet the warmth with which teachers refer to sixth-form learning, the extremely good evidence of lively and often deep thinking and sound knowledge given by the sixth-formers interviewed, and the surprisingly frequent reference in the middle-school papers, from 'Y' as well as 'X' forms, to the joy of encountering new knowledge and disciplines, to some extent counterbalance this omission. What we might cautiously conjecture is that well-qualified grammar-school teachers, feeling themselves a little on the defensive, conscious of the many matters, from dinner-money to broken homes, that they must constantly keep in mind, wearing examination blinkers largely of their own making, and unable from the nature of their occupation to see clearly the inner effect of learning on their pupils, are denying themselves a zest and an idealism that they might often legitimately feel. This is part of the intellectual's disheartenment – a disheartenment that we should acknowledge as a serious problem of contemporary society.

The pupils give a picture of themselves and their education that is largely but not entirely complementary to the teachers' view. For the most part they wish or can be persuaded to learn. Many of them enjoy learning: when they do not enjoy it, they are usually willing to admit with a sigh that it is 'good for me'. They seem to be as ready as their teachers to recognize that temperamental and moral qualities are associated with information and skill in the process of education. Their estimates of the purpose of a grammar-school education show the variation we now expect: to be a 'scholistic man', to learn good manners and decorous behaviour, to pass examinations, to get a good job. It is interesting to see that they insist more frankly and simply than do the teachers on the essentially theoretic and disciplinary nature of grammar-school learning. It may be that in them the old notion of an 'educated person' runs the more purely because the less rationally. When they reject it, as some of them undoubtedly do, they seldom criticize it in itself: they say, '*I* am not suited to it, because I am not an abstract reasoner, or do not want to accept the burden of study, or refuse to acquire manners and an outlook that will separate me from my family and companions.'

But the pupils' answers also show certain facts that, if not ignored, are at best inadequately appreciated by teachers and administrators: the immense burden of homework, reference to which is too persistent (and too reasonably expressed) to be shrugged off as normal childish reluctance to forgo a little recreation; the high significance attached to all the social aspects, helpful and unhelpful, of school life; the appreciation of teachers who deal with them as individuals and 'see their point of view' and corresponding resentment against those who will not explain or listen; the overwhelming importance they attach to personal relationships, demonstrating that they indeed 'learn by contact'; and the sometimes serious strain caused by conflict between the assumptions of home and school. This last, though recognized by teachers at its most spectacular, is probably often overlooked in the forms it usually takes: ambivalent criticism of the grammar-school ('there's a grammar-school girl for you'); expectations pitched too high and too unreasonably; crude or subtle deprecations of grammar-school interests and knowledge revealed at home; continual adjurations to take part in family duties and activities (often no more highly organized than minding younger children, running errands or getting father's tea); jealousy of time and attention given to homework or school societies. Finally, there is abundant evidence of the seriousness with which these adolescents take themselves and the extent to which they ponder, though frequently with a detachment that is the reverse of morbid, on their personality, appearance, gifts and social adjustments. They are understandably aware, not without anxiety, of their sexual development, and their expression of this awareness suggests a range from frankly physical preoccupation to shy, fantasy-coloured, commonsense or – sadly – cynical estimates of their relations with the opposite sex.

It is time to summarize this varied evidence of the academic and social assumptions which add up to the process of grammar-school education. On the academic side, teachers are seen for the most part to assume that they must have a sound knowledge of their subject, but to be less sure that they need study the art of education. They search for curricular authority less in the theoretical assurances of this art, or in their own spontaneous conviction, than in the requirements of examination bodies. Hence they are apt to regard their immediate assignment as preparing children for examinations, rather than as stimulating them to disinterested learning or as acquainting them with knowledge and skills directly selected and framed to serve what they think are the pupils' personal needs. They realize, but only in a rather too objective way, something of the complexity of the circumstances that affect children's learning-processes; and according to temperament they tend to ignore, lament or palliate adverse forces. So teaching-approaches and techniques show a comparative uniformity which does not attempt to match the wide diversity of the children's attitudes. But teachers care for academic standards, even if these standards are rather narrowly measured. And since this regard offers the best hope in our present society of countering suggestion and preserving a sense of transcendent values, we should prize it, though its over-formal expression holds dangers and disappointments for some pupils.

Some parents, themselves grammar-school products, remember the tradition of hard work and are ready to assume that the school's demands for study are necessary – or even to complain that it has grown too lenient. They do not cause conflict through their inability to understand an academic curriculum, but are apt to overpress their children and overstress the harder disciplines of learning. Other parents have an anxious new pride. They will support the demands of school, but without much understanding, and may often unintentionally place a burden on children through their immoderate appraisals and expectations. Beginning with this pride, they may become as immoderately disappointed, again with unfortunate effect. Many parents of all classes assume that academic success is to be measured in terms of subsequent career, and will openly or tacitly discredit studies that are not demonstrably 'useful'. Some fear to see their children 'growing clever' and moving away from them, and this fear is accentuated when school studies and interests are made the battleground of the conflict between the generations which comes with adolescence. Some, unused to strenuous thought, and with folk-memories of 'brain fever' and 'over-study', are genuinely afraid for their children when intellectual disciplines show any severity. Some lack the slightest interest in things of the mind. Though they will not refuse a grammar-school place for fear of missing something good, they have no intention of giving up time, convenience or money in the interests of their children's study and, when they see that school is not likely to be the means of turning the children into a lucrative investment, will meet all its demands either with fierce jealousy and resentment or with apathy.

Children, naturally, reflect their parents' attitudes. Some, fairly secure in the old tradition, move easily through the school, being prepared in advance for the ups and downs of school life, and accepting them as no more than the normal lot of human kind. Others – 'so intelligent, and so new to it all', as a distinguished headmistress has described them – find undreamed-of intellectual satisfaction and realize the aspirations of those reformers who placed their faith in the widening of educational opportunity. Some who in a happy congruence of circumstances would have been quite well enough endowed to succeed, have not the intellectual strength to be won over wholly to the love of learning for its own sake and suffer from the lack of parental tradition. Some again are bewildered by the conflicting expectations of which they feel themselves the subject and are afraid of the scorn that may meet them as intellectuals unsupported by social security. These are the children who in educational, not religious, terms 'spring up quickly because there is no depth of soil and, because they have no root, they wither away'.

On the social side, comprising manners, behaviour, mutual attitudes and morals, teachers are seen to be less sure of their position than they used to be. There is a partial collapse of the old easy teacher-pupil relationship (though, as the questionnaire replies show, many pupils still feel it and value it highly) and the teachers' uneasiness is seen in their occasional oscillations between authoritarianism and matiness. Sometimes insecurity is reflected in their automatic attachment to such externals as uniform, regulations and punishments. (That any or all of these may have their uses is not disputed, but many teachers do not seem to understand their importance as *symbols*.) As to teachers' own social assumptions, many have not an unquestioned knowledge of what is 'done' and so cannot convey this explicitly or, better, implicitly, to their pupils. Uncertainty arises partly because some teachers, not born into the older tradition, are themselves the product of too hasty and shallow an education. Partly it derives from the general contemporary casualness and lack of definition, in both manners and morals. Teachers are also quite evidently uncertain, in face of the blurring line between the duties of family and school, of how far their writ runs. They no longer know what to assume as a clearly parental responsibility, and are ignorant of the extent of their duties towards sex education and social morality. Moreover, nearly all teachers fail to recognize that certain sanctions formerly assumed in grammar-school education have totally disappeared. Few, for example, fully accept the fact that the grammar school has nowadays as much obligation as has any other type of school to deal with a socially unsatisfactory pupil.

Parents of the older tradition, missing the strength of the humane relationship that would formerly be assumed, sometimes condemn the contemporary grammar school for severity; but they are as likely to condemn it for slackness if they miss the clear-cut certainty of the old measurable aims. 'New' parents may think the school harsh, particularly if they belong to a social group that generally lacks home discipline; they may also recognize certain strictures or prohibitions as tacit criticisms of themselves. On the other hand, those accustomed to enforcing

their will with a blow or an oath – the number of grammar-school
children with such parents is not negligible – may think the school
ridiculously 'soft'; so too may those who vaguely hope that school will
compensate for their own disciplinary deficiencies. Many are aggrieved
and some genuinely embarrassed by direct and indirect demands for
money, and, of course, communicate their discontent to their children.
They are, in any case, feeling the effects of a sharp decline in the tradition
of moderation and sacrifice, a decline currently attributed in exaggerated
degree to the 'Welfare State'.

Some conventional parents are alarmed – not without reason, as evidence
given in earlier chapters has shown – by the danger of undesirable social
influences coming from other pupils: not the children with unpolished
accents or shabby clothes, but the adolescents acquainted with the street
corner and the public house, the social group of the juke-box and the
sordid paper-back. Some other parents are hostile to the manners taught
by school; they fear snobbery and affectation, and assiduously teach their
children to believe that Jack's as good as his master. They may even be
hostile to its morality because their own does not recognize its standards.
The 'new' parents' contacts with the school may be aggressive: they will
defend their children against all comers, and will march into the school,
ring up the head, or write an abusive letter, whereas parents of another
tradition assume (and are usually firmly told by their children) that it is
not done to question the school's authority or indeed demand any
personal attention except in matters of life and death. Contrasted with the
aggressive parents, there are the socially timid: those who are afraid to
appear at school functions, fail to give even necessary personal information, and are sometimes obsequious towards the school. The grammar
school was acquainted with the parents of the old 'scholarship' pupils;
though the odd boy or girl had a drunken father or came from an unsympathetic home, the majority of the parents were recognized as 'decent
and striving'. Such parents, of course, continue to exist and present no
problem: but most of the new types described above do not enter into the
school's traditional assumptions and it has no formula for dealing with
them.

The children reflect the fluctuations of home, school, and the standards
of the outside world. They are often less sheltered and in many ways more
vulnerable than their predecessors, and stresses are set up, especially when
the 'old' tradition, with its good manners, its high morality and its
conceptions of social service, is strong enough to be felt but not strong
enough to sweep them along. When the conflict is one of manners or

apparently trivial opinion it is heavy enough. When fundamental moral assumptions are called in question it can be nearly intolerable. If some readers doubt whether social tensions really do reach this stage, it can be quite definitely stated that severe breakdown, precipitated by such tensions, sometimes occurs; and that many partial solutions to the conflict are not recognized as such only because they take such familiar forms as slight ill-health, middle-school apathy, 'naughtiness', inattention or a falling-off in work.

This, then, is the pattern of instability. It remains to be seen whether, where the grammar school is concerned, the pattern will lead to 'superior reorganization' or to 'disappearance of the type'.

15

Observations and Suggestions

THE grammar school is not dead. New schools continue to be built and many old schools flourish and are expanding. Yet it would be manifestly foolish to ignore the assault that has been made on the grammar school as an institution and the many changes that in consequence have been introduced into the organization of secondary education.

First, we must consider dissatisfaction with the 'eleven-plus'. The stock arguments against the selection examination which until very recently almost all local education authorities conducted need no elaboration. The examination, it is said, cannot select perfectly, and misfits are unhappy in both grammar and modern schools.[1] Despite the limited amount of coaching that suffices to give the maximum improvement in test performance[2] primary schools cannot be dissuaded from coaching heavily for intelligence tests, as also for the standardized tests in English and arithmetic that are generally associated with them. In this they are strongly supported and indeed coerced by a large proportion of parents, many of whom supplement the school's efforts by securing private coaching for their children. The resultant atmosphere of strain at school or at home or both is bad for children. Preparation for the tests also has a disastrous effect on junior-school education in limiting the curriculum, for the brighter children at any rate, virtually to arithmetic, English and 'intelligence', and this at the very stage in children's development when the curriculum ought to be at its most adventurous. The form of the tests

---

[1] 'We find that of every 1,000 children 122 may be expected to have been wrongly allocated, sixty-one to grammar schools and sixty-one to secondary modern schools . . . We are referring only to statistical probabilities . . . On educational, or other grounds, it could be argued that the 35,800 who remain in grammar schools, although, by our criteria, they may be regarded as having been wrongly allocated, may nevertheless derive benefit from their experience.' *Admission to Grammar Schools* by Alfred Yates and D. A. Pidgeon. Published for the National Foundation for Educational Research in England and Wales by Newnes Educational Publishing Co. Ltd., 1957.

[2] 'My own suggestion is that all schools should be authorized to apply a practice test and to coach on it for three to four hours, so that all children would come to the critical examination thoroughly familiar with the test they were to take . . . There seems to me convincing evidence that any teacher or parent who spent longer on coaching would be wasting time and possibly even reducing the pupil's efficiency.' Professor P. E. Vernon: letter in *The Times Educational Supplement*, 1st February, 1952.

leads to very undesirable teaching even within these narrow limits, encouraging in English, for example, one-word answers, or writing that expresses no individuality and possesses no imaginative overtones. Children enter the modern school already labelled as failures, and grammar-school pupils have been selected by a test that takes no account of qualities such as persistence – those qualities, that, perhaps as much as intelligence, make for ultimate success. Finally, wide discrepancies in the proportion of grammar-school places maintained by different authorities make nonsense of any assumption that there is a distinguishable minority of children who are fitted for a grammar-school education.

Given the best possible selection, however, many think it undesirable to concentrate pupils in different types of school. Since an examination conceived as distributive inevitably becomes competitive, intellectual snobbery is encouraged: the successful pupils enter the grammar school with an artificially high morale, while modern-school pupils have a corresponding sense of inferiority. Class distinctions and social dissatisfaction are exacerbated for two reasons: in the first place, as research has demonstrated,[1] children of members of the professional and managerial classes, and those of skilled workers, stand a much better chance of obtaining grammar-school places than do those of working-class parents, and children of unskilled workers in particular have the dice heavily loaded against them; in the second place, dissension arises when children from the same district, perhaps from adjacent homes, are allocated to different schools. A third argument, subsidiary to the second but politically weighty, is that the products of the grammar schools, having good cause to feel complacent, tend to be on the side of the Establishment; and, since they are likely because of their intelligence to be in a position to lead and influence public opinion out of all proportion to their numbers, they will constitute a perpetual brake on progressive thought and action. In addition, during the impressionable years of adolescence young people are being conditioned to an exclusive society, whereas they should be learning that important and difficult art of mingling with all sorts of people which democracy entails.

[1] See the Ministry of Education report *Early Leaving*, 1954: 'The comparison leaves little doubt that by the time the local education authorities hold their allocation examination at 11 the children of certain social groups have as a whole begun scholastically to outstrip those at the other end of the scale, and that the same process is continued among those selected from [? for] grammar schools during their time there. We do not assume that this is solely due to environment ... The deterioration which has caused many who were placed in the top selection group at 11 to be found by 16 in the lowest academic categories is most common among the children of unskilled workers (54·0 per cent) and semi-skilled workers (37·9 per cent).'

It is further argued that, whatever the theoretical provisions for transfer between schools, transfer works only to a negligible extent in practice. Therefore selection at eleven forces children into a mould for which many of them are later found to be obviously unsuited, either because gifts not apparent at the earlier age have subsequently emerged, or because pupils have not fulfilled the promise they showed at the time of selection. Critics also adduce evidence to show that the grammar school is not achieving conspicuous success even in what it is supposedly fitted to do: the number of passes at G.C.E. 'O' level is not as high as it ought to be, and the statistics of premature and early leavers show that it is failing to hold, for the full course, many pupils who would clearly be capable of benefiting from seven or eight years of secondary education.

Before considering the proposals and actions to which these criticisms have given rise we must pay brief attention to the selective technical school. So far my account has proceeded as though, for purposes of the 'selection' argument, this type of school can be ignored. Such an assumption is substantially correct, chiefly because selective secondary technical schools have been and seem likely to remain an extremely small proportion of the secondary schools of the country, though the number in existence includes some highly successful, indeed distinguished, representatives. But it is not smallness of numbers alone that makes the case of the technical school virtually irrelevant. There is also the fact that it is difficult, if not impossible, to find a 'pure' secondary technical school. Though technical studies may give significance and unity to the curriculum, and will of course occupy a larger share of the curriculum than in other types of school, those in control of the technical school are anxious – and are indeed obliged – to see that their pupils receive a balanced general education. Inevitably, therefore, the selective secondary technical school in many ways approximates to the grammar school. Conversely, many boys' grammar schools are becoming 'bilateral' grammar-technical schools, in fact if not in name. If they continue to receive a selected population and to provide an education designed for abler children, most of the reflections relevant to the grammar school can also be applied to them.

To return, then, to the unrest and its results. These, again, are fairly well known, and need only be enumerated without elaboration. There are powerful advocates of comprehensive secondary schools, and many local education authorities are wholly or partially committed to a policy of such schools. Many, perhaps most, authorities are experimenting with 'multilateral' or 'bilateral' schools – 'grammar-technical', 'modern-technical', 'grammar-modern', for example. Some, having accepted not merely with a good grace but wholeheartedly the principle of G.C.E. and other public-examination courses in secondary modern schools, have either abolished or reduced the importance of the selection examination: while retaining their grammar schools they have encouraged 'biases' in other secondary schools and have freely invited and supported parents' choice in allocating a child to a particular school. In consequence, many parents who formerly would have shown great anxiety do not even wish their children to go to a grammar school and find in other schools a purposeful and satisfactory education. Others again, in suitable districts, are closely associating with each other a grammar and a modern school, to which children are in the first instance allocated in accordance with their primary-school heads' recommendations and their parents' wishes. Transfer from one school to the other will be possible during the first three years. By the fourth year a clear choice has to be made, those who guarantee to stay at school for at least three more years entering or remaining in the grammar school, those who wish to leave at fifteen going to the modern school. Other authorities have had for some years 'selective secondary' schools – very much like the former central schools – providing public-examination courses, and from these transfer to a grammar school at the sixth-form stage is fairly frequent. Under yet another authority, all children in certain chosen areas spend their first three secondary-school years in a common high school. Those who undertake to spend at least another two years at school then go to the grammar school, the others stay till the age of fifteen or sixteen in the high school. For most children the transfer to the grammar school takes place at the age of fourteen, but for a small number of clever children, exceptionally admitted to the high school a year early, it takes place at thirteen. This experiment, creating a structure which closely resembles that of the American junior and senior high schools, has attracted a good deal of attention and is likely to be followed in the near future by similar experiments in other areas. In concluding this review of modifications advocated or practised we must not forget recommendations that the grammar school should be for the intellectual *élite*, that small minority – estimated at between five and eight per cent of the population – designated as 'high fliers' or 'fizzers'.

It may be readily allowed that no examination, whether by standardized tests or otherwise, can ever select perfectly. This is not only because selection must be immensely complicated and because the nearer we approach the borderline the more difficult it is to distinguish one pupil's total performance from another's, but also because the idea of pupil and school being perfectly fitted for each other is a bloodless construction, useful and necessary for purposes of argument and planning but nowhere even approximating to an actual situation: if it did it would at once deny the autonomous flexibility of human lives and institutions. For similar reasons, no two schools can or should be precisely alike. Indeed, schools rightly resemble one another much more in common assumptions than in actual functioning.

But, granted that selection must be imperfect, what do we conclude? A moment's examination will show that this assertion has little necessary bearing one way or the other on the 'tripartite-comprehensive' question, unless its authors also assert without reservation that there should be no differentiation into mutually exclusive groups for learning within the school (in other words, no 'streaming'). Given selection of some kind, what this protest does is to emphasize that the membership of any selective unit must have a range of tolerance that is sufficiently, yet not too, wide. But is it so imperfect in what it claims to do? As long as we assume that general intelligence or native wit, rather than attainment, is to be the determining factor of grammar-school selection (let us call it raw material rather than the first completed stage of a whole product), then most grammar-school teachers, as the inquiry amply confirmed, are agreed that the selection examination is efficient. They disapprove not of the reliability of the machinery, but of its underlying assumption. During this inquiry a headmaster, lamenting his inability to get rid of an unsuccessful thirteen-year-old boy, said that it would be useless to present him for a further test *because the same intelligence that carried him through the eleven-plus would carry him through the thirteen-plus*. His complaint was quite simple and representative – that the boy hadn't worked.

Objections that the examination is the occasion of unwise pressure from home and school and also of illiberal teaching in the primary school are in general justified. But to allow these objections is one thing – to suggest how they should lead us to modify the system of secondary education is another. Suppose we could prove (it is not suggested, of course, that we can) that in every other respect it was clearly best to maintain a so-called tripartite system: should we not then try by every means in our power, as some authorities seem to be doing, to minimize the ill effects of the examination? But if all these efforts failed, if it were found that open, formal examinations were the only satisfactory form of test, and primary schools proved to be quite incorrigible (neither of which results need be presumed), even then we should have to consider whether or not the secondary system were intrinsically desirable enough to be worth the preliminary disadvantages. When, and only when, we had concluded that nothing could possibly compensate for the harm done by earlier pressure (*and such a conclusion would automatically condemn most public, preparatory and direct-grant schools*) should we be justified in taking this set of objections as decisive.

To say that children frequently enter modern schools with a sense of failure is true, and reflects small credit on parents or schools, or indeed on public opinion as represented by certain newspapers and stimulated by certain television series. This fact, however, in itself is no more decisive than the preceding, especially when we remember that in almost every district a school[1] can be found that quickly dispels the sense of failure. Nor is the objection concerning the variable proportion of grammar-school places decisive, since to say that there are too many or too few of such places is by no means tantamount to saying that there should be none. It points, nevertheless, to an inexcusable state of affairs. While it would be impossible to represent by invariable percentage the true proportion of pupils suitable for grammar-school education, it is quite absurd to suppose that in any circumstances the present range is justified.[2] It is urgently necessary to ascertain on educational grounds alone, the permissible limits and to introduce legislation to enforce them. This inquiry gives many grounds for supposing that such a range should not be difficult to determine.

Objections not directed primarily against the selection examination are based, it will be remembered, on allegations of intellectual snobbery, of the intensification of class distinctions and social dissatisfaction, of the tendency of grammar-school products to maintain the *status quo*, of the failure to teach democratic living, of the demonstrated unfeasibility of transfer, of unpredictable later development, and of the failure of grammar schools, taken as a whole, either to achieve full academic success or to retain their ablest pupils for advanced study. These must now be met first at a fairly superficial level and then, since they conceal unexpressed but more fundamental problems, to include their deeper implications.

The high morale which, it is said, characterizes pupils when they enter the grammar school, is artificial to the extent that it is the product of anxiety and strain, which are perhaps not *necessarily* the accompaniments of any system of selection. But in part it is natural. The children are at an

[1] An admirable account of such a school is given in *I Work in a Secondary Modern School*, by R. M. T. Kneebone (Routledge and Kegan Paul, 1957).

[2] In the Report *Admission to Grammar Schools* (1957) Yates and Pidgeon say that the smallest percentage of admission to grammar schools given by local authorities in response to their inquiry was 10·4 and the largest 30. The high figure of about 40 reported on one occasion in the present inquiry represented the intake for one area, not the average for any whole local authority.

ebullient age. They are glad to feel that they are taking a clearly marked step towards maturity. If the school has a good tradition they look forward to its society, its games, its unknown new experiences. And if they also look forward to its intellectual struggles and feel that here they are on their mettle and can meet the challenge, is that a cause for regret? Has our country really such a plethora of good thinkers that we can dispense with the temperament that welcomes the prospect of becoming one? It could, however, be argued that, whatever the mood of children on entry, the grammar school is the very place in which to lose any undue feelings of intellectual self-assurance, in that many children, having carried all before them in a small primary school, quickly find themselves outpaced and lose their confidence. This is a fault, but a fault committed by the average grammar school at least as often as it promotes intellectual arrogance.

It is undoubtedly true that the mathematical probabilities of grammar-school entry are strongly class-biassed. This is another way of saying that at present, and perhaps in the foreseeable future, those who are suited to an academic education are likely to be drawn in higher proportion (*not* higher absolute numbers) from the classes mentioned earlier. It certainly does not mean that the grammar-school population is likely to be made up exclusively of these classes, for the working classes are so much more numerous that they are bound to constitute a fairly large proportion of this population. Many people indeed maintain that the average grammar school, since it represents such a wide variety of classes, admirably promotes social mixing. But in any case it is quite unjustifiable to speak as though the existence of grammar schools constituted some kind of conspiracy to preserve for pupils from certain sections of society the monopoly of academic education. It is outside the scope of this book to inquire into mathematical probabilities. What is important is that, whether we lament it or not, in any system of education so far devised these are the pupils who will drift in greater proportion – even though in smaller actual numbers – to the academic side, who will stay at school longer and who will go to universities. As for neighbourhood jealousies – these admittedly are regrettable, but are to some extent the product of tensions that the school system may uncover but can neither prevent nor cure: tensions that, if the system were revised, would find other expressions. If a child is deprived of chances of education and a career for which he is fitted, this is a legitimate source of grievance. We must recognize plainly, however, that no revision of the system will give a child abilities and aptitudes that nature has denied him. The fact may be galling: it is also inescapable.

There may be something in the suggestion that the grammar school produces a certain bourgeois complacency. Yet it would be very difficult indeed to establish that the grammar school was in its total effect destructive of progressive thought. Prominent representatives of all the main political parties, except Labour men of an older generation, have for the most part been educated either in public schools (as were, for example, Lord Attlee and Hugh Gaitskell) or in grammar schools. No one will dispute that men like Ernest Bevin, had they been born half a century later, would have been allocated to a grammar school. Nor are undergraduates at our modern universities, who are almost entirely drawn from grammar schools, noticeably reactionary in their political outlook. It should also be said that in their free comments, which they were encouraged to make, the boys and girls who answered the questionnaire gave much completely unprompted evidence that the knowledge their education had brought them had caused them to think critically on subjects such as war, nuclear weapons, international relations, the colour bar, social inequalities, housing, underdeveloped countries and other matters of profound human significance. Beside such expressions the occasional evidence of snobbery and narrowness, revealed in some of the papers quoted, seems pale indeed.

As for the argument that the grammar-school society does not constitute a 'democratic mixture': if by this term we mean the inclusion of every kind of endowment and attitude from the very dull to the most intelligent, from the brutal and disaffected to the scholarly and co-operative, then certainly any grammar school provides a somewhat restricted experience – though, the questionnaire returns have shown, not nearly as restricted as might be supposed. But in these respects no school is fully comprehensive. The gravely delinquent are, when possible, educated in special kinds of schools. So are those below a certain level of intelligence – and they too have their borderline. By the same criteria every school is to some degree comprehensive.

That no selection test is likely to predict perfectly may be granted: so may the fact that, from various inherent and environmental causes, children develop at different rates. Transfer, too, has admittedly proved to be difficult. It may be that the common school is better fitted to deal with this particular problem – though experience in many grammar schools suggests that transfer to a lower 'stream', even within fairly narrow limits, is often difficult, and that for various administrative and other reasons free movement within a common school (which to the outside observer seems one of its most attractive features) is neither so simple nor so frequent as might be expected.[1] But until it has been proved both that schools must be of such mutually exclusive types that transfer of pupils is the only answer, and that transfer must necessarily always work as badly as it has generally done so far – and neither has as yet been proved – there are no grounds here for attacking the grammar school as a separate institution.

To say that many grammar schools do not attain complete academic success, measured either by public-examination results or by their ability to retain all their able pupils for the maximum course, is true. Before drawing simple administrative conclusions, however, we should have to satisfy ourselves that this partial failure was due directly to the system – which would be very difficult to establish. Anyone knowing the situation from the inside is indeed likely to be surprised not that the schools have some failures, but that they succeed as often and as much as they do. Those who would arraign the grammar school seem to be unaware of the facts so often mentioned in this discussion – the burden of family responsibilities, unco-operative or uncomprehending parents, the attraction of early employment (still a force to be reckoned with, in spite of the 'bulge' in the adolescent population), the shortage of teachers – particularly in certain important subjects – the frequent immaturity and inexperience of school staffs, a commercially fomented teen-age culture, and the restlessness and uncertainty of youth, from which the intelligent are certainly not exempt, and which it is not always possible to foresee and provide for – facts which in their turn sometimes bring discouragement, with consequent loss of power, to even the most dedicated and capable teachers.

Yet, in spite of all these impediments, the situation is improving, not deteriorating. If comprehensive schools developed from former grammar schools[2] have recently shown an increased percentage of examination successes and increasing sixth forms, as is triumphantly claimed, so have the grammar schools. There was scarcely a school visited for this inquiry that could not point to marked and sometimes striking improvements, and all agreed that the peak of their difficulties – estimated as occurring somewhere between eight and twelve years before – had been passed. Finally it must be remembered that there is not the slightest evidence to

---

[1] 'Ease of transfer has been a catch-phrase of the comprehenders . . . The sceptic always doubted this. There seemed, for instance, a simple difficulty in moving a child who had done no Latin into a stream that had. The A.M.A. report (*Teaching in Comprehensive Schools* Cambridge University Press, 1960) brings this sort of difficulty out squarely.' Leading article in *The Times Educational Supplement*, 22nd January, 1960.

[2] This detail is in itself significant.

suggest that the present failures (judged by these criteria) would, *as people*, have emerged as successes under another régime. Some pupils outside the original selection may be drawn, as has been demonstrated, to this kind of success – but for the most part they move in to fill the vacuum created by the failures. There is no evidence whatever that they represent a probable net gain.

Wise after the event, we can now see that the refusal of the grammar schools to take the General Certificate of Education in the spirit of its foundation has contributed powerfully to dissatisfaction with modern schools; for if grammar-school teachers cannot do without the assurance of achievement that the 'O' level gives, teachers denied this assurance feel and indeed are thought to be inferior; and if employers cannot be dissuaded from regarding '*the* G.C.E.' as a leaving certificate (which, we must remember, it was expressly designed *not* to be) of course pupils in a school that was at first forbidden to take the examination feel frustrated and humiliated, and interested parties raise the cry of 'Privilege'. No wonder that a movement to make the examination available to modern-school pupils, and another to find an alternative to the tripartite system, have both had so much success. It would be poetic justice if the fuss that schools made about the 'iniquitous' age limit should prove to have been defensive tactics that in reality brought about the extinction of the species. Let us trust that the fate which presides over education will be neither so logical nor so cruel. While the present unhappy conservatism and timidity prevail, one cannot but concur with Professor Dent in his decision that modern schools must not be excluded from the examination.[1] But what a Barmecide feast it is likely to be! Already a cry has gone up that the examination is unfairly hard for modern-school pupils. Is it too late to hope that we may yet see a movement, led by the grammar schools, to give the original G.C.E. policy a proper trial – to recapture what Sir James Robertson, addressing the Education Section of the British Association in September, 1959, called 'a brief moment of sanity'?[2]

As we have seen, it is tolerably easy to find debating-points against most attacks upon the grammar school. That these points are not made – or, if

[1] 'Children in secondary modern schools who appear capable of securing G.C.E. passes have, I think, the right to require that they be prepared for the examination.' *Secondary Modern Schools: An Interim Report*, by H. C. Dent (Routledge and Kegan Paul, 1958).

[2] 'What are our schools for?' Presidential address to the education section of the British Association, 4th September, 1959. In the same address Sir James said:

'It profits nothing to tear a passion to tatters over the invasion of the secondary modern school by G.C.E. and other examinations: educationally it is folly, but by other criteria amply justified.'

made, are found unacceptable – is due to various causes, the chief being that the opposition is not primarily rational and therefore is not amenable to rational argument. The current debate has indeed ludicrous as well as ironical elements. To a dispassionate and uninformed stranger, precipitated suddenly into the present situation, it might seem that in many parts of the country the opportunity of strenuous learning was being given behind closed doors to a minority of the population (a minority, moreover, some of whose members were unfitted for it), while outside those doors clamoured a throng thirsty for erudition, longing for a culture denied them, and only anxious to be initiated into its discipline. Yet, if he looked at the British public – its reading-matter, its radio and television programmes, its ways of spending money and leisure, its usual aspirations – he might well be puzzled to reconcile what he saw with his former impression.

What complicates the matter is that within living memory there were indeed those who had a desperate thirst for education and little prospect of assuaging it; and the memory of this vain hope lives on in the minds of many people who feel that they are striking a blow against privilege. 'We cannot go back now,' said an honest and idealistic fighter the other day; 'the door has been burst open.' He forgot (or did not admit) that in most areas there is not much of a door to burst. As we saw earlier, the Ernest Bevins of the past would have been in grammar schools had they been boys today. Those who are on the wrong side of the fence still are nearly all, as far as human ingenuity can judge, within the middle, not the very highest, ranges of intellect; and for the occasional misplaced 'lover of learning'[1] it is surely possible to devise an easier means of access without remoulding the whole system. Since the secondary-school controversy is now most unfortunately a political controversy, what should have been a delicate, flexible argument has been simplified and hardened along opposing party lines, and no politician can propose or allow a modification without loss of face. But even within this situation it is ironical that while the party that has taken up the cause against the grammar schools contrives to suggest, if it does not explicitly say, that it is championing working-class aspirants against entrenched privilege, the 'have-nots' who are most wholehearted in their feeling of deprivation are not these, but the middle-class parents of undistinguished children.

The dissatisfaction of the post-war years is compounded of many ingredients: the startled outcry of the dispossessed, who before the war in some areas – not in all – could for a moderate fee have bought in the

---

[1] Not always to be exactly equated with the most intelligent.

secondary grammar school pretty manners and a small coinage of learning for their children; the chagrin of those who, having been promised secondary education, confusedly expected it to bring the status, the certificates, the jobs and the money hitherto seen as highly desirable perquisites of secondary schools and, when it did not, felt that they had once more been cheated and supposed the secondary grammar school to be obstinate in holding on to a good thing, now dimly thought somehow to reside in the curriculum and the public examination; the disillusion of the newly academicized, who found that 'the scholarship' was not an end, but the beginning of a toilsome and often exceedingly dull path; and the genuine frustration of the few true students for whom the new scheme made inadequate provision. To the extent that politicians are cynical – and that there is some cynicism and opportunism in politics few would deny – one party may be seen as cashing in on the muddled dreams of common people, and the other on the selfish desire of the 'little man' to hold on to what he has got and guard it from intrusion. That this opportunism is on both sides entangled with genuine convictions is only typical of the usual mixture of human motives. With considerably more opportunism and less idealism, professional publicists have been quick to fan the flames and to create and maintain an educational myth. And the camp-followers of education – the coaches, the writers and publishers of 'eleven-plus' cram-books and specimen papers, and the promoters of an encyclopedia (who cajole mothers with a picture of a little boy being welcomed by a benign and gowned headmaster at the gates of a grammar school)—have not been slow to profit by it.

The foundation of this whole analysis has been the belief that education cannot exist without certain assumptions. That is, no one can say 'I will teach' or 'I will learn' without an assumption of what he means by teaching or learning, of what he is to teach or learn, and usually of the kind of person who will fulfil the complementary role of pupil or teacher. Usually too there is implied some contract between the parties or their proxies, and education proceeds more smoothly and less wastefully if all those concerned have a large measure of common assumptions. Assumptions are seldom wholly conscious or wholly rational. When they appear to be, the rationality may cover deeper and usually less commendable foundations. Generally speaking, the less conscious an assumption is, the stronger its influence. Educational assumptions are not often made provisionally. They tend to be regarded as manifestly necessary, and questioning of them is likely to be met with anger and even panic. Thus it is often assumed, in boys' grammar schools particularly, that hard work – just like that, without qualification – is self-evidently justified. Yet if all concerned with grammar-school education – teachers, parents, officials, politicians, the public – are neither to be dangerously blind traditionalists nor to fall into instability and uncertainty surely they cannot do better than to see that as many of their assumptions as possible are both conscious and provisional, and to review them from time to time not under pressure of some crisis but of settled habit.

Because one of the origins of the grammar-school heritage is the propagation of pure scholarship, and because the true scholar's approach to learning is humble and assiduous, one persistent assumption of grammar-school teachers is that a proper kind of pupil shows industry and zeal. This may be justifiably expected of the born students and may also be appropriate to those who, not being born students, come of families who so unquestioningly assume the need for these qualities that the pupil cultivates them without reflection. But what of the fairly intelligent pupil who is not in the tradition? If grammar-school learning presents itself to him as pure intellectual striving dissociated from such things as career and status-value, what is there in it for him? 'Must give – for what? – for lead?' Such a child will not necessarily need to be given a 'vocational incentive'. But he (or she) will need to be studied with far more deliberation and patience, and to be met more explicitly as a human being, than the other child of comparable intelligence. As one mistress of long experience said during the investigation, 'There are some children who have to be almost loved into learning.'

Yet the matter does not end even here. For the scholarly teacher often has most refined professional scruples and is safeguarded from some of the snares that beset less single-minded colleagues – not least the faint dishonesty of making a personal intrusion into the integrity of the pupil, in the avowed interests of learning. The pure scholar may be merciless – though in justice it must be said that the very best grammar-school teachers (still, fortunately, fairly numerous) are able to combine brilliant scholarship with exquisitely perceptive and skilful modulation of their guidance of children, accomplishing daily an act of artistic integration that would be staggering if it were not so familiar. But even 'mere scholars', through their very assumption of the intrinsic importance of learning, may ultimately kindle some vision in the most recalcitrant of learners. It is no small gain at the present time if *l'homme moyen sensuel* has in his growing up at least caught a glimpse of a world of values concerned with the things of the mind.

Unfortunately, there are also teachers who, themselves having been safe but undistinguished students, feel no compulsion to fire others with the joy of discovery. Nor do they conceive it as being any part of their duty to make a disciplined study of the very complex human situation with which they have to deal. Themselves conditioned to examinations, they assume it to be their function to prepare pupils for examinations. This they do conscientiously, but because they themselves lack vision and because they also assume as their right a docility and co-operativeness on the children's part that belong properly either to a different social system or to a different concept of learning, there is frequently for them and their pupils an undue amount of boredom, disappointment and incomprehension.

As for that fairly large proportion of its pupils which corresponds with the former secondary-school population – a population whose members, whatever their differences, had the highly important common factor that their parents wanted them to receive this kind of education – the grammar school has few problems with it beyond those, concerned with the rapid changes and complications of the world, that make all education nowadays an increasingly difficult task. Nor, with few exceptions, is it finding undue difficulty with those 'new' pupils (i.e. those who would not have entered under the old régime) who are of first-rate intellect. Though, very occasionally, a highly intelligent person unacquainted with a scholarly tradition does not wish to learn, for the most part gifted children cannot resist the stimulus of fresh knowledge and experience. In this new environment they are likely to respond adequately in comparison with their fellows, though this is not to say that a careful study of their situation and possible difficulties might not lead to higher achievement and less waste.

The greatest problem concerns those children, encountered over and over again in the course of this investigation, who, while quite safely within the supposed grammar-school range of intelligence, 'haven't a clue'. They will not be stretched or hacked to fit the procrustean bed of the old secondary-school assumptions. They are rough and noisy, or insolent, or quietly uninterested, or, after a good start, they fall back in their work; or they may work well enough, because easily, till the end of the fifth year: then, persuaded with difficulty to stay in the sixth, they suddenly collapse at the prospect of real study. At the more advanced stage some have been known to show, almost without warning, signs of severe strain; or the bright little boy or girl becomes the dull pedestrian slogger. Many such children, of course, never reach the sixth form. They leave, sometimes prematurely, to become hairdressers, shop assistants, typists, garage mechanics; and their teachers, watching them go, sigh for the old fee-paying pupils (they remember only the co-operative) whose parents knew what education was about.

But there are other children, equally clueless at first, who, gradually or suddenly, see the significance of education, and declare for school with its strange mixture of interest, boredom, companionship, manners, vocational preparation and impractical standards. Though the change may come at any time, experienced teachers agree that it tends to be late – often quite as late as the fifth year – and many sixth-formers, looking back, also say that it was somewhere about their sixteenth year that they first learnt 'seriousness' (in a Keatsian, not a sanctimonious sense). These children, it must be said with emphasis, are one of the chief justifications of the grammar school as a separate institution. For they are not going to be among the great thinkers: far from having a divine discontent, they are at first satisfied enough with the world of football pools, refrigerators and easy reading. It is likely that if common schools became the rule (instead of the privileged and exciting exceptions most of them still are) most of these pupils would not have the slightest call to withstand the 'tyranny of the majority', as Mill called it. It is also doubtful whether the 'two-tier' system would capture them. For one thing, they would be in a common school for the important years in which impressions are silently working their effect; for another, the gentle cumulative pressure of up to five years would not be there and, faced with the necessity of decision at the critical age of fourteen, they would probably shrink from the challenge. But five years in a school that, despite its defects, still preserves strenuousness and a regard for abstract values, have at last their effect. The child is drawn into its orbit, and another common citizen is preserved for dissatisfaction with a candyfloss world.

A headmaster was quoted in a previous chapter as saying that he assumed the function of the grammar school to be 'to protect children against Vanity Fair'. Such a claim is easy enough to ridicule. Many, noting that the school has lost none of its efficiency in preparing pupils for well-paid posts, and seeing it as still a very well-defended stronghold of privilege, would regard the statement as unbearably smug, and hypocritical as well. Others would see in this protected area a breeding-ground for those intellectuals whom Sir Charles Snow calls 'natural Luddites'. Others again would assert that grammar schools, inheriting by chance[1] the tradition that was formed first to be a technical training for clergy, then to

---

[1] The chance, for example, that in the first decade of grant-aided secondary schools Robert Morant was Permanent Secretary of the Board of Education.

provide the accomplishments of gentility, then to maintain the framework of bureaucracy, have no call to give themselves airs. *They* were not born to the purple.

Yet the headmaster's assumption is valid, and to maintain it may well be one of the most important services that can be rendered society today. For the civilization of this century, on to whose stage the common man has, in Ortega y Gasset's phrase, 'erupted', needs these things above all: a sense of history, the imaginative leap that carries the sciences as well as the arts, appreciation of both the comedy and the tragedy of the human situation, and a capacity for disinterestedness. These are delicate growths that may not survive if left untended. The plant that is brought on with care at first has a better chance later, not a worse, to hold its own in the open garden. Those who are intelligent and perceptive are not perhaps more vulnerable than those who have little insight, but differently vulnerable. It is probable that these children's strong sense of the succour of the like-minded – far more important to them than similarity or difference of class – springs from a deeply felt intuitive need.

It may seem, then, that the obvious policy is to restrict schools to the 'five per cent', to whom the argument outlined in the foregoing paragraph is supremely applicable. But there is a selection of temperament as well as of intelligence, and it is also necessary to cast the net wide enough to include those critically important pupils already described, whose initiation is slow. Not all of these will become real thinkers, nor is it even desirable that they should, for teachers and pupils alike benefit from a certain mixture of temperaments and abilities. One of the headmistresses questioned, describing the career of an extremely brilliant pupil, said that she had no doubt that the girl had been both balanced and strengthened by being educated in an atmosphere 'not too heavily academic'. Nor are these other pupils to be regarded as appendages to the intellectuals. They are in the school, souls in their own right, and to do them justice grammar-school teachers must be willing to devote more conscious study to social and personal development, and to the curriculum as 'activity and experience', than many of them have hitherto been prepared to give.

16

Democratic Minority

WHAT is the equality to which education aspires? Genetically, each individual is unique: there is no equality of birth. If we put all our faith in nurture we encounter, outside the school, other formidable difficulties. May not a common school, then, minimize social inequalities? Not necessarily. Let us look at the population of a large town. In such a town the common secondary school will almost inevitably be a neighbourhood school, covering approximately the same area as would a 'zoned' grammar school and having, socially, a comparatively homogeneous population. That of a corresponding school in another part of the town will also be fairly homogeneous but of a markedly different character. In contrast, though some grammar schools also have neighbourhood characteristics, others show a much stronger tendency, because of their selectiveness, to draw their pupils from a wide area. (This provides one argument against the 'zoning' of grammar schools.) Even a neighbourhood grammar school, because it represents the social range of the district but approximately equalizes the proportions, may be regarded as an agent of social unity. It thrusts members of different classes into close proximity, and emphasizes that they are one in the interests of a transcendent object. But the more freely chosen grammar school shows an especially high degree of social mixing, as may be illustrated by the following list of occupations of fathers of fourth-year girls in one of the most selective schools included in the inquiry:

Carpenter and joiner, master painter, local-government officer, pharmacist, sorting clerk (G.P.O.), ironmonger, organ builder, civil engineer, wholesale manufacturer of clothing, headmaster, lorry driver, teacher, motor engineer, insurance agent, medical practitioner, minister of religion, warehouseman foreman, skilled labourer, school caretaker, police constable, insurance agent, bus driver, solicitor, commercial traveller, guard (British Railways).

Total equality is an illusion; we have to define our objectives. If the objective is to attain social equality by mixing classes we must recognize that in several areas a common-school policy will mean that in any given school there will be moderate homogeneity of social assumptions together with a very great range of intellectual ability, while over the district as a whole there will be a strong social stratification, geographical differences being accentuated by the educational system. (This is readily apparent if we observe primary schools.) Schools with a comparatively narrow range of intellectual ability, on the other hand, will tend to have a distinctly wider range and variety of social background. The range was great, though the distribution uneven, before 1944. Since then it has been even greater, with better distribution.

For historical reasons, English society is quite extraordinarily differentiated. Theoretically, this need not be a bad thing: it could make for richness and efficiency in the body politic. It is bad, however, if it breeds feelings of arrogance or frustration. One form of social equality is accessibility – members of two or more groups being able to meet with mutual respect, competent to speak one another's language while preserving their own. This is a matter with which education is deeply concerned. In spite of the immense development of techniques and the importance attached to end-products, we still have an intuition that education means more than know-how: that it also has a connexion with refined sensibilities, width of vision and depth of knowledge. Such education, rare in any section of society, has hitherto more frequently been the mark and the possession of the 'privileged' classes than of others. Quoting, in his *Notes towards the Definition of Culture*, C. E. M. Joad's description of the spirited and gifted group of Balliol undergraduates of fifty years ago, T. S. Eliot writes:

The conditions . . . were not brought about by equality of opportunity. They were not brought about, either, by mere privilege, but by a happy combination of privilege and opportunity, in the *blend* he so savours, of which no Education Act will ever find the secret.

Nor is this surprising. A single human existence is short and subject to many accidents. It saves time and strain if a person has not to start from scratch in the task of acquiring within one lifetime what has taken centuries to evolve. Nevertheless, we must hope that Mr. Eliot is mistaken. The course can be run from scratch – by the intelligent, the sensitive, the apt for learning: especially if they are fortified by a school that knows the language and is practised in the modes of this kind of education. The word 'language' is used advisedly. Let no one underestimate the difficulties of the task. It is not a coincidence that grammar-school staffs in their evidence lay so much emphasis on the poverty of vocabulary, as well as the narrowness of view, of many even of their abler pupils. For the task is one, both literally and metaphorically, of learning a language; and many intelligent and successful girls and boys have envied, at the university or in later life, the ease with which far less intelligent contemporaries, products of the highly civilized home and the public school, could recognize an allusion or call up the requisite complexity of reference – could, in fact, talk the language of the initiated.

It is true that some of the first generation from municipal secondary and 'county grammar' schools have been inclined to romanticize the world of the educated, and to be disillusioned when they observe that products of public schools, as of other schools, can be rogues, snobs or dolts. On closer acquaintance, too, they may find that the flattering charm of manner, which sometimes covers a more inherent insolence, soon palls; they can quickly grow weary of that accomplished ease of communication and unquestioning trust in one's own *mores*. They feel that they could tell their knowing and confident colleagues a thing or two about real life and are maddened by these colleagues' quiet assurance that they hold the prescriptive right to all that is worth knowing. The girl or boy from the grammar school may look back with new and deeper appreciation to the warm loyalties and forthright speech of home and neighbourhood.

Yet it also remains true, as the more perceptive children in this inquiry have in a different setting seen and stated, that a common interest in the world of the mind can resolve the tension of social differences; can set people free to observe them with detachment and even sometimes with pleasure. Grammar school boys and girls, taking a greater strain than those in either public or modern schools, are a true bridge between the two worlds. They have, as the survey has shown, brothers, sisters and friends not educated at grammar schools. Their own schools – for the most part without the benefit of residence, generous staffing-ratios, tutorial sets, the Industrial Fund, and the confident assumption of pupils' familiarity with books, music, pictures, politics, sophisticated travel – are contriving to bring them within an educational tradition recognizably similar to that of their more favoured contemporaries. Furthermore, if in their schools are some who 'haven't a clue', in those same schools are others who are already more securely within the tradition than they are themselves.

If such education is so valuable, why cannot all be initiated? First it must be said that, given the contemporary framework of social assumptions, this particular kind of education is only for the intelligent, though it need not and should not be, as some have thought, confined to the small minority of the outstandingly intelligent. True, the finest flowering of combined scholarship and grace can only be achieved by rarely gifted people, whatever their social *milieu*, in any age. But below them is a varying number of those who, through more deliberate and skilful teaching, can also acquire refined sensibilities, width of vision and depth of knowledge. Who are they and what are their limits? We are somewhat in the dark about this, but it may be roughly correct to say that the more alien the knowledge and discipline proposed, the more intelligence is required to master it. The danger-point is reached when what is to be learnt can be acquired but only as formula or technique.

This general statement is too simple. We must remember that emotional states can affect the amount of 'intelligence' that is usable or apparent, and also that pleasure has an intimate connexion with learning and remembering.[1] The greater the skill and sympathy of the staff, the farther down the scale of initial sensibility, intelligence and social assumptions will there be found children who can accept with insight the education of letters and strenuous thought. But we can hardly doubt that there is a limit.

Two further observations should be made. If the danger-point is marked by the acquisition of learning-material as mere formula and technique, that point, on the testimony of both staff and children, is being passed by some children in grammar schools. Furthermore, since a too exclusive concern with public examinations conduces to this kind of learning, the spread of examination courses not only in grammar but also in modern schools neither constitutes grounds for simple rejoicing nor is necessarily justified by the fact that many modern-school children pass the examinations.

Not all, then, are sufficiently intelligent for the learned tradition. This assertion is not, in England, seriously disputed. Certainly comprehensive schools do not dispute it, though many of them try to extend the tradition to a larger number. But the second answer to the question 'Why cannot all be initiated?' is the plain statement that by no means all wish it. Indeed, though many in all classes of society would like the material or social advantages of 'a good education', few are anxious to be fully awakened or to court the pains of thought. A grammar-school type of education

---

[1] 'The influence of the personal emotional element is so powerful that it can select and reject patterns of responses by its peculiar capacity to facilitate what is advantageous to the individual. Hence the alarming powers of this personal reaction factor which are exerted from birth onwards.' From *The Physiology of Learning*, by W. Ritchie Russell, C.B.E., M.D., M.A., D.SC., F.R.C.P. (The Morison Lecture for the year 1957 delivered in the Hall of the Royal College of Physicians in Edinburgh.)

is neither universally appropriate nor universally desired. But if it is only suitable for the minority, why not give it in a school designed for those to whom it is appropriate? To give it is not so easy that the teacher can afford to dispense with the powerful aid of an environment designed for its mediation.

In yet another important way, the continuance of the grammar school makes for social equality. There has never yet been any serious attempt to abolish all independent and partly independent schools, nor is there likely to be such an attempt in the foreseeable future. But as long as these schools survive as enclaves of privilege there can be no formal equality of institutional type. In this situation the grammar school can be seen as the only institution that holds a position intermediate between the rigidly exclusive and 'the rest'. As things are at present, many people who – whether because of a sincere value for things of the mind or because of social ambitions – desire the 'best' education for their children, make every effort to send them to a public boarding school or to a good independent or direct-grant day school. If, however, there exists within reach a highly respected grammar school, such people are coming in increasing numbers to accept it as providing the kind of education they want. To the cynic this means that, if their children are selected for grammar-school education but do not obtain a free place in the local direct-grant school, they will regard the maintained school as a highly satisfactory alternative, and will send their children to it in preference to paying fees in the other school. But it often means much more than this. Good fee-charging day schools do not exist in all districts, and many parents who do not wish to send their children away to school will gladly send them, if they have obtained a place, to the local county grammar school. Moreover – and this is the most significant development – in more than one district there is a fully maintained grammar school of such high and growing reputation that in each succeeding year more middle-class parents with a regard for education make it their first choice for a grammar-school place in preference to the local direct-grant school.

If selective maintained schools ceased to exist – a remote possibility, it must be hoped – there is at least a probability, regrettable though we may think it, that most of the children in the category just mentioned would cease to attend any maintained school. Even more parents than at present would make desperate efforts to send their children to public schools. And there would be even more competition for the fee-paying, as well as the free, places in direct-grant schools. Good independent schools would flourish and would probably see a rise in the average intelligence of their entrants;

new independent schools would be founded, somewhat as the nineteenth-century public schools were founded, in response to rapidly increasing demands; and inferior independent schools would receive a greater boost than they received after the 1944 Act. Direct-grant schools would be the only grammar schools within the State-aided system, and the comparatively few working-class children who gained free places in these schools would be making a social leap rather like that of the scholarship children in the old days of fee-charging secondary schools.

It may be said that if all this were to happen – and there can be no proof that it would – the maintained schools would be well rid of the children of such pitiful snobs. Let them, if they will, refuse the opportunities offered them, and make themselves miserable chasing an expensive education which may well turn out to be inferior to that which they could have had for nothing. The fact remains that if the selective maintained school disappeared, the traditional grammar-school ethos would not cease to exist – it would merely be once more associated, as in the past, with wealth or class. But at present the children of the lorry driver, the doctor, the clergyman, the solicitor, the policeman and the labourer share the same lessons and games and feel they are meeting for a common purpose. The modern grammar school is a great social unifier.

Some will object that these arguments take no account of existing comprehensive schools, most of which are characterized by high morale, good social feeling and considerable academic success. But the great achievement and value of many, perhaps most, existing comprehensive schools is not in dispute. As nearly always in English education, it is the single school that counts, and a dedicated staff can make a success of a school almost irrespective of its place within an official system. Existing comprehensive schools are also in a special position. They have been the object of much thought, planning and financial expenditure. Their heads and staffs are carefully chosen, and include some extremely gifted people whose very attraction to a comprehensive school suggests that they are actively interested in their professional art and willing to experiment. Moreover – an important detail – some of these schools are so placed at present as to be the object of deliberate parental choice; some, too, have been grown from the stock of a long-established grammar school with a reputation sturdy enough to survive many vicissitudes; all are on their mettle and eager to prove their worth. Can we believe that, if virtually every secondary school were 'just another school', this peculiarly beneficial tension would continue? The present argument is far from maintaining that there should be no comprehensive schools. It is directed against the abandonment of the grammar school, and the mechanical application of a principle of uniformity that might well destroy the best features of the comprehensive school itself.

Others may say that the 'two-tier' system of junior 'high' school and senior 'grammar' school would meet many of the difficulties inherent in both selective and comprehensive systems. There are pedagogical arguments for and against the two-tier system (the predominant 'for' argument being its noticeably good effect on the quality of primary-school teaching). But to the problem of social equality with which we are here concerned, this system does not offer an obvious solution. Already there are parents who send their children to private schools, avoiding the common high school, until they are old enough to join the grammar school. One can discern signs of a resettlement – along the old lines of social-intellectual division – that seems to be the reverse of progressive.

There are also dangers, it must be remembered, in a too unrestricted parents' choice. In order to allow for the capture of the uncommitted – those whose failure to work to their full powers can so easily be masked – there must be some conscious acceptance of the casual and the accidental: the deliberate admission, in sufficient numbers, of children whose parents 'thought they'd let them come'. But the two main types of school will have to reorientate themselves. Since no line of exclusion can ever be quite definitive (even the five per cent school has its 'borderline'), obviously education for some miles inside each territory, though it will be differently centred, should be almost indistinguishable in its approach and in the opportunities it offers from that on the other side of the boundary fence; and as long as examinations on the 'grammar' side are so unhappily important, they must not be denied to the 'modern' side.

Both grammar and modern schools, then, must accept their own degree of 'comprehensiveness'. There should be a well-marked difference between them in the average intelligence of their pupils, and those of the highest ability will be found in the grammar school as those of lowest ability in the modern school. But there may well be pupils in the modern school somewhat more intelligent than some in the grammar school. Nor should it be assumed that such pupils are necessarily misplaced. It has been repeatedly said that schools are, rightly, individual. To suggest the continuance of grammar and modern schools is to suggest not so much two distinct species as two large groups of individual schools, the groups having different centres of attraction.

It is evident now that the assumption of 1944 – that abilities and aptitudes, properly tested, were a sufficient guarantee of correct selection for secondary education – was too ingenuous. Ingenuous, too, were the assumptions of the Norwood Report, castigated by Sir Cyril Burt,[1] that children could be categorized according to three main human types that conveniently bore a rough correspondence with already existing forms of post-primary education. Equally ingenuous is the assumption of many grammar-school teachers that certain 'qualities of character' such as interest, concentration or industry need to be somehow added to abilities and aptitudes to make up the requisite educational mixture.

Yet, though the fashion is to disparage the Norwood Report, it is difficult to improve on its definition of a grammar-school education:

> The grammar school upholds an ideal of disciplined thought promoted by an introduction to the main fields of systematic knowledge, which is valued first for its own sake and later invoked to meet the needs of life . . . In the grammar school the pupil is offered, because he is capable of reaching towards it, a conception of knowledge different from that which can be and should be envisaged in other types of school.

To this may be added the comment of a headmaster, made in the course of this inquiry:

> The central purpose of the grammar school is to give training of a specifically moral kind, but the process is rather complicated: it is an education which uses intellect as the material with which moral training is accomplished.

and of a headmistress already quoted:

> Grammar-school education is an essentially abstract form of learning – learning organized in subjects. It consists in the acquisition of a wide moral attitude, first in the abstract subjects, then in life itself. It is a training to use one's powers of thought in any capacity, however humble, and is a preparation of that part of society which should have opinions.

Nor is this view weakened by pointing out that the grammar-school tradition was and is 'vocational', producing clerks in the Middle Ages, administrators in the nineteenth century, nuclear physicists and managers of industrial concerns in the twentieth. There is a wide difference between the kind of education which, although it may indeed be the avenue to certain positions and professions, regards the acquisition of learning and growth of certain personal qualities as good in themselves, independently of their acknowledged relation to these professions; and that which treats its task as the development, at however exalted or lowly a level, of an instrument – human, but therein interesting only as being more

[1] In *The British Journal of Educational Psychology*, Vol. XIII, 1943 (pp. 126/140).

complicated and more potentially efficient. The second conception should not have a place in any type of school.

The love of learning need not already be manifest in a grammar-school boy or girl. We may properly suppose that it is part of the school's function to awaken that love, though that all people have the capacity to pursue and enjoy systematized thought is almost certainly untrue. Differences of temperament and function as well as of intelligence must surely continue to characterize human society. 'The quiddity of Ens and Prima Materia will scarce please a soldier,' said Sidney. But it is those who are capable of reflection on the quiddity of Ens (or on mesons and the quantum theory) who provide the definition of grammar-school education. They, however, are at the centre of a magnetic field which is not infinitely extensive but can nevertheless exercise a considerable pull on others much nearer the periphery. And it is these marginal children who in one sense are the justification of the separate grammar school. For they are the children who, as has been shown, feel most strongly the pulls from other centres. In a vital school with a good sixth form many of them become, if not necessarily better, undoubtedly different from what they would have been in another kind of school. If grammar schools were to disappear, other, perhaps compensatory, characteristics would develop in these children. It is certain that something would be lost; for grammar-school education cannot and should not be the norm of an unselective school.

Though the norm of the grammar school is systematic study for those whose gifts and temperament predispose them towards it, this is an abstraction, an ideal more useful as providing a standard of reference and aspiration than as indicating any methods of practical teaching and learning. It does not, for example, justify aridly academic teaching, nor the rejection of pupils who cannot take such teaching. Moreover, though exactitude and rigour of scholarship are an integral element of this type of education, its fruits are not merely, or even primarily, aggregations of knowledge or intellectual skills, but certain personal qualities developed through the fervour, discipline and self-denial associated with strenuous study.

'Because he is capable of reaching towards it.' We must try to define the suitability of pupils for such education; and this is no easy task. We may however assume that very high intelligence is evidence of suitability. Great eagerness for the content of the curriculum, so far as this can be separated from mere social or careerist ambition, will give a child of considerably lower intelligence a good chance of success. There will be a limit of intelligence below which eagerness and co-operation are unlikely to achieve success, and an upper limit of unco-operativeness for which moderately high intelligence cannot compensate, though very high intelligence may do so. It must also be remembered that there are fairly intelligent pupils – initially dissociated or antagonistic – who, given time, sympathetic teachers and sufficient flexibility of approach, come to accept with enthusiasm what they formerly resisted.

Grammar-school teachers now stand at the intersection of polar axes. Through them flow the expectations of society, the needs of the labour market, the graces and glories of tradition, the preoccupations of home and the aspirations of scholarship; and they themselves are the fixed points to which all may be referred. They are haunted by many questions. What are the principles, in both learning and morals, on which I take my stand? What internal or external forces impede learning in my pupils? Is the swiftest learning necessarily the best? Is there any warrant, other than convention, for studying certain elements of my subject in their usual order? When advising on a programme of studies, what proportionate weight do I give to employment and career prospects for the pupil; national needs; the child's intellectual capacity; his emotional development? If communication is one of the chief functions of teaching, is my criterion to be 'between whom?' or 'of what?' – or is there a point at which the two questions become one?

These are important matters. It is also important to recognize that whether in practice the policy of the school seems to lean more towards a 'balanced curriculum' or 'liberal specialism', it is in the mind of the teacher that unity and generality of studies have first to be perceived. Teachers must therefore be more analytic and at the same time more spontaneous than ever before. How is this to be achieved at a time when many professions are open to the able graduate, and grammar-school teachers, like their pupils, are no longer such a closely selected group? Nor are teachers any longer supported either by the comforting consciousness that certain branches and forms of knowledge are by common consent right for them to teach, or by the body of middle-class assumptions that in the past ensured at least a modicum of docility and acquiescence on the part of parents and children. It is necessary to be fully, sensitively and constructively aware of the immense network of forces to which nearly all children are subjected and which manifest themselves in aberrations of learning and behaviour. Education is communication. We must come to regard as an exciting challenge to the utmost resources of our art the child who, though apparently intelligent, is not on our wavelength.

For it really is time to stop 'writing off' a minority of grammar-school children. Nor should we accept too readily the pronouncement that six per cent are wrongly placed within the school. Why should performance in public examinations, and teachers' judgements, be the only criteria of suitability for grammar-school education? Among the malcontents of the present inquiry are some who clearly are not working up to full strength. Pauline's French mistress rejected her at a critical moment. No one is setting herself to give Jean necessary confidence. George, torn by adolescent longings and with some poetry in his make-up, is seen only as a disloyal, defiant boy. William hates writing pages of notes. Professional life is busy, and perhaps no one is to blame for not discerning these children's problems. But, though some of them will fail, it will not be because they could not have succeeded. On the other side, the testimony of staff, sixth-formers and children has again and again made it clear how apparently fortuitous matters – a chance visit, a change on the staff, the release of some private worry – above all, the finding of the right companionship – has changed for the better the course of a child's school career. To capture some of these boys and girls involves neither sentimentality nor the abandonment of proper scholarly standards. But it may mean more place in the school for the tutor and counsellor; a subtler knowledge of sociological influences than is represented by the labels 'a good home' or 'a bad home'; and, in teaching, some abandonment of what Whitehead called ideas of 'necessary antecedence' and the revision of many conventional assumptions of pace and timing. The very children who want to escape from the challenges of thought and work may be those who beneath the surface are intelligent and perceptive enough to feel them as challenges, while their less able but better-adjusted companions 'jog along happily because they do not know it is difficult'.[1]

Teachers, too, are members of society. They have many personal adjustments to make, deliberately and clear-sightedly, before they can devote themselves to the art of teaching. They have to decide, for example, just how far the notion of disinterested learning continues to be appropriate in a world clamouring for particular skills. One of their most necessary and difficult duties, perhaps, is to keep their own eagerness and love of intellectual pleasures. The best test of both attitudes and standards may remain in Francis Bacon's words:

> But the greatest error of all the rest is the mistaking or misplacing of the last or farthest end of all knowledge: for men have entered into a desire of learning and knowledge, sometimes upon a natural curiosity and inquisitive appetite; sometimes

[1] See page 60.

to entertain their minds with variety and delight; sometimes for ornament and reputation; and sometimes to enable them to victory of wit and contradiction; and most times for lucre and profession; and seldom sincerely to give a true account of their gift of reason, to the benefit and use of man: as if there were sought in knowledge a couch whereupon to rest a searching and restless spirit; or a tarrasse, for a wandering and variable mind to walk up and down with a fair prospect; or a tower of state, for a proud mind to raise itself upon; or a fort or commanding ground, for strife and contention; or a shop, for profit, or sale; and not a rich storehouse, for the glory of the Creator and the relief of man's estate.

The distinction between 'grammar' and 'modern' education is not that between 'liberal' and 'vocational', nor 'pure' and 'applied', nor even difficult and easy – though all of these elements are apt to enter consequentially. The modern school is not by definition, as some of the grammar-school pupils think, a school 'where they play all day', 'for those who are good with their hands', 'where the lessons are easy'. It may be primarily, however, for those who need a shorter rhythm of learning not in the daily programme but in the general design, who must not be asked to suspend judgement too long, and who need clear and circumscribed assignments. It need hardly be added that some pupils working in this mode, especially those near the grammar-school borderline, may become good students. But they are different from the majority of grammar-school pupils: those who, though absorbed in the current activity, can take time, can postpone, can reflect, can await results – though some of them may need to be brought to this point by way of leisure, patience and successful weaning. These last, so easily confused or distracted, need the support of a community that may be socially comprehensive, but whose ultimate educational aims are not too widely dispersed.

It is a curious reflection that if society as a whole treasured both as a possession and as an ideal that which grammar-school education, at its best, stands for, the question of whether the maintained grammar school should be a separate institution would cease to have much importance. But this is not the present attitude of society. Paradoxically, only if grammar schools achieve near-perfection in their complicated and delicate task – that is, if they can show to an ever-widening society that thought is to be admired and loved – may they render themselves unnecessary. Such a possibility is far distant. For education becomes in the deepest sense comprehensive not through administration, but in the unity of a single civilized perception.

Appendix

d, and the consequent mingling within one age-group of young people
re physically men and women with those who are still children – a situation
amiliar to teachers of third- and fourth-year forms.

more misleading is the unqualified assertion of the earlier emotional develop-
of girls. It is true that girls develop, on the average, earlier than boys – but
n the average. There is plenty of evidence in my material that many boys
l as girls have, as early as the second year, a well-advanced interest in the
ite sex, an interest doubtless due to social as well as physiological causes.
s illustrated too by some of the teachers' opinions that I have quoted; cer-
the assertion that 'for boys, a personal interest in girls is usually still in the
when they leave school, though only just over the horizon' would find
upport in the schools I visited.

report indicates clearly the relevance of sexual ethics to secondary education.
s its finger on the present problem:

Education can only function within the broad directives of right and wrong
ich society gives.'

ps it was hardly within the Committee's assignment to make precise sugges-
about ways in which the schools should work for the application of their
admirable principle:

t seems to us quite possible to imagine a society in which teenagers had their
sent freedom to live their own lives; but in which they were not deprived
the security which comes from a well-understood knowledge of what is
at and what is wrong.'

ere as elsewhere, they do not sufficiently stress that in the grammar school
lay, almost as much as in other secondary schools, it is necessary to make
it many attitudes and standards that could formerly have been assumed.

section on *Women's Education for Marriage and Employment* (paragraphs 43 to
of great importance, and not least for grammar schools. The report recognizes
is 'increasingly possible for marriage to mark not the end, but simply a break
oman's career'. For the grammar school this means, though the report does
at it so plainly, that it should now be possible to give girls active inducement
ntinue their studies and gain qualifications without either provoking the
ion 'What's the use? I shall soon be married' or making them feel that they
riously increasing their chances of spinsterhood. It is also recognized that,
se of the earlier age of women's marriage, if girls' full-time education is to be
ued it must help them to 'learn to behave and to react as adults'. As the
truly says,

t is not calf love, but the love which leads to marriage that they feel.'

this promising beginning, however, the report gives little guidance to the
nar school:

APPENDIX I

THE CROWTHER REPORT

The Living Tradition was completed just as Volume I of the Crowther report appeared. Since much of my book concerns the experiences, thoughts and feelings of boys and girls aged 12 to 14, it may in one sense be regarded as a prologue to the study of the older adolescents. But the book is by no means confined to a survey of these younger pupils, and in another sense it should be seen as a critical examination of the type of school, as distinct from other places and institutions, in which the Crowther age-group is at present most likely to be found. From either point of view it is interesting to note ways in which the book and the report supplement, complement or differ from each other.

The Crowther report asserts, on the authority of the Committee's social survey of boys and girls aged 16 to 19, that neither parent of two-thirds of the present-day grammar-school population was educated at a grammar school. My inquiry gives an average figure of 39 per cent, and even if 'don't know' answers were all equivalent to 'no' – which is most unlikely – the percentage would hardly be raised above 50. I am confident of the reliability of the answers I received. However, since the 'X' form pupils – whom I found to be significantly more likely to have had parents who had been educated at grammar schools – outnumber the 'Y' formers by 1,052 to 924, my 'first-generation' figure may be on the low side for the population as a whole. I should also emphasize that I make no claim to have based my survey on a scientific sampling of the whole population. Indeed, half of my sample population was in the south-west of England,[1] where, as the Ministry's publication *Early Leaving* demonstrated, a higher percentage of the school population remains after the age of 15. This may point to a higher than average proportion of grammar-school parents, even though the south-western schools (some of which, incidentally, are nearly 100 miles apart) are well distributed along my 'first generation' scale.

On the other hand, compared with the social survey, my inquiry was made rather more recently, and among children still at school. There is an average difference of five years in the actual ages of the two sets of young people considered – and those five years happen to be of critical importance. If we assume 30 to have been the average age of parenthood, the father of a boy aged 17 in 1957 would have reached the legal school-leaving age in 1924. The father of a boy aged 13 in 1958 would have been 14 in 1929. But opportunities of grammar-school education were increasing with every year of this period. The argument is

[1] This was because my cross-section of schools under one city authority happened to be made in that part of the country.

strengthened if the age of parenthood, particularly of the younger group, is lower than 30; and there are in fact definite suggestions in my evidence that many of the pupils are the first-born of wartime and even post-war marriages, which may well have been of younger people. We may recall, too, the impression of more than one school head that the 1957 entry was of slightly higher social status.

If, then, we wish to look at the country as a whole, my estimated proportion of 'first-generation' pupils – between 39 and 50 per cent – should be somewhat raised. I would, however, suggest with caution that the figure of social the survey may still be high. For if all the former grammar-school pupils questioned were aged between 16 and 19, and all had left school some two years previously, few could have been sixth-formers, and almost certainly none was an undergraduate. * Since sixth-formers are more likely, and university students considerably more likely, to have parents who were educated at grammar schools, the Crowther figure of 'first-generation' pupils may show an excess roughly equivalent to the deficiency of mine. Perhaps we may estimate that the average 'first-generation' figure for the whole country is now something between 50 and 60 per cent.

More important than average figures is the very uneven distribution of 'first-generation' pupils – a fact given little attention in the Crowther report but clearly demonstrated by my inquiry. It is misleading to write as though, in virtually any maintained grammar school, two out of every three pupils come of a family with no grammar-school tradition. We have to envisage, rather, a number of schools in which nearly all pupils are of this kind, others in which such pupils may be only four or five in a class of thirty, and others again in which the balance is about even. Obviously the task not only of social integration but also of disposing pupils to learn according to the traditional mode will differ greatly in the three groups. Schools of all these types, whether determined according to parents' preference or to 'zoning', may exist together under one large city authority. There are also, in general, well-marked differences between single-sex and co-educational schools and between different parts of the country – the industrial north, for example, and the suburban south.

Nor must it be forgotten that the phrase 'first generation' is used much too glibly. As I have pointed out, the earlier maintained secondary schools had an appreciable number of pupils of the first generation, many of them in fee-paying places. The problem of today is not entirely quantitative. It also consists, first, in a social temper which, though valuing technical mastery and tangible products, gives little general esteem to scholarship or reflection; secondly, in that appreciable minority of 'new' parents who, if not apathetic or hostile to the grammar school, yet have no concept of the disciplines of serious study or of the 'pupil-product' of the earlier tradition.

In a second respect the report's reliance on averages is misleading. 'By 1938', we read, 'the majority of places in maintained secondary schools were free.' It takes a moment's reflection to realize that this majority is only *just* a majority – 53 per cent – and is very unevenly distributed. For if, as the Ministry's figures for

---

1938 state, all places were free in 29 per cent of the scho… remainder probably averaged over 60 per cent. Again, in … extreme variation. Though, by 1938, over a quarter of th… anticipated the situation created by the 1944 Act, in near… majority of pupils were fee-payers, and many schools must s… minimum quota of special places. While, then, we must no… must we underestimate the effect of the Act on a large number…

The report rightly devotes much attention to the nature and… and makes some wise observations, reminding us, for exampl…

> 'children are not the "supply" that meets any "deman…
> They are individual human beings, and the primary co…
> should not be with the living they will earn but with the…

It is in the light of such principles that it studies the effects … and recognizes that:

> 'if . . . there is a greater demand for education, it is a condi…
> for an education that seems to the boys and girls themselves…
> needs.'

It hints, as my inquiry abundantly confirms, that general socia… very rapid increase of adolescents' earnings can have an unse… studies of even intelligent young people, and it properly r… contemporary isolation of the individual and the powerful tec… media as important considerations in the education of the adol…

Adolescence is a theme that seems to have power to stir ev… curiously romantic eloquence. The Hadow report has its pa… 'There is a tide which begins to rise in the veins of youth .… Committee write of:

> 'the frequent mood swings, and mingled brashness and tend…
> and deep uncertainty – all that April weather of the soul whic…
> adolescence.'

In a sense this is true – there is, I suppose, plenty of evidence fo… from which I have quoted. But the note is false. There was e… variability in the responses of these boys and girls – yet I was re… their robustness and their extraordinarily cool appraisal both of t… and of the adult world.

On sexual development in adolescence the report's reliance… more gives rise to some misleading generalizations. There is… for the statement that the onset of puberty is earlier than it used to… the existence of great individual variations is conceded, the… attention to the very wide time-span within which puberty may…

'Where the intellectually able girls are concerned, it is difficult for the schools to adjust to this sharpening contrast between career interests and personal demands, for most of what they learn in school is related to their professional training and to entrance into the universities and other institutions where it is pursued. There is not much scope – in school hours, at least – for giving them any education specifically related to their special interests as women.'

So the grammar school girl is to be left to struggle on unaided, for lack of time to consider her as a woman. But this will not do. There is no need to restrict to the modern-school girl the comment:

'Though the general objectives of secondary education remain unchanged, her direct interest in dress, personal appearance and in problems of human relations should be given a central place in her education.'

Some intelligent girls, as this book has shown, are impatient of a school régime that seems to them to have little to do with their main interest in life and to be prolonging intolerably the status of childhood. Others express their ardent and very proper longing for school or parents to give them some clear and sympathetic guidance in finding and following the road that leads to love and marriage. This is no light assignment for the grammar school, nor should it be undertaken casually. But it cannot be evaded by conscious and unconscious attempts to 'keep the girls young'. I am not making a frivolous proposal to substitute the beauty parlour for the physics laboratory or to introduce naïvely self-centred courses. But the femininity of the intelligent girl must somehow be reconciled with her academic ability, not only in order to preserve 'woman-power' for the professions but also – and this is more significant – because of the need for educated and cultured wives and mothers, in the interests of that very preservation of the family to which the Crowther report so rightly attaches importance. In connexion with this whole matter we should remind ourselves that the presence on a school staff of mature and happily married women is an invaluable asset.

In its consideration of grammar-school successes and failures the report takes full account of the social factor. Commenting on the figures presented in *Early Leaving* it says:

'Indeed, if the objective were to reduce failure rates in the G.C.E. without regard to the total yield, the easiest way to do it would apparently have been to introduce a social element into selection.'

Thoughtful attention is given to the relative failures:

'Many of those who disappoint come from homes which . . . cannot give their boys and girls much assistance beyond elementary work. It may well be that some of these pupils, who fall back relatively in their progress, do so not through lack of general ability, but because some of the things they are asked to do –

foreign languages, for example – are intrinsically more difficult for them than for the others for reasons arising out of their home surroundings.'

This conjecture is fully confirmed by my evidence, both in the verbal testimony of teachers and pupils and also in findings such as the high figure of unpopularity and high estimate of difficulty in foreign languages:

'The important thing to realize is that these boys and girls are not stupid.'

The report considers the problem carefully and constructively and surveys possible solutions – a course leading to Ordinary level at 17 instead of 16, more weight given to subjects such as workshop practice or art, or transfer to the kind of full-time education, closely linked with the world of industry, that forms part of the future pattern of education envisaged by the Committee. It is suggested, too, that many such pupils would have done better in technical or comprehensive schools.

Yet here as elsewhere the report regards the situation in a somewhat external and mechanical way. It considers these pupils, however sympathetically, as misfits in the grammar school, and seeks a remedy in modified curricula or in transfer. But is this not to accept that very social determinism which the Committee have seemed implicitly to reject? As the report itself suggests, many pupils may be socially rather than inherently predisposed to find certain subjects difficult. In that case, unless we are indeed to introduce a social element into selection – which would be most readily achieved by a return to pre-1944 procedure – surely the grammar school must accept responsibility for intelligent children who find the atmosphere alien. My investigation has convinced me that many of these pupils attach immense importance to personal relationships and often look to their teachers to give them the reassurance and sense of significance in their studies that neither their parents nor society can give. Methods undoubtedly need modifying and much imaginative understanding is necessary. But we must not too hastily decide that such pupils are incapable of abstract thought or of initiation into a verbal culture.

In its survey of the curriculum and of the school structure and in its comments on the sixth form, the report in many ways agrees with the findings and conjectures of *The Living Tradition*. The Committee observed, as I observed, the unfortunate effects of the choice of 'sides' that is forced on pupils, particularly boys, sometimes as early as their fourteenth year. We are in agreement that the squeezing out of aesthetic and humane studies in the middle school has developed over the very period during which a school population has arisen that probably needs them more than any of its predecessors (though I have also briefly referred to strong signs of far more care for liberality, grace and general culture than is often credited to the grammar school). My survey, like the report, found evidence of the undesirable split in co-educational sixth forms, with boys almost invariably choosing science and girls arts. Both book and report note with regret the tendency to push more and more sixth-form pupils towards three 'A' level passes and deplore the elaboration – and confusion – of university entrance requirements. (The report deals with this last matter in much more detail).

On the other hand the report is in many ways less disposed than I am to question current practice. The Committee readily accept, for example, the policy of 'express' routes. Having taught for many years in a highly selective school where these routes were often followed apparently without harm, I began with little prejudice against them. Yet my survey suggests to me that they rob the uninitiated of joy and make it hard for them to grow into the strange tradition even though they can do the work.

Again, the report easily accepts the break between main school and sixth form and, though it recognizes 'bypassing', apparently regards it as inevitable that the great majority of pupils will be examined in several 'O' level subjects before entering the sixth form. It also takes little notice of the immense and on the whole stultifying effect, noted and analysed in this book, that G.C.E. examinations at both Ordinary and Advanced levels have on thought and teaching.

In much of its praise of the sixth form the report is at one with *The Living Tradition*; but it does not sufficiently consider – as some members of staff reported by me have considered – whether the 'intellectual discipleship' that marks the good sixth form could not exist much further down the school. On the attitude of the able sixth-former to specialization the Crowther Committee's opinions are very much those of the teachers I questioned. As the reader may see, though, the responses of the sixth-formers themselves – some of them very gifted people – make one by no means so certain that able boys and girls at this age are almost invariably anxious to 'get down to the serious study of some one aspect of human knowledge which, with the one-sided enthusiasm of the young, they allow for a time to obscure all other fields of endeavour'.

Though more sophisticated than the Norwood report, the Crowther report seems to have swung further back towards the attempt to distinguish types of mind, rather than grades of ability, than would have been generally approved a dozen years ago. It is particularly interesting to read of

'Dr. Ethel Venables' demonstration that the non-verbal mind, when its basic intelligence is assessed by a test appropriate to it and not by tests designed for verbal minds, is not so inferior to the academic mind as is sometimes supposed. It may be that a similar demonstration could be made of some of the other types of mind that we have been attempting to distinguish.'

Such authoritative statements may support my suggestion of the 'centres of attraction' of the grammar and the modern school (though my distinction is based more on ability than on distinguishable 'types'). At the same time I am convinced, and have tried to show, that we have much yet to learn about the emotional conditioning that, in two people of apparently equal ability, may make learning easy for the one and hard for the other.

On both the quality and the supply of grammar school teachers, the report, though more detailed and less impressionistic, confirms very closely the opinions expressed in this book. A comparison of the two, however, raises some interesting questions. If, for example, it is as important as the report suggests to ensure that there is no unnecessary waste or extravagance in the disposition of people capable of teaching the sixth form, how far should we or must we concentrate our most scholarly teaching at the top end of the school? What, in fact, is the exact and proper compromise in present circumstances to be made with the principles stated in *The Living Tradition* – the refreshment of teachers by alternation of work, the early and economical initiation of the young into proper scholarly habits, and the giving to even first-year pupils a glimpse of the end of their school road? Again, the bold proposal to attract able graduates into the grammar schools by means of salary differentials may be read in conjunction with my analysis of the effect on staffing of the 1944 legislation. What would become of 'parity of esteem' if the Crowther proposals were followed? This principle, as I have suggested, has cost the grammar school something. But if it is now to be abandoned we must know what we are doing.

I have attempted to justify my faith in the institution that in this century has mediated the tradition of strenuous learning and immaterial values to a wider population than ever before. At the same time I have tried to see the complicated structure of grammar-school education in terms of the men and women, boys and girls who compose it. If the Crowther report has located the field in the larger map, perhaps I have made it 'a field full of folk'.

* *I based my statement on the summary of the contents of Volume II, given at the end of Volume I, which stated the age range of the social survey as 16–19. Volume II, since published, gives the range as 16–20 and it is now clear that the survey covered a proportion of university and college students.*

It is perhaps more important that the selective schools of the survey included technical schools (with a probably higher percentage of first generation pupils). My figures refer only to the maintained grammar schools.

APPENDIX II

Table I

LENGTH OF SERVICE AND DISTRIBUTION OF THE MAJORITY OF THE TEACHERS WHO RETURNED QUESTIONNAIRES

Service

Under 5 years : 18	
5 to 9 ,, : 24	
10 ,, 14 ,, : 21	
14 ,, 19 ,, : 11	Average length of service: 16 years
20 ,, 24 ,, : 9	
25 ,, 29 ,, : 19	
30 ,, 34 ,, : 13	
35 ,, 40 ,, : 5	
120	

Number of teachers

Pre-war teachers: 46	Boys' schools: 36	Men: 55
Post-war teachers: 57	Girls' schools: 46	Women: 62
	Co-educational schools: 38	Not stated: 3

Diagram I

SUBJECT-INTERESTS OF TEACHERS WHO RETURNED QUESTIONNAIRES
(A few are represented by more than one subject)

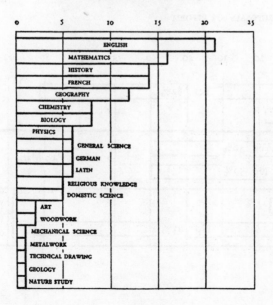

Diagram II
TEACHERS' ATTITUDES TO THE G.C.E. EXAMINATION AT 'O' LEVEL

OPINIONS ON EFFECT AT 'O' LEVEL

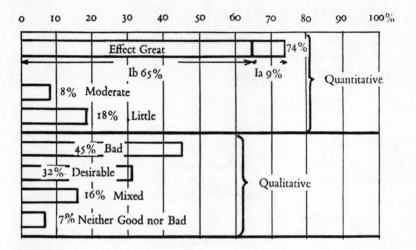

OPINIONS ON PROPOSALS FOR REFORM

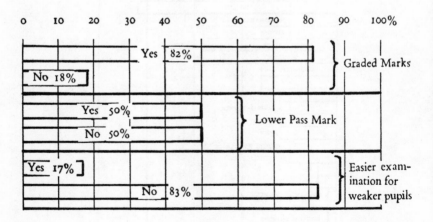

Diagram III

TEACHERS AND THE SIXTH FORM

I. Use made of published examination questions. (Percentages are of *teachers*.)

II. Estimate of sixth-form pupils: (*a*) can think for themselves; (*b*) have little originality, but can for the most part learn and follow instructions carefully and accurately; (*c*) take their work rather casually. (The estimated percentages refer to *pupils*.)

III. Estimate of pupils' attitude and performance in sixth form, compared with previous stage. (Percentages are of *teachers*.)

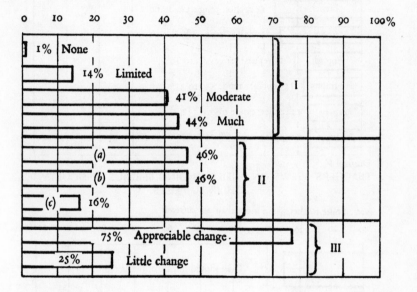

Diagram IV

TEACHERS' AVERAGE ESTIMATES OF PERCENTAGES OF PUPILS FINDING SERIOUS DIFFICULTY IN CERTAIN SUBJECTS

Note: This has no statistical significance, but is an illustration of the wide fluctuations of opinion.

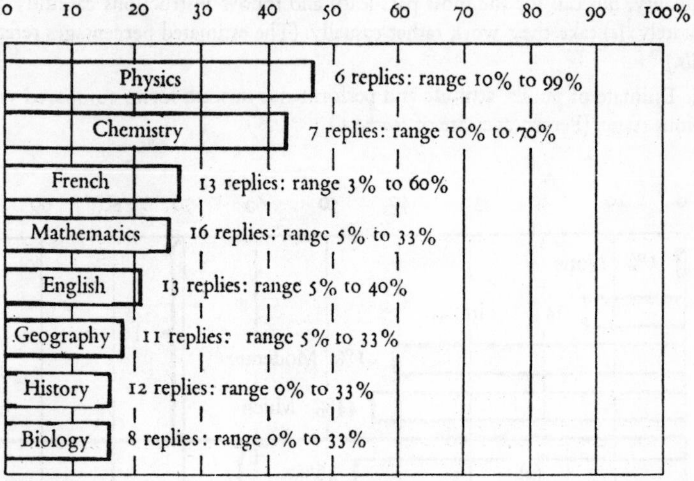

| 0 | 10 | 20 | 30 | 40 | 50 | 60 | 70 | 80 | 90 | 100% |

Physics   6 replies: range 10% to 99%

Chemistry   7 replies: range 10% to 70%

French   13 replies: range 3% to 60%

Mathematics   16 replies: range 5% to 33%

English   13 replies: range 5% to 40%

Geography   11 replies: range 5% to 33%

History   12 replies: range 0% to 33%

Biology   8 replies: range 0% to 33%

Diagram V

TEACHERS' VIEWS ON PUPILS FINDING SERIOUS DIFFICULTY IN THEIR SUBJECTS

Note: Some teachers gave more than one answer.

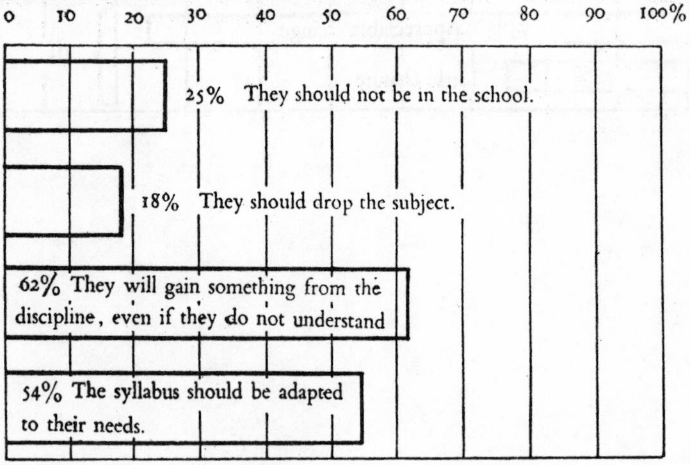

| 0 | 10 | 20 | 30 | 40 | 50 | 60 | 70 | 80 | 90 | 100% |

25%   They should not be in the school.

18%   They should drop the subject.

62%   They will gain something from the discipline, even if they do not understand

54%   The syllabus should be adapted to their needs.

Diagram VI

TEACHERS' VIEWS ON PROPER SCHOOL ATTITUDE TO UNIFORM, TABLE MANNERS, MONEY-EARNING BY PUPILS, MEMBERSHIP OF YOUTH CLUBS, FRIENDSHIPS WITH OPPOSITE SEX

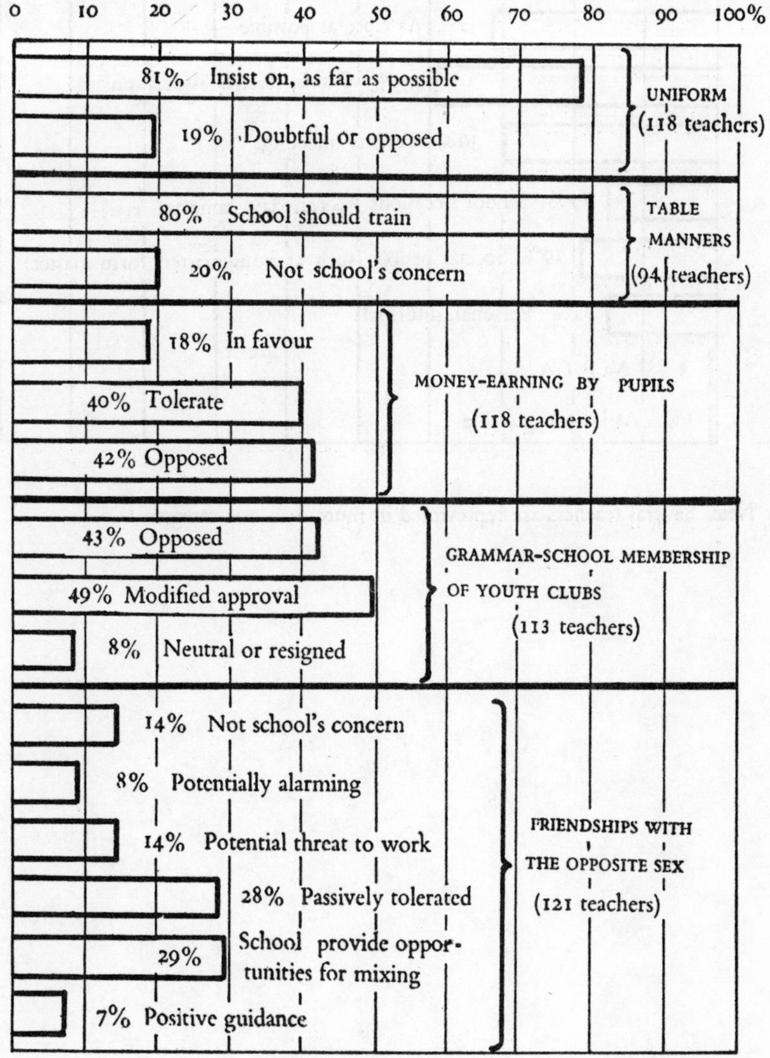

0   10   20   30   40   50   60   70   80   90   100%

81%   Insist on, as far as possible
19%   Doubtful or opposed

UNIFORM
(118 teachers)

80%   School should train
20%   Not school's concern

TABLE MANNERS
(94 teachers)

18%   In favour
40%   Tolerate
42%   Opposed

MONEY-EARNING BY PUPILS
(118 teachers)

43%   Opposed
49%   Modified approval
8%   Neutral or resigned

GRAMMAR-SCHOOL MEMBERSHIP OF YOUTH CLUBS
(113 teachers)

14%   Not school's concern
8%   Potentially alarming
14%   Potential threat to work
28%   Passively tolerated
29%   School provide opportunities for mixing
7%   Positive guidance

FRIENDSHIPS WITH THE OPPOSITE SEX
(121 teachers)

Diagram VII
TEACHERS' OPINIONS OF DESIRABLE EXTENT AND KIND OF CONTACT OF SCHOOL WITH PARENTS

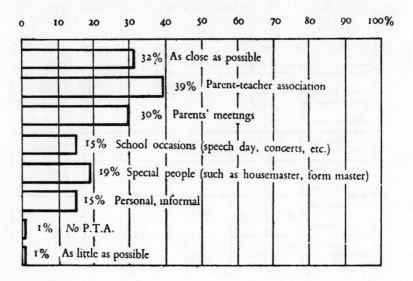

| 0 | 10 | 20 | 30 | 40 | 50 | 60 | 70 | 80 | 90 | 100% |

32% As close as possible

39% Parent-teacher association

30% Parents' meetings

15% School occasions (speech day, concerts, etc.)

19% Special people (such as housemaster, form master)

15% Personal, informal

1% No P.T.A.

1% As little as possible

Note: Several teachers are represented in more than one category.

Diagram VIII

TEACHERS' JUDGEMENTS (EXPRESSED IN PERCENTAGES) OF
PUPILS IN 1958, COMPARED WITH 1948 AND 1938, IN RESPECT
OF INTELLIGENCE, HOME BACKGROUND, INTEREST IN WORK,
ABILITY TO CONCENTRATE

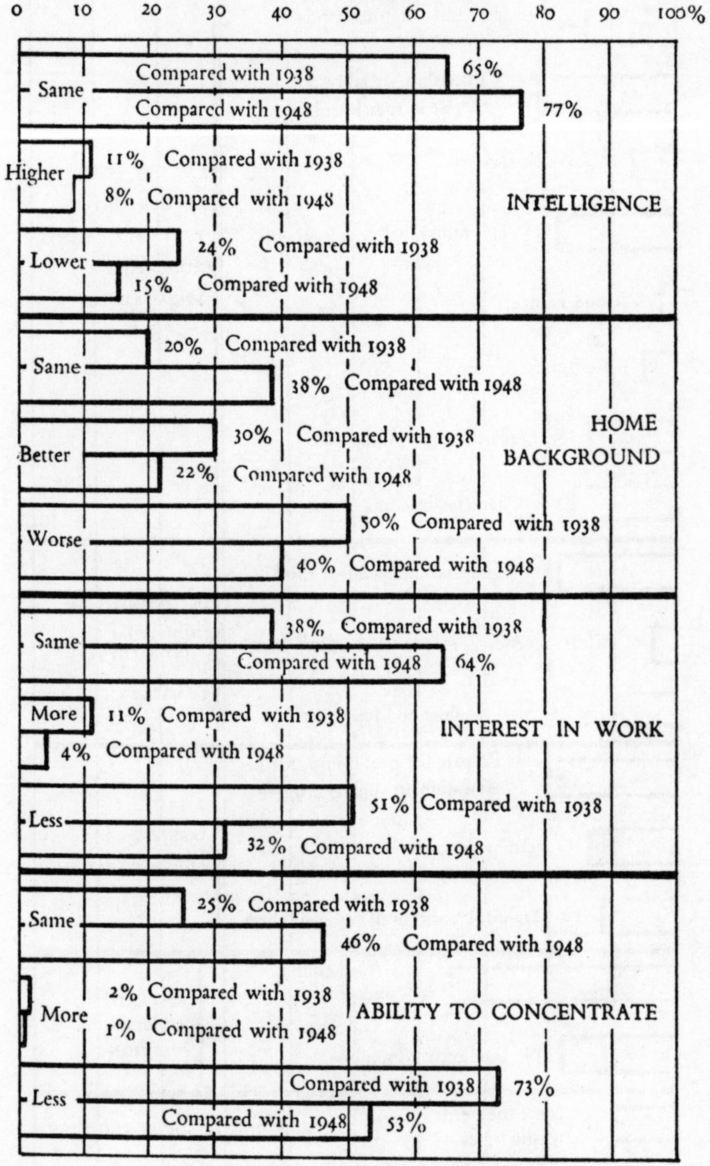

Diagram IX

126 TEACHERS' VIEWS OF THE FUNCTIONS OF THE CONTEMPORARY GRAMMAR SCHOOL

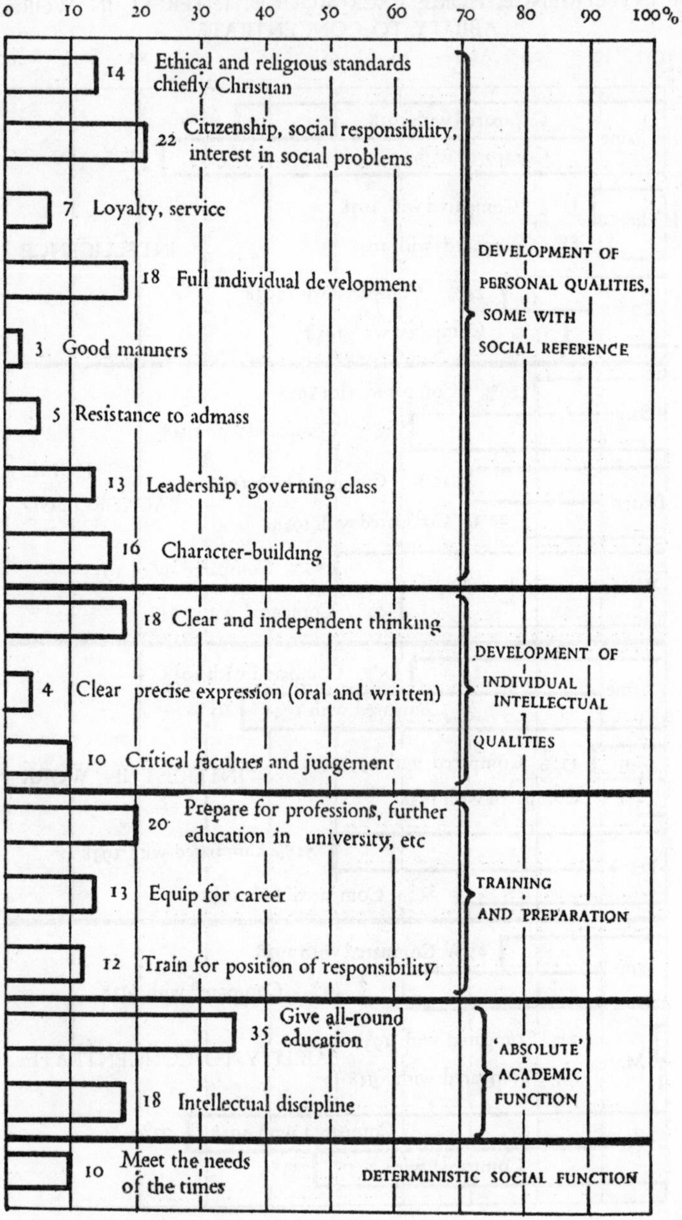

0   10   20   30   40   50   60   70   80   90   100%

14 Ethical and religious standards chiefly Christian

22 Citizenship, social responsibility, interest in social problems

7 Loyalty, service

18 Full individual development

3 Good manners

5 Resistance to admass

13 Leadership. governing class

16 Character-building

DEVELOPMENT OF PERSONAL QUALITIES, SOME WITH SOCIAL REFERENCE

18 Clear and independent thinking

4 Clear precise expression (oral and written)

10 Critical faculties and judgement

DEVELOPMENT OF INDIVIDUAL INTELLECTUAL QUALITIES

20 Prepare for professions, further education in university, etc

13 Equip for career

12 Train for position of responsibility

TRAINING AND PREPARATION

35 Give all-round education

18 Intellectual discipline

'ABSOLUTE' ACADEMIC FUNCTION

10 Meet the needs of the times

DETERMINISTIC SOCIAL FUNCTION

Diagram X

DISTRIBUTION OF THE 2,055 PUPILS WHO COMPLETED QUESTIONNAIRES

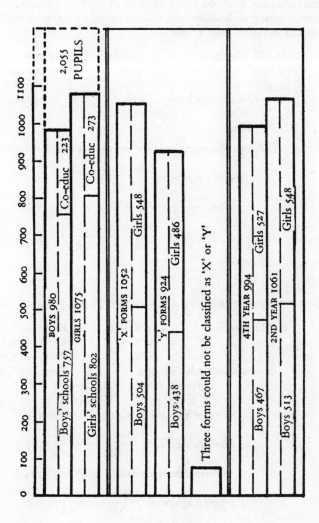

Table II
PERCENTAGES OF PUPILS *NEITHER* OF WHOSE PARENTS ATTENDED
A GRAMMAR SCHOOL

Note: 'Don't know' answers – a total of 268 out of 2,055 – were omitted from the reckoning. Thus, the total number of all pupils was assumed to be 1,787, and corresponding adjustments were made in the total number of pupils in groups of schools and in 'X' and 'Y' forms.

In ALL schools	39% [S.E. = 1.1][1]	Range: 15% to 72%
„ boys' „	34%	Range: 24% to 52%
„ girls' „	32%	Range: 15% to 52%
„ co-educational schools:	57%	Range: 49% to 72%
„ 'X' forms:	35%	
„ 'Y' forms:	43%	

Difference between single-sex and co-educational schools: 24%

$$[\text{Highly significant.} \quad \frac{\text{Difference}}{\text{S.E.}} = \frac{24}{2.7} = 8.9]$$

Difference between 'X' and 'Y' forms: 8%

$$[\text{Significant.} \quad \frac{\text{Difference}}{\text{S.E.}} = \frac{8}{2.4} = 3.3]$$

[1] S.E. = Standard Error.

Table III
PERCENTAGES OF PUPILS WHO SAY 'I LIKE SCHOOL VERY MUCH'

In ALL schools:	50% [S.E. = 1.1]	Range: 22% to 80%
„ boys' „	47%	Range: 29% to 67%
„ girls' „	52%	Range: 22% to 80%
„ co-educational schools:	49%	Range: 28% to 67%

Year II: 56%   Year IV: 42%
'X' forms: 56%   'Y' forms: 41%

Difference between boys' and girls' schools: 5%

$$[\text{Perhaps significant.} \quad \frac{\text{Difference}}{\text{S.E.}} = \frac{5}{2.5} = 2]$$

Difference between Year II and Year IV: 14%

$$[\text{Highly significant.} \quad \frac{\text{Difference}}{\text{S.E.}} = \frac{14}{2.2} = 6.4]$$

Difference between 'X' and 'Y' forms: 14%

$$[\text{Highly significant.} \quad \frac{\text{Difference}}{\text{S.E.}} = \frac{14}{2.4} = 5.8]$$

Diagram XI

PERCENTAGES OF PUPILS NEITHER OF WHOSE PARENTS RECEIVED
A GRAMMAR-SCHOOL EDUCATION (NPG) COMPARED, SCHOOL
BY SCHOOL, WITH APPROXIMATE PERCENTAGES OF BROTHERS
AND SISTERS OVER 11 HAVING, OR HAVING HAD, A GRAMMAR-
SCHOOL EDUCATION (BSG)[1]

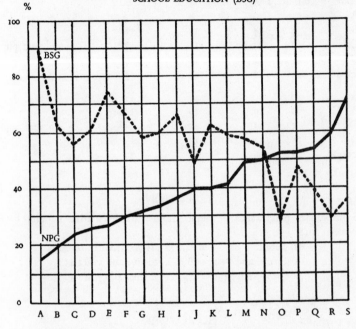

[1] The raw numbers were obtained from a show of hands, after a careful explanation.
Note: The local percentage of grammar-school places will have some effect on the
proportionate numbers of brothers and sisters educated at grammar schools.

Table IV   FAMILY, FRIENDS, SCHOOL

Comparative percentages of (1) pupils *neither* of whose parents received a grammar-school education; (2) brothers and sisters over 11 with a grammar-school
education; (3) friends not attending a grammar school; (4) pupils expressing strong
appreciation of school.

SCHOOLS

	I	II	III	IV	V	VI	VII	VIII	IX	X	XI	XII	XIII	XIV	XV	XVI	XVII	XVIII	XIX
(1)	24	34	37	40	52	26	27	15	30	32	52	40	20	41	54	49	72	50	59
(2)	56	60	66	49	28	61	74	89	67	58	47	62	63	59	39	57	35	54	29
(3)	57	65	67	61	60	48	33	41	56	51	54	53	49	62	69	58	56	66	66
(4)	67	61	56	44	36	29	41	80	64	80	27	22	47	47	32	64	28	67	66

Note: (*a*) Figures relative to line (2) were obtained, after careful explanation,
from a show of hands. (*b*) Figures relative to line (3) are dependent on an arbitrary
interpretation of children's answers to the question: 'Have you many friends who
are not at grammar schools?'

Table V   BEDTIMES

Bedtimes (shown in approximate percentages) of pupils in 2 girls' schools (A, B) and 2 boys' schools (C, D).

School	Before 9 p.m.	9–9.30	9.30–10	After 10 p.m.	
A	71	19	8	2	⎫
B	34	44	15	8	⎪
C	42	44	11	3	⎬ 2nd year pupils
D	27	54	12	7	⎪
Average	44	40	12	5	⎭
A	10	30	44	15	⎫
B	7	19	59	16	⎪
C	5	25	35	35	⎬ 4th year pupils
D	10	29	35	25	⎪
Average	8	26	43	23	⎭

Table VI   TELEVISION

Approximate percentages of pupils' homes (representative sample) having television, 1958.

> All pupils: 66%; Boys: 70%; Girls: 62%
> 'X' forms, 2nd year: 66%; 'Y' forms, 2nd year: 45%
> 'X' forms, 4th year: 38%; 'Y' forms, 4th year: 56%

Table VII   HOMEWORK

Distribution (shown in approximate percentages) of rooms in which homework is done by a random sample of pupils.

	'X' forms		'Y' forms	
	Boys	Girls	Boys	Girls
Suggesting special provision:				
Own room, study, office, etc.	5	5	3	3
Suggesting possibility of solitude:				
Dining-room, drawing-room, spare room, quiet room, front room, room without T.V.	50	37	25	33
Doubtful:				
Bedroom	27	18	22	19
Suggesting presence of others:				
Sitting-room, living-room, lounge, kitchen	13	40	44	45
Suggesting absence of any provision:				
'Any room', 'none specially'	5	0	6	0

Table VIII   SUCCESS, FAILURE, PREFERENCE (1)

'Best' and 'weakest' subjects and 'lessons enjoyed most' and 'lessons liked least' (pupils' estimates, expressed in approximate percentages).

Note:

1. The children were asked to name the *two* lessons they enjoyed most and the *one* lesson they liked least.

2. 'Best/weakest' refers to *subjects*, but 'most enjoyed/least liked' to *lessons*.

3. Percentages, being approximate, sometimes make a total of more or less than 100.

	'Best'	'Most'	'Weakest'	'Least'	
English	13	10	10	6	
History	11	10	8	9	
Geography	9	10	6	5	
Religious Instruction	2	1	3	5	
Foreign Languages	16	11	26	28	All Pupils
Mathematics	19	10	25	19	
Sciences	16	20	12	12	
Practical Work	4	8	2	3	
Arts	7	9	8	9	
Physical Activities	4	12	1	3	

Foreign Languages: chiefly French, but also Latin, German, Spanish.

Practical Work: woodwork, metalwork, technical drawing, needlework, domestic science.

Arts: music, painting, pottery.

Table IX   SUCCESS, FAILURE, PREFERENCE (2)

'Best' subjects and 'most enjoyed' lessons. 'Weakest' subjects and 'least liked' lessons,

	Same	Different	Same	Different
School T (Girls)				
4'X'	18	7	14	10
4'Y'	20	12	16	15
2'X'	22	8	16	14
2'Y'	18	6	15	10
School U (Boys)				
4'X'	22	5	11	14
4'Y'	17	9	10	16
2'X'	23	4	13	14
2'Y'	19	6	12	12

(It should be remembered that two 'most enjoyed' lessons were named, so that there was a greater chance of correspondence in the first category than in the second.)

Table X   'BEST' AND 'WEAKEST' SUBJECTS
(Pupils' estimates, expressed in approximate percentages)

| | All | | 'Best' | | 'W'kst.' | | 'Best' | | 'W'kst.' | | 'Best' | | 'W'kst.' | |
| | | | Year | | Year | | | | | | | | | |
	B	W	II	IV	II	IV	'X'	'Y'	'X'	'Y'	B	G	B	G
English	13	10	13	13	11	10	12	14	12	8	10	16	12	9
History	11	8	12	10	9	6	10	12	8	8	13	9	7	9
Geography	9	6	9	9	6	6	8	10	6	6	9	10	7	5
Religious Inst.	2	3	1	2	4	2	1	2	4	2	1	3	2	3
Foreign Languages	16	26	16	15	21	31	19	12	25	27	14	17	30	23
Mathematics	19	25	20	17	24	26	20	17	22	28	20	17	18	31
Sciences	16	12	13	19	9	14	19	12	12	12	20	12	13	10
Practical Work	4	2	4	3	3	1	3	5	2	1	4	4	3	1
Arts	7	8	7	8	11	4	6	9	9	7	6	8	8	8
Physical Activities	4	1	4	3	1	1	1	6	1	1	4	4	1	1

Table XI
'LESSONS ENJOYED MOST' AND 'LESSONS LIKED LEAST'
(Pupils' estimates, expressed as above)

| | All | | 'Most' | | 'Least' | | 'Most' | | 'Least' | | 'Most' | | 'Least' | |
	M	L	II	IV	II	IV	'X'	'Y'	'X'	'Y'	B	G	B	G
English	10	6	10	10	6	5	9	11	5	6	7	13	6	5
History	10	9	11	10	10	8	10	10	7	9	10	10	8	10
Geography	10	5	10	10	5	6	9	11	6	5	8	11	6	5
Religious Inst.	1	5	1	1	6	4	1	1	6	5	1	1	5	6
Foreign Languages	11	28	12	9	27	30	13	7	32	26	9	12	36	22
Mathematics	10	19	11	9	19	19	12	9	16	21	11	9	13	25
Sciences	20	12	16	23	9	15	25	14	13	11	26	15	12	12
Practical Work	8	3	8	8	4	2	6	11	3	4	8	8	4	3
Arts	9	9	9	9	10	7	7	10	9	9	7	10	9	9
Physical Activities	12	3	15	9	3	4	9	16	4	3	13	11	3	4

Table XII   SUCCESS/FAILURE IN SCIENCE

Proportions of single science subjects within total pupils' estimates of 'best' and 'weakest' for science (given in approximate percentages).

	'BEST'					'WEAKEST'					
	All	B	G	'X'	'Y'	All	B	G	'X'	'Y'	
General Science	37	14	23	25	12	32	8	23	14	18	
Chemistry	17	15	2	13	4	31	21	9	20	11	Year II
Physics	23	20	2	11	11	15	9	5	11	4	
Biology	21	5	15	13	8	21	8	13	12	9	
Nature Study	2	2	—	1	1	2	2	—	—	2	
General Science	12	4	8	7	6	17	4	13	2	15	
Chemistry	32	28	5	27	6	36	28	8	18	18	Year IV
Physics	18	18	—	13	5	27	19	8	20	7	
Biology	37	15	22	20	18	21	8	13	11	9	

Table XIII   PREFERENCE IN SCIENCE

Proportions of single science subjects within total pupils' judgements of 'most enjoyed/least liked' for science lessons (given in approximate percentages.)

	'MOST'					'LEAST'					
	All	B	G	'X'	'Y'	All	B	G	'X'	'Y'	
General Science	31	11	20	18	14	30	6	24	16	15	
Chemistry	24	20	4	17	7	22	10	12	16	6	Year II
Physics	17	16	1	11	6	12	9	3	6	6	
Biology	26	12	13	15	11	29	8	21	17	12	
Nature Study	2	2	—	1	1	6	6	—	—	6	
General Science	10	3	7	7	3	16	1	14	4	12	
Chemistry	30	23	6	24	6	29	21	8	19	10	Year IV
Physics	23	21	2	18	6	38	25	13	29	9	
Biology	36	15	22	20	17	18	8	10	8	10	

Table XIV   FRENCH AND LATIN

Proportions of French and Latin in 'best/weakest' and 'most enjoyed/least liked' estimates of 2nd and 4th year 'X' forms for foreign languages (expressed in approximate percentages).

		'Best'		'Weakest'		'Most'		'Least'	
		F	L	F	L	F	L	F	L
Year	II	83	11	60	40	61	31	51	48
Year	IV	71	22	55	42	54	32	49	47

Note: Unexpressed percentages are accounted for by other languages such as German.

Diagram XII

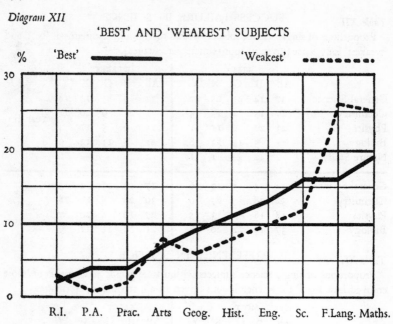

'BEST' AND 'WEAKEST' SUBJECTS

%   'Best' ━━━━━━━   'Weakest' ▪▪▪▪▪▪▪

R.I.   P.A.   Prac.   Arts   Geog.   Hist.   Eng.   Sc.   F.Lang.   Maths.

Diagram XIII

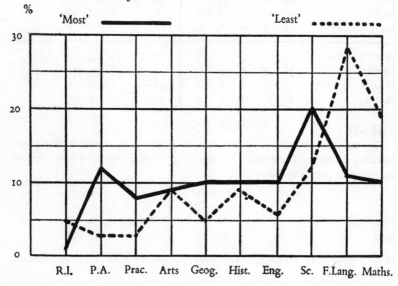

'MOST ENJOYED' AND 'LEAST LIKED' LESSONS

%   'Most' ━━━━━━━   'Least' ▪▪▪▪▪▪▪

R.I.   P.A.   Prac.   Arts   Geog.   Hist.   Eng.   Sc.   F.Lang.   Maths.

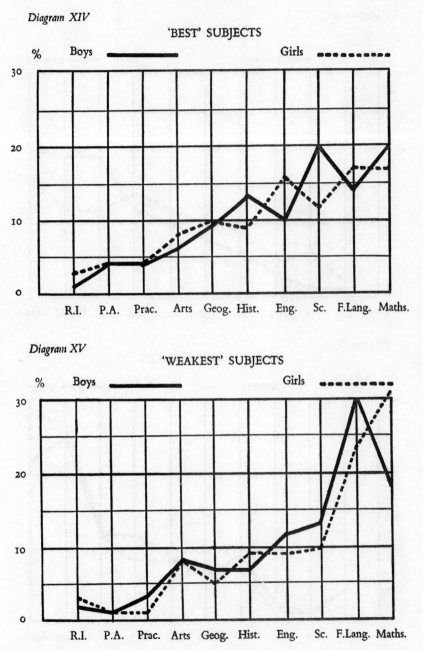

Diagram XIV

'BEST' SUBJECTS

% Boys ———— Girls ----------

R.I. P.A. Prac. Arts Geog. Hist. Eng. Sc. F.Lang. Maths.

Diagram XV

'WEAKEST' SUBJECTS

% Boys ———— Girls ----------

R.I. P.A. Prac. Arts Geog. Hist. Eng. Sc. F.Lang. Maths.

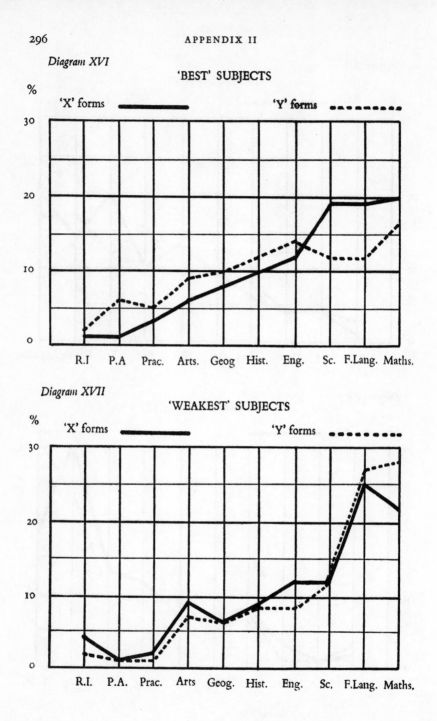

Diagram XVI

'BEST' SUBJECTS

Diagram XVII

'WEAKEST' SUBJECTS

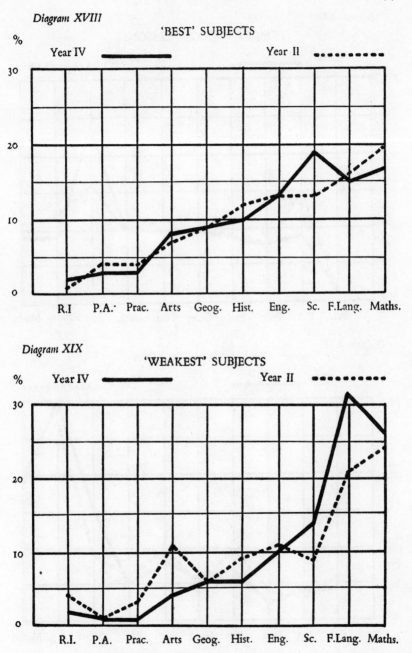

Diagram XVIII

'BEST' SUBJECTS

%

Year IV ━━━━━━━ Year II ▪▪▪▪▪▪▪▪▪▪

30

20

10

0

R.I   P.A.   Prac.   Arts   Geog.   Hist.   Eng.   Sc.   F.Lang.   Maths.

Diagram XIX

'WEAKEST' SUBJECTS

%   Year IV ━━━━━━━   Year II ▪▪▪▪▪▪▪▪▪▪

30

20

10

0

R.I.   P.A.   Prac.   Arts   Geog.   Hist.   Eng.   Sc.   F.Lang.   Maths.

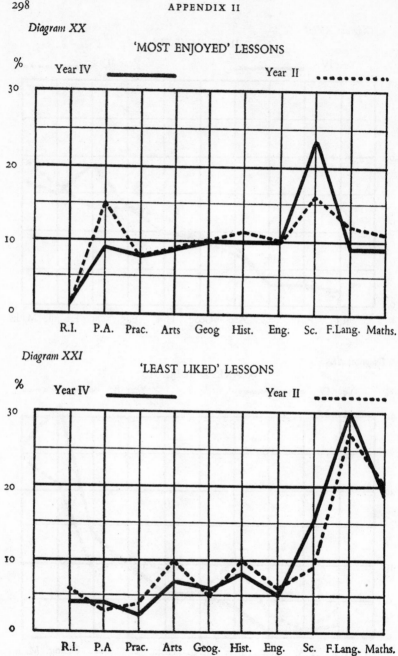

Diagram XX

'MOST ENJOYED' LESSONS

%

Year IV ────────　　　　　　　　Year II ••••••••••

30

20

10

0

R.I.　P.A.　Prac.　Arts　Geog　Hist.　Eng.　Sc.　F.Lang.　Maths.

Diagram XXI

'LEAST LIKED' LESSONS

%

Year IV ────────　　　　　　　　Year II ──────────

30

20

10

0

R.I.　P.A　Prac.　Arts　Geog.　Hist.　Eng.　Sc.　F.Lang.　Maths.

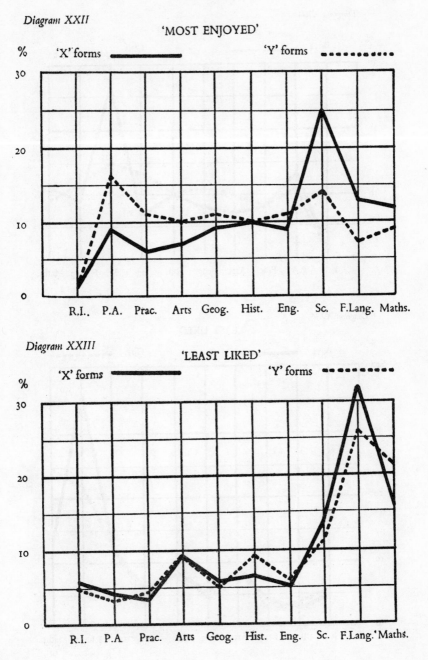

Diagram XXII

'MOST ENJOYED'

%   'X' forms ━━━━━   'Y' forms ●●●●●●●●●●

R.I.   P.A.   Prac.   Arts   Geog.   Hist.   Eng.   Sc.   F.Lang. Maths.

Diagram XXIII

'LEAST LIKED'

%   'X' forms ━━━━━   'Y' forms ●●●●●●●●●●

R.I.   P.A   Prac.   Arts   Geog.   Hist.   Eng.   Sc.   F.Lang. 'Maths.

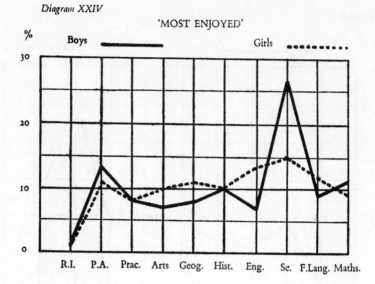

Diagram XXIV

'MOST ENJOYED'

Boys ——————   Girls ············

R.I. P.A. Prac. Arts Geog. Hist. Eng. Sc. F.Lang. Maths.

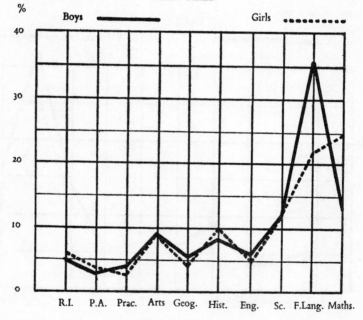

Diagram XXV

'LEAST LIKED'

Boys ——————   Girls ············

R.I. P.A. Prac. Arts Geog. Hist. Eng. Sc. F.Lang. Maths.

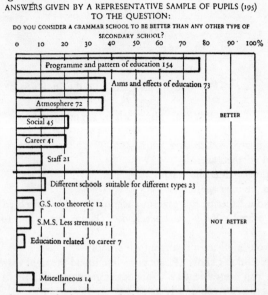

Diagram XXVI
ANSWERS GIVEN BY A REPRESENTATIVE SAMPLE OF PUPILS (195)
TO THE QUESTION:
DO YOU CONSIDER A GRAMMAR SCHOOL TO BE BETTER THAN ANY OTHER TYPE OF
SECONDARY SCHOOL?

Programme and Pattern of Education includes: Better educational standards, intellectual quality, hard work, selectivity of topics, cultural education, more subjects, work at uncongenial subjects, homework, G.C.E., length of school life.

Aims and Effects of Education includes: Preparation for adult life, understanding of the world, ability to converse, good manners, maturity, choice, responsibility, independence of mass media, development of mind and character, encouragement of self-confidence.

Atmosphere includes: Discipline, organization, uniform, relaxed relationship, community, tradition, reputation, moderate punishment, 'tone', better games.

Staff includes: Better-qualified teachers, individual attention, helpfulness of teachers.

Social includes: Class, better friends, intelligent companions.

Career includes: Scope of career, better jobs, road to university.

Different schools suitable for different types includes: Grammar schools suitable for the intellectual, but *only* for them, technical schools better for technically minded.

G.S. too theoretic includes: G.S. subjects useless, curriculum too narrow, S.M.S. facilities for practical and domestic work.

S.M.S. less strenuous includes: Ease of S.M. schools, less competition in S.M. schools, no homework in S.M. schools.

Education related to career includes: S.M.S. just as good preparation for job, different schools related to different careers, early earning for S.M.-school pupils.

Miscellaneous includes: Public school preferred, comprehensive school preferred, buildings and equipment, games, personal attention.

APPENDIX III

THE GRAMMAR SCHOOL (PUPILS)

BOY/GIRL (please delete as appropriate)

1. How many brothers have you?
2. What are their ages?
3. How many sisters have you?
4. What are their ages?
5. Did your father go to a grammar school? (It might have been called a secondary school.) Yes/No/I don't know. (Please put a line round the right answer.)
6. Did your mother go to a grammar school?
   Yes/No/I don't know. (Please put a line round the right answer.)
7. Have you many friends who are not at grammar schools?
8. What time do you usually go to bed?
9. Is there television in your home?
10. In which room do you usually do your homework?
11. Which is your best subject in school?
12. Which is your weakest subject in school?
13. Which two lessons do you like most?
14. Which one lesson do you like least?
15. What do you enjoy best in school life?
16. What do you dislike most in school life?
17. Which of the following statements comes nearest to your feelings about this school? (Please put a line round it).
    I neither like it nor dislike it much / I like it very much / I dislike it very much.
18. Can you give a reason for your answer to question 17?
19. Do you consider a grammar school to be better than any other type of secondary school? Give full reasons for your answer.
20. How much did your parents want you to come to a grammar school?
21. What do they feel about it now?
22. What is your greatest interest outside school?
23. What do you do in your spare time?
24. Do you often feel bored? If so, in what situations do you feel most bored?

FOR THOSE UNDER 13 ONLY
25. In what ways is this school different from your last school?
26. How long do you hope to stay at school?

27. What do you feel about leaving school?
28. After leaving, what would you like to do if you had unlimited choice?
29. Is there any obstacle to your choice? If so, what?
30. What will you probably do?

FOR ALL
31. Thinking of your home, your school, and the district where you live, what special difficulties or advantages has coming to this school brought into your life? (Please answer as frankly and fully as possible.)

THE GRAMMAR SCHOOL (STAFF)

It will be appreciated if you will answer the questions below as fully and precisely as your knowledge and experience permit.

MASTER/MISTRESS (*please delete as appropriate*)

1. How many years have you taught in a grammar school?
2. How many years have you taught in your present school?
3. What subject do you teach?
4. To which aspects of it do you get the best response?
5. Which parts do pupils find most difficult?
6. What effect upon work in your subject has the G.C.E. examination at 'O' level?
7. What would be your attitude to graded marks at 'O' level, with the pass mark lower than at present? How would you justify this attitude?
8. What would you think, as far as your subject was concerned, of the introduction of an easier public examination than the G.C.E. 'O' level for the weaker pupils in grammar schools?
9. Approximately what percentage of pupils find real difficulty in tackling work in your subject?
10. Which of the following remarks most nearly describes your opinion on these pupils? (More than one remark may be included.)
    (*a*) They should not be in the school. (*b*) They should drop the subject. (*c*) They will gain something from the discipline of studying it, even if they do not understand it. (*d*) The syllabus should be adapted to their needs.
11. In sixth-form work, what kind of teaching use do you make of published examination questions set in past years? (Please be as specific as possible.)
12. How many sixth-form pupils (all years together) have you? What proportions of them: (*a*) can think for themselves; (*b*) have little originality, but can for the most part learn and follow instructions carefully and accurately;

(c) take their work rather casually? (It is realized that category (c) may overlap the other two!)

13. Do you wish to extend or modify anything said in answer to question 12?

14. Do you find that the attitude and performance of a pupil in the sixth form almost invariably correspond closely to that pupil's attitude and performance below the sixth? If not, what variations have you found? (Please be as particular as possible.)

15. How should the grammar school regard: (a) uniform; (b) friends of the opposite sex; (c) youth clubs; (d) part-time money-earning; (e) table manners?

16. What extent and kind of contact with parents should the grammar school have?

17. What differences, if any – in respect of intelligence, home background, interest in work, ability to concentrate, etc. – do you find between pupils of the present day and those of: (a) ten years ago; (b) twenty years ago?

18. What should be the main function of a grammar school today? Does your answer differ in any important respect from what it would have been, say, twenty years ago?